op

Amer (South)

6.50

POTO M R

Bath
(Berkeley Sps.)

R. R.

Harper's Ferry.

Shannondale Sps.

RIVER

Jordan White Sulphur
Winchester

Capon Sps.

Washington

orkney Spr.

New Market

Alexandria

River

Rawley Spr.

Warrenton

Harrisonburg

Fauquier White Sulphur

Rappahannock

Aquia Cr.

Stribling Sps.

Shenandoah

River

Fredericksburg

Orange C. H.

Aquia Creek was
the landing for
steamboats from
Washington

Staunton

Gordonsville

Bath Alum Sps.

Virginia Central R. R.

Charlottesville

Goshen.

Rockbridge Baths

dge
n Sps.

Lexington

D

Kanawha Canal

Buchanan

River and

River

James

James

Richmond
Huguenot Sps.

Buford's

Lynchburg

VIRGINIA
Sic Semper Tyrannis

Amelia Sps.

Petersburg

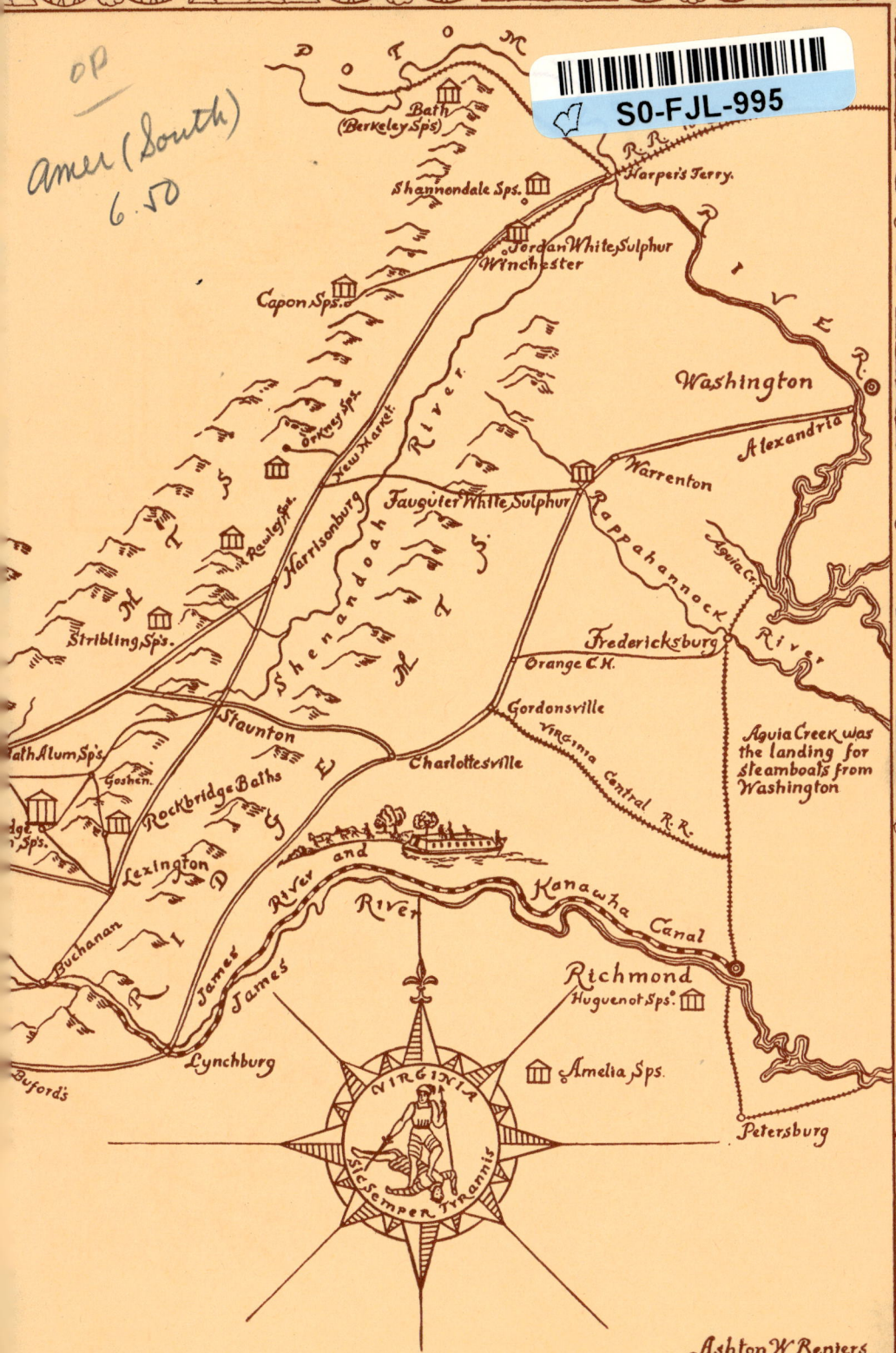

Ashton W. Renters

THE SPRINGS OF VIRGINIA

The SPRINGS of VIRGINIA

Life, Love, and Death at the Waters

1775–1900

By

PERCEVAL RENIERS

CHAPEL HILL

The University of North Carolina Press

MCMXLI

TYPOGRAPHY, PRINTING, AND BINDING IN THE U. S. A. BY
KINGSPORT PRESS, INC., KINGSPORT, TENNESSEE

To Ashton

Whose Enthusiasm and Industry

Prepared the Way

CONTENTS

LIST OF ILLUSTRATIONS

IN COLOR

LIST OF ILLUSTRATIONS

THE SPRINGS OF VIRGINIA

Watering places all over the world are much
alike—a general muster, under the banner of
folly, to drive care and common sense out of
the field.—

CAPTAIN MARRYAT, *Diary in America*.

I

Mr. Featherstonhaugh Makes A Visit

WHEN George W. Featherstonhaugh, F.R.S., F.G.S., arrived at the White Sulphur Springs in August, 1834, he was possessed by an idea. The idea was, when the coach stopped, to leap out ahead of all the other passengers, and the object of that was to beat them to the "man in brown." Forewarned was forearmed. Over at the Warm Springs the Kentucky lady had told him how it would be. The White Sulphur was crowded to repletion, she said, and no matter how respectable you were, if you didn't come in your own carriage you were turned away without ceremony. The only possible way to get in at all was to wring the promise of a cabin from the man in brown. He controlled everything. And, said the lady from Kentucky, "if he wasn't the biggest liar that ever belonged to Virginia there was a great one to be born yet."

No matter how much of a liar he was, if he had to be tackled it would certainly be better to tackle him first than last. For over forty miles of hard jouncing, Mr. Featherstonhaugh had faced the facts with the resolution of a true Britisher. First out would be first served.

The coach topped a rise, rolled gently down past some neat white cottages, turned right through a large white gate and pulled up before a building that looked like an ark. This ark, the only structure of any size in the place, was the dining room, and underneath it in the basement story were the receiving rooms, the post office and the bar. Mr. Featherstonhaugh did not wait for the driver to open the door and he did not wait for the steps to be let down. He was indeed the first out of the coach and he landed in a dusty arena in the midst of a crowd of people.

At stagecoach time the space before the receiving rooms was always swarming: Negro baggagemen, hostlers, countrymen, clerks, children and mammies, and clean crisp ladies and gentlemen searching the coaches for their friends, the ladies in fine muslin with enormous puffed sleeves, the gentlemen in blue swallow-tails with brass buttons, fawn colored trousers, high choking stocks around their necks, all fresh as daisies. And here, dusty, bedraggled, excited, aching and bewildered the new arrivals milled about like the lost and the damned, most of them without a place to lay their heads that night.

Immediately in front of him Mr. Featherstonhaugh found a clamoring circle of humanity pressing around a short heavy-set gentleman, the "man in brown" himself, topped off with a tall brown greasy beaver which he wore tilted at such an angle that the wonder was it stayed on at all. The clamorers were obviously suing for the stocky one's favor. They argued and expostulated. They tried to impress him with their importance, their distress, the desperate state of their health, but the gentleman under the dirty beaver did not look impressed. He only looked as if he wished the lot of them to hell. Just now he stood with arms akimbo and his round pugnacious face was annoyed.

Still ahead of his coachmates, the Britisher elbowed his way through the levee around the man in brown and demanded where he might see Mr. Anderson. The man in brown turned a look of insolent indifference on the Fellow of the Royal Society.

"I reckon I am Mr. Anderson," he said.

So it was that Mr. Featherstonhaugh made the acquaintance of Major Baylis Anderson, unquestionably in those days the most important personage in the South. The most important, that is to say, while the Springs season was on, which was during July and August and part of September. From Baltimore down to New Orleans, from St. Louis to St. Augustine there was not another man so courted and so vilified, so autocratic and insolent, so talked about and written about, so burdened and so chivvied and withal so little appreciated as Major Anderson.

"You behold him," said one of the Richmond ladies, "upon whose breath the fate of hundreds, nay, it has been said thousands depends, the Minister Plenipotentiary and Envoy Extraordinary of the Calwells. To him Senators bow, legislators, judges, professors are supplicants, flattered beaux and flattering belles sue for his high permission, without which all is lost." Harry Humbug called him "the little Grand Vizier." It was the fashion to speak of him as Metternich of the mountains or simply as Metternich. "There is a sort of major domo here," related Captain Marryat, "who regulates every department: his word is law, and his fiat immovable, and he presumes not a little upon his power; a circumstance not to be surprised at, as he is as much courted and is as despotic as all the lady patronesses of Almacks rolled into one. He is called the Metternich of the mountains."

At the moment what the Major was trying to do was to get these people to go away. There wasn't any room for them here, the place was packed to the gates. There wasn't a bed or a mattress or a blanket or a bench or a row of three chairs that did not have its nightly occupant. It didn't matter how important they were or how sick, that was the situation. Let them go to the boarding houses within a mile or two of the Springs. Let them go on to Lewisburg, nine miles west, or to the Blue Sulphur Springs, twenty-two miles west, where there was always plenty of room. There they could wait their turn and he would accommodate them when he could. The certain thing now was, they would have to get on away out of here.

Mr. Featherstonhaugh introduced himself to the Major. He was, he said, George W. Featherstonhaugh of London, geologist, and he was now on a commission for the United States Government to report on geological deposits in the Mississippi Valley and he was looking for a place to leave his invalid wife while he went into Tennessee. He had been "induced" to come here, he said, by assurances that Major Anderson would procure lodgings for himself, his wife and his grown son yonder in the stagecoach. He had a friend who had great influence with the proprietor, Mr. Calwell, a friend who came here "in his own carriage," and he had every reason to suppose that his friend had made the necessary arrangements and that his lodgings were waiting.

"Look ye, Mister," said Major Anderson with some asperity, "I haven't got room for a cat, to say nothing of your family."

By the time mid-August came around the Major had reason to be fretful. Hour after hour and day after day and week after week all summer he had this business to go through, listening to people trying to wedge themselves in because they were important or had influential friends. He had reason to know what real importance was. Just now he had as his guests two United States Senators, one of whom was Henry Clay; various members of the House, one of whom was George McDuffie; three Commodores of the Navy, one of whom was Biddle; three Judges of the Virginia Court of Appeals, one of whom was Cabell; and the American consul to London, Colonel Aspinwall. He knew the real thing from bluff, and bluff got to be very annoying.

It wasn't only the clamor at the gate that wore him down. To that was added the constant drubbing he got inside: people demanding to be moved at once and vociferating the charge of "fleas," people who couldn't stand being so near the kitchen, people who had to be turned out of the best cottages when the Southerners who owned them swept through the gates in their huge creaking coaches and claimed their abodes. The dispossessed who had to exchange Paradise Row for Flea Row set upon him like furies.

Not three days before, he had been compelled to move a family into one of the unfinished cabins of Virginia Row. It was still in process of construction, had only half a roof. When a mountain downpour hit the Springs the unfortunates were washed out. The young lady of the family took the revenge of the witty. She nicknamed the new row Compulsion Row and now everyone was calling it Compulsion Row and giving it a bad reputation.

Ladies and gentlemen harried him for leaving their baggage out under the trees all night. What was he to do? He had no room for either the ladies, the gentlemen or the baggage. The coachmen chucked it under the tree, not he. And the people who were "doing quarantine" in the neighborhood, as the phrase was then, came back and hounded him all day long for rooms, sitting on the porch in front of the dining room like birds of ill omen, taxing him with favoritism, reproaching him for taking in the planter families with private coaches and six horses before he accommodated the poor wights who had come with the public stage. As though it was any of their business how many private carriages he admitted or why. Truly in the great and crowded month of August there was almost more to contend with than a man could bear.

Mr. Featherstonhaugh felt as though he had been slapped. "Not room for a cat, to say nothing of your family." Could there possibly have been a more insolent way of putting it? He had still another shock when he turned around and saw the stage driver removing his luggage from the boot and ordering his family out of the coach. The Fellow of the Geographical Society considered that these Americans were singling him out for especially bad treatment.

"Here, then, we were without friends or lodgings or sympathy from anyone." After all, it had done no good leaping out of the coach ahead of everyone else. Others were there before him anyhow. That crowd pressing around the Major had been discharged at him from another stagecoach that had pulled in just ahead of Featherstonhaugh's. The fellow who had lept out of *that* coach first of all hadn't got anywhere either.

It was no use looking for comfort to the Springs folk who had gathered to see the arrivals. They had all gone through this themselves, and if they did have any room to spare, if they knew of a cot or a trundle bed, they were guarding it jealously for a friend. They must have looked with cheerful indifference upon the humiliation of the gentleman from London, for he was quick to sense their lack of feeling. He formed a low opinion of them. Most of them, he said, were "dirty, spitting, smoking, queer looking creatures." For the new arrivals, too, as well as for Major Anderson, the tribulations of the month of August were almost more than a man could bear.

Suffering quarantine in the neighborhood was no better than it sounded. Each day coachful after coachful either started in with this course of purgatory or gave it up altogether and went away to some other Springs. The *Southern Literary Messenger* reported that in this same summer "almost every house for miles on the roads leading to the springs was thronged with persons who had been turned off at the hotel." Featherstonhaugh and his family took quarters at the house of a blacksmith turned tavern keeper, and from this base of operations he laid siege to Major Anderson, persistently and with mounting British choler, for five days.

After the fifth attack (on which occasion the gentleman from London threatened the Major with physical violence) the Featherstonhaughs found themselves in possession of a cottage in Alabama Row. It was a one-room cottage. As Featherstonhaugh calculated, it was "about 12 feet long."

Actually it was 14 feet long and 11 feet wide. There were two doors, one in front and one in back, and there were two low bedsteads. It had been built and furnished not for fastidious foreigners but for the devil-may-care bachelors. Immediately he was admitted to the company of the blessed in this earthly paradise, the Fellow of the Royal Society was faced with a new and critical problem. The problem was, how to get any sleep on a rough plank bed that humped up in the middle like a camel, and with a pillow full of hard mysterious knots?

✿

The little village of the White Sulphur, gleaming with white paint and red brick, was nestled in an upland cradle of the mountains, a long shallow cradle, a swag in the earth. The two sides rose gently from a central spread of lawn and the upper end rose likewise gently to a hill. The lower end of the cradle was knocked out. This open end faced westward and was guarded on either side by two shoulders of earth where the high sides dropped off abruptly. Midway between these shoulders and down on the green stood a circular temple, twelve stout columns supporting a domed roof. The roof was painted a dull red. This temple might have been expected at Marathon or in the Roman Campagna but it was startling to find it here, so white against the dark green American forest.

It was, as it would have been in Hellas, a symbol of great faith on the part of the communicants, of great power on the part of the deity. The goddess that these people worshipped was Hygeia, daughter of Aesculapius, high priestess of healing. This was her temple and coming out of the earth directly under the dome was her medicine, welling up in a reservoir several feet deep, the extraordinarily clear water of the White Sulphur Spring itself. The whole miniature valley, the cradle of earth and the trees and the little houses therein tipped gently and reverently toward this spot.

The resort was roughly in the form of a hollow square, rows of cottages ranged along both sides and joined at right angles another row that connected them, thrown across the little vale half way to its head. Even now the carpenters were busy extending the sides of the square with new cottages. Shortly it would be a square no longer but an oblong. Count Arese, Louis Napoleon's Italian friend, was to find this arrangement and its irregularities quite charming. Featherstonhaugh thought it had the look of a "permanent Methodist camp meeting."

Moving about through this little village were perhaps four hundred people, swarming in and out of the cabins, over to the dining room on the turnpike side, down to the spring below, up to the ballroom, a separate two-story building with a double-decker porch. The flood and ebb tides of this movement were fairly regular, since the worshippers of Hygeia enjoyed doing the same things at the same hours. They moved through the day's glad ritual together and one day was much like another: the same three mass attacks on the springhouse and on the dining room, the same plantation lull every afternoon ("evening" in their language), the same leisurely promenade after siesta, the same drift to the ballroom after a supper which was usually called "tea."

Into the action of this forest opera the Featherstonhaugh

family was at last admitted. Their cottage was No. 29 Alabama Row, directly overlooking the springhouse, but No.
29 did not detain them long. Mrs. F.'s bed was not so bad
but Mr. F.'s was hopeless, even with the help of all the spare
articles in his wardrobe. Besides, one of his neighbors, an
old friend of the quarantine days, reported that he had found
in his pillow the heads of two chickens and one duck. Mr.
F. did not wait to look into the lumps of his own pillow but
hastened over to the receiving rooms and executed a rear
attack on the Major. It resulted in their being moved to No.
31 Alabama Row.

No. 31 did not suit because the steps were too high, so
the Major (by now the desperate one) hastily shunted them
once more, up to No. 3 Compulsion Row. The carpenters
were still pounding there but it was new, it had a porch, it
smelled fresh, and it had two rooms. If it was not, in its unfinished state, the habitation of the elect, it was at least the
abode of those cast out of Paradise and Carolina Rows to
make way for the elect. That alone gave it distinction. The
Featherstonhaughs would now be out of the public stagecoach crowd and in the private carriage crowd, those ladies
and gentlemen of the South who brought their own slaves
to wait on them, who had their own cottages, who never
seemed to worry about money, and who travelled in the
grand manner.

Genteel was the siren word. But for the fact that gentility
was generally supposed to frequent the White Sulphur in
greater quantity than any other Springs, the Featherstonhaughs and the Marryats and the Martineaus and the Buck-
inghams and the Areses would not have suffered their hu-
miliations and discomforts in order to touch the hem of its

garment. Such phrases as "this model of a courtly company," "first society," "gay and finished aggregate," "Almack's of the South" had blown far and wide like milkweed seed. A gentleman who called himself Harry Humbug put the case precisely. "All who visit the mineral region are bound by a law more absolute than that of gravitation to wend to this favorite spot. It is the great magnet which alike attracts the valetudinarian and the votary of fashion. It is the Almack's of watering places."

To see how the planter nabobs and their ladies dressed and ate, took the cure, played their whist, gambled at faro bank, consumed juleps and sangaree and gum ticklers, chewed tobacco and smoked segars, flirted, courted and arranged a marriage (for this was the marriage market of the South), all this was considered worth a little purgatory.

The new cottage was a double one, two rooms to a side. Across the front there was a common piazza; inside, the main partition had been left unfinished and above it the whole building was open to the rafters, a state of affairs that promoted a certain intimacy between the Featherstonhaughs and their neighbors. The first tenants on the other side of the partition were two tract society gentlemen. The world was utterly depraved, everybody in it would be damned; but they themselves were pure and would be saved. They vented their spite on their wicked fellow man through the afternoon, through the evening, and began again early next morning. They hawked and they spat. The language they produced in praise of Sunday schools and temperance societies was vulgar and ignorant. They were missionaries and what they were doing in Compulsion Row was a mystery.

The "canting jackasses" were exchanged the next day for

three stalwarts of the South, one from Virginia, one from Kentucky and one from Louisiana. They were Democrats and strong State Rights men. The first thing they were State Rights about was bacon. The Virginian declared there was no bacon in the whole world like Virginia bacon. The Kentuckian allowed Virginia bacon might be tolerable but it wasn't to be compared, not for the beginning of a thing, to Kentucky bacon. Kentucky land was a sight finer than Virginia land; it raised better corn and, naturally, better corn made better hawgs. Whereupon the Virginian shifted ground. Anyhow, said he, Virginia had more real luxuries than Kentucky or any other State, yes sir, more than any other place in Christendom. Did Kentucky have oysters, for instance, or clams? No, sir, she did not. And as for land, what about Southampton County? Why, there wasn't any finer land in the whole world than in Southampton County. At which point the Louisianian roused himself. Fine land in Southampton County, was there? Well, sir, what about sugar, could they grow sugar in Southampton County? And as for oysters, had the Virginian ever tasted a New Orleans oyster? Why, the New Orleans oyster could knock the Virginia oyster into its ninety-ninth year any day.

"I reckon they get that from the yellow fever," said the Virginian.

The Featherstonhaughs were surprised. The society of Compulsion Row was not at all what they expected.

❦

Another visitor without friends at court was the stout party who chose to conceal his identity under the *nom de plume* of Harry Humbug, and like Featherstonhaugh he had made up his mind to see this circus of gentility if it killed him. It was twilight the evening he arrived with his large portmanteau and a lurking idea that his experiences here might be worth setting down for the edification of the readers of the *Southern Literary Messenger,* which they were. Tea was over, there was nothing to eat, but he got in and that was nourishment for his spirit at least.

"To me the stars were propitious," he wrote when the time came for putting it to paper, "and when the little Grand Vizier tipt me the nod of assent, I was elated. I followed the guide to my dormitory with as light a heart and as elastic a step as if I had been appointed an ambassador." His dormitory turned out to be one of the chambers over the ballroom and he swore it was not more than eight feet wide. There were two cots, one on either side of the door, and there were two chairs, one washstand and "a fractured mirror about the size of the Jack of Spades." That was all. It was nightfall and he retired early, hoping for better things in the morning.

He was awakened out of a sound sleep by a noise directly beneath him which he took to be the shrieks of the Bacchae. It was in fact the music of the band; eight-thirty had struck and the regular evening ball was under way. In no mood to appreciate good music, Humbug proclaimed it just so much "clamor and screeching." But it was all over down there by ten-thirty and he got to sleep again, only to be wakened at midnight by the arrival of the saturnine stranger who was his roommate. He thought his initiation into the Springs life was unusually difficult.

The morning was damp and cold, a chill fog seeped

through the cracks. There were no fireplaces in the rooms over the ballroom, and the servants always told the gentlemen that they would find a fire on Mr. Plum's hearth, Mr. Plum being the Englishman who kept the bar at that time. So Humbug trundled his great weight to this refuge of the low-in-spirit under the dining room, at the lower corner toward the springhouse where the ground dropped off, which would put the bar in the "basement story." All the bars at all the Springs were in basement stories.

Sure enough, Plum had a fire. The difficulty was to get near it, for the room was packed with such close knots of drinking and disputatious gentlemen that a man of Humbug's girth could make but little headway. As he tried to wedge through, he heard on his right a grandiloquent oration on the recent discoveries in the moon. On his left there was a loud denunciation of abolitionists, with some particular maledictions laid upon two chaps named Tappan and Thompson. If they would only come to the White Sulphur, what a trouncing they would get!

Since the fog was thick outside, the popular drink inside was an anti-fogmatic, and an anti-fogmatic was a drink of any straight unadulterated liquor. It was stimulating to political discussion, and just ahead of him our friend Humbug heard the very worst about the then Secretary of State, Mr. Van Buren of New York. Making a trifle of progress he came upon some of the tenants of Fly Row (just below the kitchens), eaten alive by fleas and abusing the proprietor, old man Calwell, and his dark angel at the gate.

Having got within hailing distance of Mr. Plum's "cabinet," Humbug discovered a group that was above political discussion, above abolitionists and above fleas. These gentlemen were applying themselves to lowering the contents of a bowl of mint julep. On such a morning they could make proper headway. But Humbug could not get near the fire. The way was blocked by men of experience who knew better than he the dangers of a foggy morning in the mountains and got down to their drinking early.

Outside, Humbug saw multitudes hastening to the spring. It was the noontime drinking hour, known as the fashionable lounge, when the circular area in the temple was crowded with the beau monde and when a serious invalid had a time of it to get hold of the common dipper. It was the second of three daily levees under the dome; the first was between six and seven in the morning and the last at the same hours in the evening. The midday meeting was the most popular and, in the opinion of one gentleman from New England, it had been taken over by frivolous drinkers who came "merely to gratify a truant disposition."

"Down I went," said Humbug, "and whilst the throng which preceded me were eagerly quaffing the delicious beverage I had leisure to survey their countenances. Upon the pallid cheeks of some wasting consumption had fixed her fatal seal. Others bore the jaundiced marks of obstructed bile. A few were hobbling victims of hereditary or acquired gout. By far the greater proportion, however, had the ruddy complexions and smiling countenances of health." As for the water, it convulsed him in agony, a bitter draught of brimstone and bad eggs. They said one got used to it, even learned to crave it. Mr. Humbug shuddered with nausea.

Featherstonhaugh was there, too, his eye peeled for the worst that America, even America of fashion, might have to offer. He saw invalids "with emaciated sallow faces, made ghastly with fever and ague." He saw people who were indifferently dressed, people who smoked and spat and people who chewed and spat, and it delighted him not.

The large bell high on its pole over by the dining room rang an hour before each meal, saying, "Prepare, drink of the appetizing water, gird up your loins for the battle that cometh." Before the hour was out the dining room piazza was packed with a mob feverish with hunger. From the excitement it looked to Featherstonhaugh "as if some extraordinary exhibition was to be presented." They were famished, for the effect of the water was to produce a violent craving for food and the more water they drank the more ravenous they became. Inside, a little bell gave the signal, waiters opened the three doors and humanity poured through them as water through a dynamited dam.

"Body of Bacchus! what a furious set-on there was," said Humbug. Pushed and torn in this avalanche were the invalids and the fashionables, the Virginians and the Creoles, Senators and gamblers, slave drivers and naval officers, planters with their wives and daughters, women both pure and beautiful who had come to the Springs for the pleasure it would give them. Some of them, knowing what it was to be wrenched from their escorts and have their toilettes knocked askew, advised their sisters to take breakfast at least in their cabins.

"If you venture to the dining room," warned one of them, "—what a rush! —what a press! —woe to sleeves, destruction to tournures!"

There were a few who brought up the rear at their leisure, little noticed in the confusion. Either they were the planter-patrons who had their private tables or they were habitués who knew that the stampede was unnecessary. The place-card system had lately been introduced, everyone's name card was at his plate, each guest could be certain of a seat on the long benches and the old days when there were no cards and there was good reason to rush were gone forever. But the multitude made a scramble of it just the same. Hunger and the habit of years were too strong.

It was a large room for those days, one hundred and twenty feet long by about forty wide. It was a prodigiously low room, too, so that the clatter and the crying after the waiters and the odors of the food rose hardly at all into the air before they rebounded from the low ceiling onto the heads of all present. The clamor was deafening.

"Who can describe the noise, the confusion incident to a grand bolting operation conducted by three hundred Americans," asked the amazed Featherstonhaugh? "It seemed to me that almost every man at table considered himself at job work against time, stuffing sausages and whatever else he could cram into his throat. What with the clinking of knives and forks, the rattling of plates, the confused running about of troops of dirty slaves, the nasty appearance of the incomprehensible dishes, the scene was perfectly astounding. Twice I tried to dine there but it was impossible. I could do nothing but stare, and before my wonder was over everything was gone, people and all, except a few slow eaters." One had to be nimble. It was all over in fifteen minutes.

Seated at the end of one of the least desirable tables (the newcomers started at the foot and worked up) was Humbug, foodless still halfway through the meal, looking about him in consternation. "At length I ventured to ask one waiter for a hot cup of coffee—of another I civilly requested a chop—and a third I respectfully solicited to hand me a roll. I might as well have addressed my language to the door post. The menials rushed by me like the whirlwind.

"I addressed myself to a juvenile looking man who was sitting not far to my right. I perceived that by a good understanding with the members of the Kitchen Cabinet he had gathered around him as many tid-bits as would have feasted a London Alderman.

" 'Pray, sir,' said I, 'will you be so kind as to help me to one of those extra dishes in your vicinity?' The youngster looked at me in perfect amazement. It seems that every mother's son of them [the waiters] had been bribed to wait on particular gentlemen."

Humbug had brought smack up against the tipping system of the White Sulphur, as everybody must who ventured there. It was like leaning their tender breasts against a row of pikes. Everybody hated and reviled it, everybody cried out against it, everybody bled because of it. No good came of complaining to Mr. Calwell for he was the one who allowed it to flourish. In a slave-holding community such a malignant growth was incredible, nobody could ever understand it.

"Bribe high and you live high; fail to bribe and you starve." Out of wisdom and experience spoke J. H. B. Latrobe. "If you have a servant of your own he must bribe the cook. If you have no servant, you must bribe one of those attached to the place. Bribery furnishes you with the best and avoids the rush," a truth which Harry Humbug sat pondering in the midst of plenty, where we shall leave the disconsolate gentleman. If he waits long enough he will be

The "Tavern," White Sulphur Springs

In the dusty arena before the dining room the weary travellers arrived and the refreshed departed. Barroom was in the basement, cemetery on the hill beyond.

From a water color after the original by J. H. B. Latrobe

fed, after the tippers have been satisfied with the first cuts.

The bar, the springhouse, the dining room,—three out of five rings in the genteel circus. The fourth was the ball-room, the most popular and certainly the most glamorous with its three crystal chandeliers and hundreds of sperma-ceti candles around the walls to play their light on the jew-els in the ladies' hair and the pearls about their throats, on the gold embroidered muslin and the silken dresses with ballooning sleeves. Of all the scenes this one alone drew from Mr. Featherstonhaugh an exclamation of pleasure. Here and here alone cleanliness and decorum prevailed, here the refreshments were neat and tasty and what was more they were *gratis;* the music was good, the best he had heard at an American watering place, and the atmosphere was positively thick with *ton.* As he explained, "The genteel families who have their private cottages always attend." In the ballroom at last he found the leaven of gentility work-ing to the surface.

But he found also the gamblers, the gentlemen of the fifth ring. Several of them were prowling near the wall, slipping an oily word of invitation to the young bucks, "And what about a little go at faro bank after the ball, sir? Always at your service, sir." And to his amazement the chief of the tribe had the effrontery to dance with a very nice young lady, having represented himself as Colonel Smith of the British Army and a veteran of Waterloo, an imposture which Mr. Featherstonhaugh himself had the pleasure of exposing.

These gamblers had their special dwellings, the pair of well-known cottages standing alone to the right of the springhouse and surrounded by a picket fence so no one could make a mistake. There in the doorway these gentlemen with too much weight of watch chain across their dirty velvet waistcoats might be seen lounging during the day and at night in a rearward den they called the cards at faro bank. Thus, said our friend from England, "every direct encouragement was given to vice, and inducements held out to the vilest fellows in the country to flock to the place for the express purpose of preying upon the company."

After two weeks the Featherstonhaughs left the White Sulphur and set their faces toward the Sweet Springs, seventeen miles south. They had made their trial of the Queen of the Springs and its five show rings and they decided to go for respite to the Sweet where the company was quieter and reputed to be more select. They fixed the morning of August 27 for their departure. Two days previous to this the head of the family reserved three places in the early coach, not only reserved them but paid for them. It was a necessary precaution, he was advised, for at this season the stage to the Sweet was always full.

Every day there were people who had taken the same good advice and paid ahead for their places in the stage and stood waiting at five o'clock of a cold misty morning, out by the roadside in front of the receiving room. The long porch was empty; the place was still asleep except for a few reluctant slaves. The moisture, sifted out of the fog by the trees, dripped from the leaves and made a dark crust on yesterday's dust. With only their reserved places to comfort them they waited under the trees beside their luggage, a little aloof from the derelict trunks that Major Anderson left out over night. And every morning some of them found out that it was all a chimera, that you could no more insure yourself against the uncertainties of departure than you could against the uncertainties of arrival.

The heavy coach that appeared around the bend and pulled up before the Featherstonhaughs with a four-horse rattle and clatter was, as usual, packed. It already had its full complement of nine, three passengers on each of the three seats. Mr. Featherstonhaugh opened the door and a general growl informed him that he wasn't wanted, there was no place for another. But, he insisted, he had reserved his places and he meant to have them. The driver shrugged his shoulders. They could ride on top. Featherstonhaugh was amazed at the fellow. A lady and an invalid ride on top! God in heaven, what a country! Getting into this place had been bad enough; was it to be as difficult getting out?

They had reckoned without their man. He looked more narrowly into the coach and in a far corner espied a mulatto-looking fellow. To him he appealed. Would he not give up his place for an invalid lady? No, the mulatto-looking fellow would not. "Upon which I called my son and told the fellow that if he did not without further delay evacuate the premises we would drag him out neck and heels." Fearing for his life, the mulatto got out and climbed up with the driver; Mrs. Featherstonhaugh got in; Mr. Featherstonhaugh rode on top with his victim and shivered in his light dimity roundabout jacket. Featherstonhaugh *fils* was obliged to walk the seventeen miles to the Sweet Springs. So much for the precaution of reserved places, paid for in advance.

The visitor from England had caught only one glimpse of gentle behavior, one scene of polite intercourse at the Springs which was called, in his time and by various persons, the Grand Emporium of Fashion; the Seat of Learning, Literature and the Fine Arts; the Athens and Paris of America; the Paradise of Enjoyment; the Great Lion of the Virginia mountains. What stumped him was, if the people who frequented the place were really the *élite* of the South and if the luxury of their homes was true to report and not just fable; if they actually moved through life with a slave at each elbow, slaves to bring them cooling drinks and keep the fly fans moving, slaves to cook their succulent meals and bring their boots and nurse their babies and smooth their pillows, how in the name of heaven did they put up with the White Sulphur?

How could they endure the crowding, the unspeakable food, the dirty table cloths, the corrupt servants, the gamblers, the shocking invalids, the stinking bar room and Major Baylis Anderson? In his own words, these waters were annually resorted to by many of the most distinguished persons of Virginia. Annually, season after season. It defeated him. It must appear incredible, he said, to others besides himself.

But the Southerner was better able to take his waters and his pleasures without flinching. Unlike many an alien such as Featherstonhaugh, he looked upon the Springs as terrain only slightly removed from heaven, in time even the White Sulphur where the going was often the hardest, and for this attitude he had his own good reasons, which shall appear in due course.

II

Taking the Springs Tour

BY THE 1830's, after more than half a century of trial and error, the Southerner had evolved his method of taking the waters: he took them in quantity and he took them seriatim. That is, he made the Springs Tour, visiting as many resorts in a season as time and money would allow. The phrase at home in the lowlands was, he was going "up to the Springs," always in the plural. He might own a cottage at the White Sulphur and expect to put in most of his time there, but he went to "the Springs" just the same; it was taken for granted that before he returned to the lowlands again he would sample the water and the company at anywhere from three to half a dozen other places, a few days here and a week there, if water and company agreed with him.

The region of the Virginia Springs straddled the continental divide, sprawling through the long valleys and over the equally long ridges of the Alleghenies. Anyone beginning at the Warm Springs, which was the northeasterly point of the region, and drawing a line around the principal watering places would have traced a lop-sided, diamond-shaped kite, a long kite pointing northeast and southwest, with Warm Springs at the top and Gray Sulphur Springs at the bottom. The central axis running between them would be about seventy-five miles long and the transverse axis, running cross country from east to west between Rockbridge Alum on the east and Blue Sulphur on the west, would be approximately the same.

Outside the lines of this region there were numerous other Springs, some large and some small but most of them not destined to come into prominence until the Fifties. Now, in the Thirties, the shadow of the kite covered all that were of importance. Down through the center lay the inner group, the fountains most strongly impregnated with minerals, heat, fashion and fame—the Warm, the Hot, the White Sulphur, the Sweet, the Salt Sulphur and the Red Sulphur. For the most part they were connected by good turnpike roads, and in order to make the circuit of the lot one had to cut back and forth across the mountains, up out of one valley and down into another, travelling in all about a hundred and seventy miles.

Almost everybody went in at the Warm Springs and came out the same way. That was natural. The first turnpike that pierced the region was laid over the top of the Warm Springs Mountain, dipping swiftly down and skirting the edge of the wondrous bubbling pool as it ran westward. That is the way the Virginians first came with their Colonial spleens out of whack and their early-Republic joints creaking; thereafter everybody from the direction of Tidewater followed in the same tracks.

Standing on his high-pillared portico, Colonel John Fry, the happy landlord of the Warm, could see each stagecoach as it appeared in the gap of the mountain up on the sky line. It stopped there to rest the horses, pay toll at the gate, and let the passengers get the view. Then it tipped its weight toward the valley and with one wheel chain-locked raced down that dizzy, zig-zag mile until it pulled up at Colonel Fry's feet, every passenger dithering from fright.

The popular thing was, to alight at the Warm and then be off again with all possible speed. That would mean overnight and not more than over two nights. When we consider that Colonel Fry's hospitality was among the best at the Springs and that it was by all odds the most amusing, it seems a grateless thing for people to have flown from it as they were accustomed to fly from the cholera.

Their overnight stay was just long enough to see the Colonel cut his pigeonwing in the ballroom and to make a visit to Charley, the colored bartender, in the basement story, where the wine was cooled in a spring and stag horns bristled from the walls. It was just time to sink like a sigh into the soft warm liquid of the pool, just time to inquire what was the news from the White and to get it. It was always bad. The White was jammed, the crowding was disgraceful, the food was worse than last year, Major Anderson had grown more supercilious, people were sleeping two on a cot, there were not enough blankets and unless someone died or was murdered not another soul could get in. This long familiar story put them in a fever to get there with as little delay as possible. If there was a seat to be had in one of the morning coaches, they were away early. If there were no seats they hired a hack.

Colonel Fry was the kind of landlord who could see them spurning the delights that he and the Almighty had prepared for them and make a jest of it. He was on hand betimes to help them into the coach or hack and he sent them off with a joke, his own precious, perennial joke. Go, said he, and get well charged at the White Sulphur, well salted at the Salt, well sweetened at the Sweet, well boiled at the Hot and then let them return to him and he would Fry them. They would return, he knew, at least many of them would. A final stay at the Warm was the last move in the game they were at with the waters. "Here ends the course of the springs," noted Wheaton Bradish in his journal. But that was weeks or possibly months away. What concerned them now was to get off, to fly from this heavenly place and its host's delicious food.

If that brief landing at the Warm could be called a stop, then the White Sulphur was the second on the Springs Tour. The belles and beaux naturally presumed that fashion had laid out this course, but fashion originally had nothing to do with it; the fashionables were merely following on in the path beaten down long since by the invalids. When the doctors and the chemical analysts got around to charting the cure on scientific lines, they readily came to the conclusion that the invalids had by happy accident stumbled on a design of Nature's.

Nature herself had arranged the springs in order for their best action on the human system, and it was Nature's inscrutable purpose that the bowels of the ailing should have the White Sulphur purge first of all. These were the preparatory waters which so readjusted the component parts of the interior machinery, so sensitized and altered them ("altered" was the magic word) that the other springs could then get in their specialized whacks with incredible efficiency. The doctors, perceiving this, sensibly fell in with Nature's plan.

You should begin at the White Sulphur, said Dr. Horner, and stay there at least a fortnight, drinking. Dr. Huntt came to the same conclusion from experiments on himself, that being the exploratory method of hundreds of medicos in that day. Dr. Huntt tried starting at the Red Sulphur but, as he soon discovered and broadcast to the world in a pamphlet, he had started at the right end for phthisis but at the wrong end for dyspepsia. So he repaired quickly to the White Sulphur and subsequently had recourse to those waters for several years with startling results. He became marvelously improved, he testified, though as it turned out his colleagues were soon thereafter referring to him as "the late Dr. Huntt."

"That most valuable of all our watering places, the White Sulphur," said Dr. Burke, and it was most handsome of him too, considering that he was proprietor at the Red Sulphur. Peregrine Prolix, a Philadelphian, reported that it was the generally esteemed practice to prepare at the White, not alone for other stomachic waters but even for the baths at the Hot. "When the complaints are such as to require the powerful action of the bath at the Hot Springs, it is extremely beneficial, first, to drink the White Sulphur water three or four weeks, to improve the condition of the stomach." Nature was an all-wise physician and they were learning to take her bitter draughts in the order she meant them to be taken.

After the White there was no hard and fast rule; which

Springs came next depended on many things and not the least of these was what the White Sulphur water had done to the working parts. The patient might now need the Sweet for the "tonic" which rehabilitated the over-purged, or he might need the Salt for its Glauber salt or its iodine. Dr. Horner, continuing his prescription, routed them first to the Salt, then on to the Red Sulphur, seventeen miles, then doubled them back through the Salt to the Sweet, recommending a week at each. By that time the animal economy, what was left of it, would be ready for the bathing at the Hot and Warm, thermal springs which Nature had so conveniently placed near the main exit from the region, just when one had done enough drinking and stood in need of a little steaming.

That was the tour that any invalid followed who wished to do a good job on himself. When it was all over he would have consumed six weeks and about twenty-six gallons of variegated mineral waters.

The beaux and the belles and the papas and mammas who rated as hearty, and all those whose anxiety lay not so much in their livers as in their wardrobe trunks and their hearts, when they took up the whirligig set going by the invalids followed no fixed course after the White either, but they kept going. Generally speaking, the turnpike over to the Sweet was the most crowded. There was an immutable law that required everybody in the fashion to converge on the Sweet for the last week in August and the first week in September, from whatever direction, whether from the White or the Salt or the Hot. There, after the unspeakable hilarity of crowding together for another fortnight, they separated, some striking straight South to Tennessee and the Carolinas, some going back east the Fincastle way, but most of them returning to the Warm for a last lingering farewell.

Mr. Featherstonhaugh, the geologist from England, had come crashing into the Virginia scene when the South, having found that Spring-going was a pastime agreeable to both its talents and its innards, was very busy enjoying it. The fact was, it was just now busier than it had ever been before. By the hundreds daily people were pouring through the mountain gaps into these long narrow valleys. Gigs and chaises, coaches, coachees and carioles, Berlins and an occasional calash, hacks and barouches and light Dearborn wagons with the baggage, some of them bright and new but most of them with a resurrected look, toiled up into this high promised land and then careered around from one healing water to another.

So many private carriages rolled into the White Sulphur that there was not enough space for them in the barns and they stood around everywhere under the trees. The guests complained that this was too much; after all, trees were not coach houses. That, somehow, was the kind of disorder that offended them.

Public stage lines were adding coaches and new routes; more "extras" were appearing from Charlottesville, even from as far east as Winchester; an extra cost double the fare of a regular coach. And the slaves in Staunton began hiring their masters' ancient hacks, leaky and loose in the joints, to such as had been too badly bruised in the cannon-balls, as the fast stages were called, or who, while recuperating, had been left in the lurch.

Not everybody when the tour had been completed went

out by way of the Warm. Those who were returning to the Deep South by steamboat departed in the opposite direction, westward toward the Ohio River, along with the Kentuckians. The Carolinians struck south from the Salt or the Red Sulphur or the Gray Sulphur, and the emigrant trains bound for Tennessee stood aside as the elegant coaches rolled heavily by. "Carolinians returning from the Springs!" said the pioneers to one another. It had a royal sound.

But most of the Springs folk wouldn't have missed the last days of parting at the Warm for anything. Colonel Fry awaited them, now that they had been charged, salted, sweetened and boiled at the other places; it was not in their hearts to disappoint him. The great scales on his portico awaited them too, those fine old scales with the seat under the beam where they had sat to weigh going in; now they must weigh going out and count the extra pounds.

During the final sad-happy week they exchanged their souvenirs and their mutual invitations for long visits; they gave each other sprigs of arbor-vitae, symbols of eternal friendship; they counted over the summer's gossip gathered from place to place and they soaked the accumulated minerals out of themselves in the delicious pool. For the last time that season they looked upon Colonel Fry and his fat wife and his fine ham and mutton and iced milk, and for the last time Charley mixed them an incomparable brandy julep downstairs. Then one September morning early Fry would help to boost them into their coaches and they would be off, toiling slowly up the steep road to the toll gate on the sky line. Until another year the Springs Tour was behind them.

III

Spa Manners: An Early Start

ACTUALLY, the South had cut its Spring-going teeth long before the 1830's, using for this purpose a spate of water larger than the crown of a hat in eastern Virginia. It was called Warm Spring, later Bath, and was a well-known refuge for rheumatics even in Colonial days. George Washington himself took to these waters with a case of rheumatic fever, at the age of twenty-nine, though he had visited them eleven years earlier as a young surveyor.

In those days there was no Springs Tour, since there was only one Spring, but there was an evolution of spa manners at Bath, of styles and customs and habits at a time when the western Springs were still in the discovery stage and the occasional hunter out there was prevented from bathing by the fear that a lurking Indian would catch him with his breeches off. Manners, like the mahogany and china and rugs and carriages, were imported, spa manners in particular, and although the pool at Bath was behind a pine stockade and the visitants lived primitively in log huts or tents, their code and their pleasures they fashioned as nearly as possible on the lines of those at Bath, England. They had only to close their eyes to imagine they were in the pump room there, listening to the polite insults of Beau Nash.

The imitation began with the name, obviously. Plain Warm Spring, also Frederick Spring, had satisfied the beginners there; it was the august Assembly of Virginia that hit upon Bath when in 1775 it provided for the laying out of a town around the spring, which had been given by Lord Fairfax. The Assembly had lots to sell at about twenty-five guineas each and to prospective customers "Bath" would mean a great many things that "Warm" and "Frederick" did not mean: swarms of fine ladies and gentlemen, adventurers, ceremonious assemblies, the theatre, plated carriages, card games, steaming hot baths and God only knew what scandals and intrigues. It was surprising how many of these visions came true in Bath Americanus. All of them, in fact, but the steaming hot baths.

A wanderer in that deep little valley during the Revolutionary summer of 1779 might have heard a female voice singing Italian songs. That would have been in the mornings when the Baroness de Riedesel gave her matinees, relieving the tedium of internment for herself and her Hessian husband. The Baroness was charming, quite plump, very handsome, they said; the Baron was a prisoner of war, paroled to Bath for the cure; he had sun stroke. They met some of General Washington's kin at the Springs, but the person they enjoyed most of all was Mrs. Carroll (of Carrollton), whom the Baroness called Mrs. Garel: "Mrs. Garel, a very lovable woman, an ardent American patriot—but reasonable."

They made a friendly group, the patriots, the wives of patriots and the Hessian prisoners. Mrs. Carroll spent most of her forenoons with the German family, and the Baroness trilled Italian arias. Captain Geismar, another interned prisoner, had brought his violin to the wars and the Captain obliged with accompaniments and solos. In its very infancy Bath was enjoying a fine dose of European culture.

Next came the theatre. Bath, England, had a theatre and a resident company of actors, playing smart and sophisticated comedies as well, or nearly as well, as they were played in London. Ergo, Bath Americanus should have a theatre, and it had. The announcement appeared in the *Maryland Gazette* just the year after the Peace of Paris.

"The American company of comedians, it is expected, will open there [at Bath], under the direction of Mr. Ryan, on the 15th of July, and is to continue till the 1st of September. It is supposed they will prove so acceptable to the Bath as to encourage the proprietor to renew his visits yearly. 'The Muses follow freedom,' said Socrates. Let us hail, therefore, their residence in America." The writer was conscious that the plan for Bath, as a spa, had for its basis "the uses of similar springs in Europe." Whether this would please the native populace, he said, remained to be fully tested. At any rate there were already built a large assembly room and a theatre, both of logs, but the plan was European.

The American company eventually gave way to an Irish company, and it was the Irish that a Frenchman, Captain Bayard, found on his visit in 1791. They were performing comedy, tragedy, comic opera and farce; the Frenchman's critical reaction to this rich repertoire was that the performers were evidently very badly fed.

It was a sporting enough crowd: they played billiards, they gambled, they had boxing matches and the ladies rode as though they had all been born on horses. But what fascinated Bayard most was the conduct of five o'clock tea, quite high tea, served meticulously every afternoon. Everything was very orderly at the tea parties, very ceremonious. The ladies were ranged in a half circle, "all grave as judges on a bench" and all strangely moved to silence on the arrival of each new guest. The equipment was of the best, an acajou table, a fine silver tea service, a large silver tray on which a slave passed tea, sugar, cream, butter balls, tarts and paper-thin slices of ham.

When it came to second cups there was a sign language with the spoons: the way the spoon was placed, when the empty cup went back, indicated to the tea dispenser whether more tea was desired or not. Bayard seems to have caught onto the business in time, but he swore that a friend of his had been the unwilling recipient of sixteen cups of tea because he kept placing his spoon in the wrong position, and only ended the agony when he put his cup in his pocket. After tea there were songs. A certain Mlle. L. was the artist on this occasion. "Her favorite song was of a certain Patrick, who absent was still to be remembered."

Such ceremoniousness and mannerisms were not what Captain Bayard had expected to find in America, the cradle of liberty; he had not supposed they would still be aping England, now they had repudiated her, with formal teas and starving Irish actors, and hanging onto that pretentious name, Bath. It was imitative, slavish, and he trembled for the future of the nation. But Bath had started that way, with the "uses of similar springs in Europe," and it kept right on.

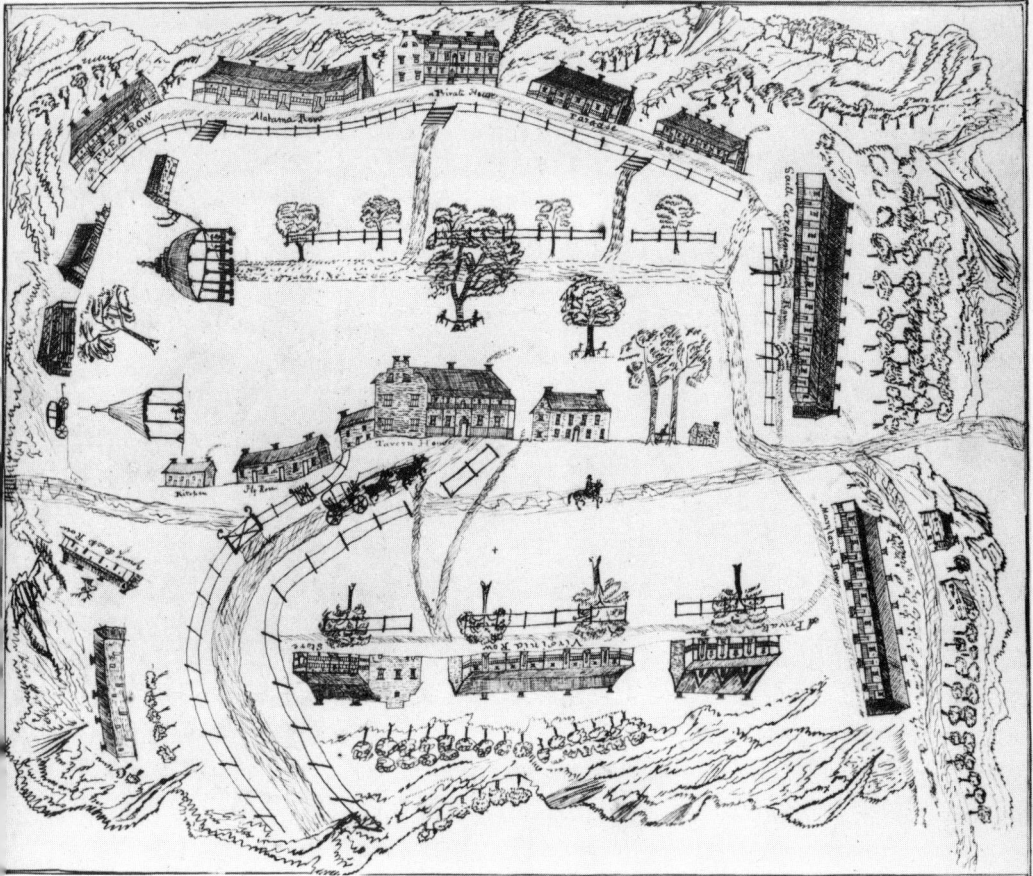

White Sulphur Springs about 1835

A puzzling drawing; the layout is approximately correct but the "Tavern" and some other buildings are alien architectural inventions. Compare with Latrobe's accurate paintings.

Warm Springs, 1832

The primitive cabin "street," from the versatile pencil of
J. H. B. Latrobe. A hitherto unpublished sketch.

In time, when they were fully in bloom, Bath manners and the composition of the Bath scene could be very pretty indeed. On the day, for example, when a New York dandy rounded a turn in the road and came suddenly upon what looked like a Provençal *court d'amour.*

"On a little greensward," he said, "skirting along the foot of a steep mountain, at least a hundred gay people of both sexes were rambling among the trees, just in the twilight of a mild summer evening. Even my philosophy shook in the wind at the view of so many fair damsels, every one of whom dressed in white, put me in mind of white fringe upon a green petticoat. . . . There was something exquisitely exhilarating, thus to break upon people resembling our accustomed associates, sporting gayly in the midst of the wild mountains."

James K. Paulding was one of the Knickerbocker wits, collaborator of Washington Irving, a literary elegant, modish, civilized and uncommonly handsome. Just arrived from a tour of the new western Springs, and a rough lot they were, the airs and graces of Bath, long and diligently tended, captured his imagination as surely as the charms of Islam captured the Crusaders.

"There is a fine drawing room here, in which the ladies meet to chat or work, and play at chess, or devise some pleasant excursion." Pic-Nics. There was "a very splendid room" appropriated to dancing. "Every night or two there is a ball." At the western Springs, whence he had come, there had been no drawing room, not even at the Sweet, the most sophisticated. A New York macaroni, a lover of the arts of society, could be bitter over such an omission. Hot baths and the most superior purgatives in the South could not make up to Paulding for the lack of a drawing room. But at Bath things were ordered differently.

You think, he wrote to his correspondent in New York, that there is nothing refined to the south of the Schuylkill, "and no watering place worth visiting excepting Long Branch. I will try to set you right in this matter. . . . In the midst of the Virginia mountains there is a little spot where is to be found all the airs, graces, paraphernalia, caprices, and elegancies of the most fashionable assembly. The truth is, these springs are as gay, as fashionable, and far more delightfully situated than any I have ever visited." There were "as many gay equipages and gay people, and almost as great a lack of variety of amusement as at Ballston or Long Branch," and that was cachet enough.

There was another side of Bath, or Berkeley, as people had begun to call it now, that escaped Mr. Paulding, so engrossed was he with its elegancies. There were faro banks and their attendant gamblers, a part of the destiny it had borrowed from England and the Continent. There were Mr. Robert Bailey, a well-known gambler turned innkeeper, and his helpmeet and mistress, Mrs. Ann Turnbull of Winchester, whom the more upright citizens of the place did not fail to stigmatize as a "notorious whore." They fill out the picture of a lively spa; they were on the saltier side.

The clientele at Bath was served by various inns and proprietors. Robert Bailey had no hesitancy in proclaiming his inn the most successful. Why, said he, gentlemen would sleep on the floor at his place, on a pallet, rather than go elsewhere. He charged $10 a week to the $7 charged by his rivals, and at that he was putting them out of business. He was taking in $6,000 a week, if one could believe him.

Richard Nash had gone to the old Bath as a gambler, to make his living from plucking geese, and there he reverted to semi-respectability as social arbiter. Robert Bailey reversed the order: he came to Bath Americanus a reformed man, a tavern keeper, having forsworn his old habits of gaming and raking (to the great relief of Mrs. Turnbull), only to backslide into his former ways when he came by too much money. But Nash and Bailey were out of the same bolt of goods; in boldness and self-esteem they had much in common.

Bailey's preparation for this life of rectitude and industry had been a career of card sharping, law breaking, whoring, running for Congress, tavern keeping, horse racing, jail breaking and wife deserting. When he had money he had lots of it and tore around the country in a splendid carriage with four fine horses, his mistress happy and proud by his side. When he was broke he turned his thoughts to more solid pursuits.

His arrival at Bath, which he had known well for many years as a visiting faro gambler, had been a sensation. He came down from Philadelphia with servants and supplies filling a whole train of carriages and wagons, he and Mrs. Turnbull first in an elegant phaeton drawn by a pair of bays; in the second carriage were the French cook and his wife and the bartender; other servants and furnishings filled the light wagons that followed, pipes of Madeira wine, Jamaica spirits, Cognac brandy, Holland gin, Burgundy, champagne, porter, tea, coffee, chocolate, cheese, segars and a variety of fanciful prints, all purchased in Philadelphia. Town and country flocked to see them. Nothing like this had ever come to Bath.

Bailey and Mrs. Turnbull gave the Springs a heady dash of America to mix with its European inheritances. Oil portraits of himself and his mistress he hung in the dining room, life size, costing $120 each in Philadelphia, and so "real," he said, that people went up and bowed to them. He bought the best of supplies and paid double for them. He bought farms, a distillery, a flour mill, a saw mill and he hired a Scotch gardener for his vegetables. The other innkeepers, discouraged by such prodigality, laid aside their aprons.

But Bailey's $6,000 a week burnt his pockets. Unable to take his own advice on giving the faro tables a wide berth, he began patronizing them himself and soon it was all over. Not only was he toppled from the pinnacle of success, he was bogged in debt and they drove him and his woman from the town. Bailey and his mistress were on the reverse side of Paulding's pretty Bath tapestry but it took a little of everything to make a spa. It had in England.

Bath finally abjured its imitative name and became Berkeley once and for all, but by that time the lions in the west had begun to outroar it and it sank back into a secondary role, like a little old lady with a past, with hosts of friends and memories but not much future. She could remember that George Washington had built a house there, which he never occupied and could not rent, and that Irving had stayed there while engaged in writing his *Life of Washington* and that the Baroness de Riedesel had long ago sung Italian airs there and that Patsy Custis had been brought when she had "spells." But she could never remember when the spring was really warm or when it had tasted strongly of minerals, and these things were against her.

It was an ill day for the old lady when word came out of

the west that a gentleman's silver shoe buckles had turned black as he was standing by Bowyer's Sulphur Spring, from the fumes, and when visitors began bringing back shilling pieces that had been tarnished *in their pockets.* The Warm Springs out there, they said, was 98 degrees and the Hot, 106. Berkeley was only 74. But even if she could not stand up to these new wonders, she could with justice say that she had been the first of the Virginia Springs and that many a Southerner had learned his spa manners at her feet.

❁

There was a social taste to the Sweet Springs water. People began using it for ennui almost as soon as they did for swollen spleens. From the beginning there gathered there "a general muster under the banner of folly," Captain Marryat's blanket definition of all watering places. The social taste had been discovered while George Washington was still riding his acres, while gentlemen still wore satin "small clothes" and cues, while shillings and pence were still the currency of the country.

Gamblers hanging around a spring were like the bush hanging over a vintner's door; they were sure signs of a convivial water. By 1790 they were thick here, they were loud and blasphemous and they were as busy as sapsuckers. During the whole of young Mr. Alexander's stay that summer, "they never intermitted their games, day or night, Sunday or workingday." By relieving one another at the tables they got down to the spring, where they mixed with the crowd and swore like troopers. "They strove to outdo one another in the rapidity and novelty of their profane expressions," filling the air with a horrid symphony. They rubbed congenial elbows with the old broken-down debauchees and they exchanged jests with the Baptists, who promised them a miserable hereafter.

Not all the scene was so raffish; some of it was positively elegant. "We had a good deal of Genteel Company," said an English traveler, "some from the West Indies. We had a regular ball every week, besides Tea parties." Bath, where there was a sign language with tea spoons, had sent torch-bearers into the wilderness. Mr. Dabney Minor, from Orange County, found the ceremony oppressive. Among fifty or so guests there were perhaps a dozen ladies "whose faces we never saw except at meal times. Stiff, formal and ceremonious in the extreme, the sight of them only served to raise sentiments of aversion and disgust. Nor were the men much better." Mr. Minor was disgusted but had he known his Oliver Goldsmith better he might have been encouraged. "Although ceremony is very different from politeness," said that philosopher, "no country was ever yet polite that was not first ceremonious." No Springs either.

Certainly the physical facilities weren't up to such high-toned manners. By 1792 there was a two-story "hotel" with eight lodging rooms above, surrounded by a number of log huts with plank floors, "rendered as comfortable as such buildings made in haste will admit." No assembly room, no ballroom, no theatre à la Bath. When the dancers required a floor they simply cleared the dining room of its long tables and pushed the backless benches against the walls.

Such as it was, the cluster of log cabins on the high ground above the spring had been built by Major John Lewis after his return in 1781 from the War of the Revolution. He dodged the griefs of innkeeping by leasing the whole outfit to professional bonifaces. Robert Bailey, later of Bath, conducted the establishment for three years. The proprietor furnished him cabins, bare floors, mattresses and even some beds, but no fixings. There wasn't even a springhouse. Guests bathed in the muddy pool and drank from it as well.

To attract the backwoods legal circuses, Major Lewis built a stone Court House, a jail and a jailer's "tenement." But it was no use; law and mineral water wouldn't mix. The ladies seized upon the Court House for a parlor. Bailey, saying he paid rent for it, put the ladies out and installed some gamblers. They soon had a faro bank humming under the judge's dais. Then the jailer was ejected from his tenement to make room for the exigent guests and some felons escaped from the jail. In the last act of this comic opera the indignant local citizens invoked the law against the gamblers, threw them out (temporarily) and moved the Court House to another part of the county, where the folks who came to take the waters couldn't get at it.

The outlay was primitive, but no matter, the water was the thing. It was "tonic," it was stimulating, it was fine for barren wives. Small wonder the crowd was frolicsome, gathered as it was about a fountain that was practically guaranteed by the medicos to increase the ardor. Of course it was good for other things, too, for debility after fever, for consumptives (in time it would be bad for consumptives, it would knock them off like ninepins, but just now it was good), for dropsical spleens, for king's evil (scrofula) and for those who had had a weakening course of sulphur water and needed bucking-up.

But there was nothing to compare with that other business, the one that concerned the ardor, and Mr. Paulding heard of many a young lady there who would not go near the pool "lest something might happen to her." They knew well enough the connection between lurking Greek water gods and babies.

Dr. Burke from Alabama, a Scotchman, was one to come out with it, flat. These waters "excite the animal passions," quoth he, "and inspire the mind with pleasurable sensations." It was only a step to the acknowledgment that this was the true fountain of youth: "aged persons will find youth and vigor at the bottom of this noble fountain." Another plain speaker was Edward A. Pollard. "In sterility the Sweet Springs water is regarded almost as a specific." Those ladies whose fecundity had been mysteriously suspended by the blighting heat of the Deep South could take hope, for here was a water that would restore them to motherhood and their husbands' embraces.

Anyhow the tone of the company was almost always blithe; there was always amusement there, whist and loo and faro for cards, an occasional duel (Bailey fought several himself), horse racing over the quarter-mile straightaway, shooting for bearskins, dancing. The Balls were mostly Virginia reels and square dances, with an occasional cotillion thrown in when there were enough sophisticates to carry it off. The South Carolina girls could rise to stardom then, being more experienced in the fashionable world than most of their Virginia sisters.

It amused Mrs. Allston of the Georgetown crowd to see the discomfiture of the Virginia belles and it made her feel superior too, a not unknown occurrence among the Rice-coast Carolinians. "I have heard a great Deal often of the Virginia Girls Dancing," she wrote her son, the future Governor, "but they sit down here and look Panic Struck, when our Girls get on the Floor—they dance nothing here but Reels and Jigs, our dancing you know is Cotilions and Country Dances, they cant go it, one young Lady got up tryed a Cotilion Blundered got Vexed and walked out the Room." Rice-coast Carolinians and Tidewater Virginians were never beyond a little social knifing; their superiorities were mutually irritating. However, the Virginians dominated the company at the Sweet, they felt a proprietary interest there. The South Carolinians took the Salt Sulphur for their own and had some reason to feel that they had the better of the bargain.

A true Virginian always thirsted for the company of his fellow man, even if it was a Carolinian. The Colonial antecedents of this Sweet Springs crowd had been known literally to go gunning for company, posting their servants on the highways of an evening to inveigle the strange traveller to their houses, sending their colored boys to the Ordinaries to look for discontented guests and offer them a more comfortable hospitality. They wanted company, they wanted talk, news of the world; they had to pay the tavern keepers for the guests snatched from under their noses, but a good talker was worth double the price.

The descendants of these men were now finding the Sweet a congenial rendezvous; the thirst for company was greater than the thirst for water. Frank Meriwether, that archetype of the Virginia country gentleman which Kennedy created for *Swallow Barn,* went up for precisely this reason. "Towards autumn it is his custom to journey over the mountains to the Springs, which he is obliged to do to avoid the unhealthy season in the tidewater region. But the upper country is not much to his taste, and would not be endured by him if it were not for the crowds that resort there for the same reason that operates upon him, and, I may add, though he would not confess it, for the opportunity this concourse affords him for discussion of opinion." In a word, to confabulate.

If they had no pump room they had the open air around the spring, and they made it serve all the purposes of an assembly hall, as any observer could see by the grand levee there each noonday. As long as the company was congenial, Virginians could make out. No ball room? Reels and jigs could be danced as well in what room there was, which chanced to be the dining room. Gentlemen as indifferent as these were in the matter of dress (many an outsider had the shock of his life) were not so particular about the equipment: the pine plank tables did very well for whist, the jail could be used for a dormitory in a pinch. The "uses of similar springs in Europe" were, in the essentials, surviving; the manners were dying in this freer atmosphere.

The Sweet Springs society grew to be thoroughly *grande dame*, looking down the nose on the groups at the other Springs as upstarts. Complacently it considered the Sweet as the oldest of all; dignified old ladies and gentlemen would tell foreigners so, and believe it themselves. "This is the oldest of all the mineral springs of Virginia," Buckingham entered in his notes. Nothing of the sort. Pioneers had steamed the kinks out of their joints at the Warm and the Little Warm (afterwards the Hot) long before the Sweet was discovered, and in the matter of spa sophistication Bath and the Bathites had a priority that was indisputable. However, it was the first of the great western group, the Virginia Springs proper, to fly the banner of society above the banner of the invalids, and that was the sort of pre-eminence that so easily displaced historical fact in the minds of the old habitués.

IV

Enter the Singletons, Well Heeled

AMONG the first of the gentlemen who nearly died from dosing himself with Sweet Springs water was a South Carolinian by the name of John Singleton, of Midway Plantation in Sumter District. Malaria ridden, he arrived at the Sweet about the middle of July, 1818, and began at once to drink that compound of stale lemonade and cream of tartar. The results were awful and the poor old gentleman faced about for home again, in his coach with two servants.

"After using the waters his complaint became so troublesome and painful it was almost insupportable for 2 or 3 days. Everything that could be thought of or heard of was applied for his relief—he got a little better the day before yesterday and on yesterday started for home. I have sent my boy with him as it is impossible that one servant can render him the attention he stands in need of. His case is truly alarming and painful—it is impossible he can live long if he don git some relief." So the old gentleman's grandson wrote home to his uncle, Colonel Richard Singleton.

Colonel Alston of Georgetown, who had come up to the Sweet that summer with eight other Alstons, big and little, thought Mr. Singleton should go right back to Sullivan's Island, the beach resort which an understanding Providence had placed right on the edge of Charleston harbor, and try the skill of Drs. Simons and Glover. Mr. Singleton himself had in mind two other doctors, Keen and Hartley. At any rate, since the waters were even worse than the doctors, he was returning posthaste to the lesser evil.

To Charleston by way of Staunton and Richmond and on south by Fayetteville would be about six hundred and fifty miles. Up to Sumter would be another hundred. It had taken him three weeks to come up to the Springs and, considering his condition, it would take him more than three weeks to go back. He would get a shaking-up that might kill him. The mountain roads were full of rock and the swamp roads were nothing but corduroy. But he survived. The trial and error system of taking the waters had given Mr. Singleton a bad fright but it was not immediately fatal. For two years longer he resisted his disease, staying quietly at home; and what relief he got came from pint bottles of Tincture of Yellow Bark at two dollars a bottle.

It could not be said of John Singleton and his contemporaries that they belonged to a Spring-going generation, that is to say, a generation that went to the Springs out of social habit as certainly as each July came around and each crop was harvested. The elder Singletons, Hamptons and Chesnuts were already old by 1820, and as a rule they toiled northward only when death began to haunt them, when the doctors were at the end of their devices and hustled them off to God's elixirs in Virginia. Except for a few people from

Charleston and roundabout, they were not quickened by any ideas of fashion or pleasure. They were sore beset by tertian fever, gastro-intestinal spasms, wasting consumption or stoppage of the bile, and they were told that in Virginia there was a water for each and every one of these afflictions. They had faith, a faith born of belief in America and its inexhaustible wonders.

It remained for the following generation to contract the only and genuine Springs fever; the waters got into their blood, the minerals went to their heads. As it turned out, it was the son of John Singleton who became the outstanding Spring-going figure of his time. For a span of more than three decades before his death in 1852, Colonel Richard Singleton was the paradigm, the bright and shining exemplar of what a Spring-going Southern gentleman should be and do. For thirty years he was the outstanding social figure at the White Sulphur, the Spring of Springs, an eminence which he achieved by his unshaken loyalty to the waters, by a gracious and unobtrusive personality and by his amiable willingness to lend money. Before he was through with lending he owned a large share of the White himself.

The Singletons were Up-country South Carolinians, of Virginia stock, in common with most of the Up-country families. Their chief plantations lay on the road between Charleston and Camden, near Sumter. Ann Royall, when she passed by the Singleton acres on that rose-scented road, thought she had wandered into Paradise. It was the largest, neatest and most beautiful plantation she had ever beheld.

"The man and the land must have been well matched," she said, "for more taste, more industry, or more beautiful fields are not to be found in America, high, rich and level.

One field lay along the road, it was paled for about two miles and must have been laid off with the compass. The field was swarming with active stout negroes with white clothes on, some ploughing and some hoeing. But the house, the gardens and the hedges of roses, it yields to none." All along that road it was heavenly. "The fences for miles were concealed with roses! they were as tall as apple trees, and inexpressibly brilliant, while their fragrance fills the air."

Not only was it beautiful, it was renowned among all who loved the sight of a race horse, as who in that day did not? The Singleton stud, said the editor of the *Turf Register,* had bred "more High Mettled Racers than almost any other in the Union." At the Charleston Jockey Club meeting of 1827 Colonel Singleton's horses won every day, a feat equalled only once before, in 1800, by a famous string of General Wade Hampton's. His pillared house, not enormous but quite elegant, with lions couchant at the head of the steps, was the nearest approach the *Turf Register's* editor had seen to the residence of "the fine old English gentleman."

In front, between the house and the post road, was an oval racecourse measuring a mile and passing so close to the high portico that the Colonel could call instructions to his jockeys from the top of the steps. Lines of forest trees radiated from the house, as hub, to the road, running like the spokes of a wheel through the racecourse and surrounding park, bringing up against the great hawthorn hedge which bordered the road. "Nothing can surpass the picturesque beauty and effect of the views obtained through the trees of the massive columns which support the entablature of the mansion," exclaimed Mr. Turf Register. Whoever viewed the Colonel's handiwork was in ecstasy over the orderliness of it, the good taste, the symmetry and the high state of cultivation to which he, and his father before him, had brought these upland levels.

The man and the land were well matched indeed; his pretty park was not more fastidiously tended than himself. His dress was faultless; it required two hours of careful work for him to equip himself for the day, the while his wife read the Bible and the newspapers. To all those humorists who thought this was not exactly efficient, the Colonel replied that it didn't matter when you got down to work so much as what you did *after* you got down. For himself, he managed to do a great deal more than most, and better too.

He was a large man with thick strong hands. His hair he wore straight up, *en brossé*. His broad, heavy chin was cradled deep in a white stock, and the collar under the stock was so high it cut across his cheek. Above the massive chin was a wide, sober mouth and the upper lip of it was long and full like the upper lip of an Irishman. There was something Irish about his eyes, too, they were so small, and the expression of them seemed to say: "We are staying open out of politeness but sad as we are it would be easier to let the lids drop down." He was a sober man, very particular in all things, and he loved his family with an almost desperate love. If he had a love of show, so did other great landowners, and his was never cheap or pretentious; it tells much of him that when he built his house he called it Home, not Singleton Hall or Home Place as others often did, but simply Home.

The role of *pater familias* which became his at the

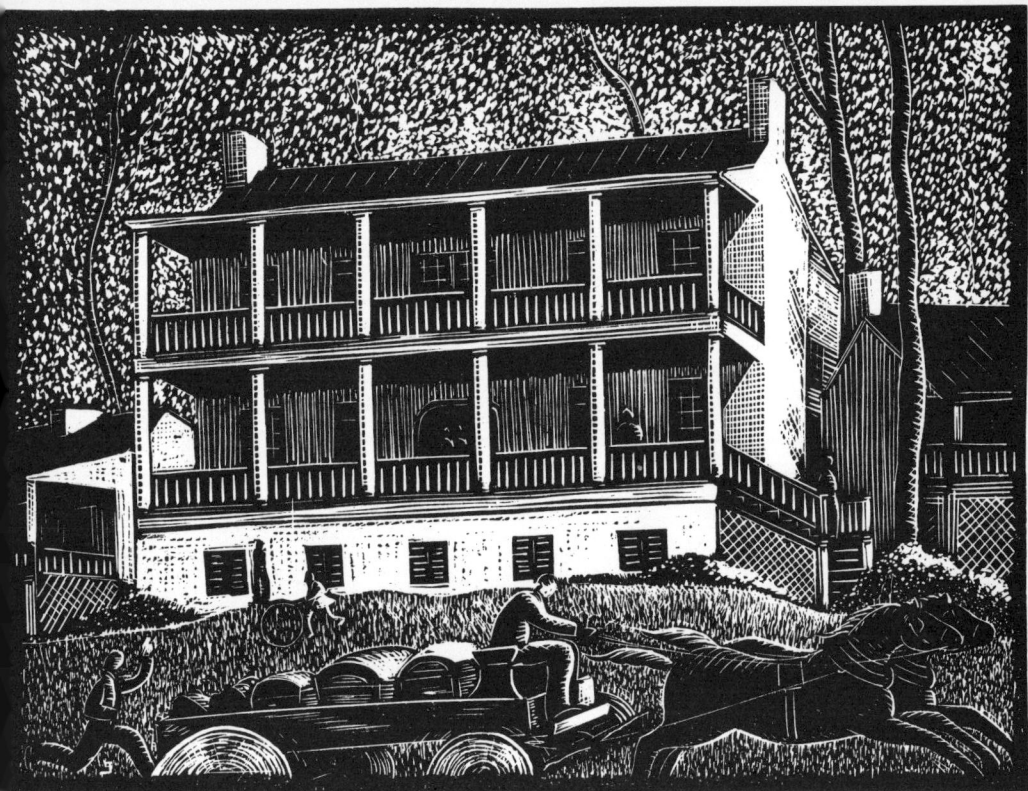

Stephen Henderson's House

Built with Louisiana gold by the Scotch millionaire, it later became the Presidents' Cottage.

Woodcut by Charles Smith

The Red Sulphur, Consumptives' Hope

Here Dr. Burke built himself into bankruptcy. Lithograph from the painting (1836) by George Cooke.

From Burke's Mineral Springs of Western Virginia

Springs he was already accustomed to in South Carolina. Neighborhood and kin looked to him for guidance, particularly when it came in the form of favors. "As I believe the time approaches when you will soon be on your way to Virginia," wrote Mary Waties, "I write to ask the favor of you to add to your list ten barrels [of Family Flour] for me and four for my mother." The local minister, A. L. Converse, also wanted some of the Virginia flour, two barrels, please, and furthermore about his salary, he realized it was not due until March, four months away, but could not Colonel Singleton oblige him by advancing his yearly contribution now? The Colonel obliged. The one-legged divine paid him back later by marrying one of his daughters and beating her, so it was said, with his wooden leg.

Kinsman Laurence Manning wrote: "My little stock of corn made by my own hands the last year is now exhausted. I therefore again trespass on your liberality by asking for a few bushel—three, four or five as may be most convenient for you to spare." Colonel Wade Hampton wanted to know, could Colonel Singleton spare Cornelius, his trainer, for a couple of months? He and his friend FitzSimons wanted to get their horses in shape for a "profitable campaign in the interior of Georgia before we meet the 'Regulars' in Carolina." As usual, Colonel Singleton obliged. Everyone came to him with his needs and was supplied.

His style of living encouraged the predatory. Did he not have in his drawing room a pedal harp that cost $450 and a Viennese pianoforte that came to a like figure? Did not his daughters go to school to Mme. Greland in Philadelphia year after year until they were young ladies of marriageable age? Did he not have a fleet of barges serving his various estates (half a dozen or more) and were not these barges always moving up and down the Santee to and from Georgetown or Charleston and was it any trouble for his boatmen to run errands and bring packages?

Besides his open-handed ways there was a quality of quiet charm about the Colonel that drew the affection and loyalty of other men. Richard I. Manning, a kinsman, wrote him: "When travelling along you conversed freely with me and discovered to me those amiable traits of character which at once exalt and dignify human nature, your utter abhorrence of whatever was dishonorable or unfair, your strict humanity and benevolence shewed you to be the man of honor and the true gentleman."

He affected men that way. His friends devoted themselves to his interests; they visited his plantations while he was away at the Springs and reported to him on his crops and Negroes. Colonel Hampton took command there in emergencies; it was a matter of course with him that he, one of the busiest planters in the South, should spend days on end looking after Singleton's business in his absence.

Colonel Singleton started his Springs career modestly enough, without benefit of retinue or hint of grandeur, without even a carriage. We catch a glimpse of him at the Warm Springs in 1818, going and coming on horseback, staying a day or two at that already ancient establishment, disappearing for another day or two and returning again for a final stay of five days. It was evidently an exploring trip; he brought only one servant, also on horseback. Earlier in this same summer his father had fled from the Sweet Springs in terror of his life; it was in the same week that Thomas Jefferson drove away from the Warm Springs totally prostrated, so weak he could hardly move a finger, both object lessons to all who were tempted to use these waters indiscriminately, and not very encouraging certainly for a man who sought a summertime refuge for his family.

Several years later Mrs. Singleton (the Colonel's second wife, Rebecca Coles that was) was ordered to the White Sulphur for her health. It seems she had a "situation." She was on her annual summer's visit to her family in Albemarle County, Virginia, with the children. In seven years she had had seven, though two of them, Richard and Matthew, were twins and that made them come not quite so close, but it was close enough. Dr. Everit of Charlottesville said her situation was bad and would require "great attention." It should not have been so long neglected, he said, and the quicker she got to the Sulphur Spring the better.

Unfortunately the Colonel was not in Albemarle but in Philadelphia to get his daughter Mary from Mme. Greland's. Mrs. Singleton wrote her husband: "He has recommended the Sulphur Springs but advices me to travel on very slow and remain there a fortnight, then visit the Sweet Springs in preference to the Warm which is too enfeebling —I hope my dear Husband that you will join me at the Sulphur Spring as soon as possible, for I fear I shall excite the commiseration and pity of every person as a 'neglected wife,' and in truth I shall feel very ill at ease, with none but a Boy as Escort, at so public a place—more I am sure will be unnecessary, to induce you to hasten to me, for I dread the Springs—but if they are to give me health I ought not to repine."

Truly it was no place for a lone female. There were by actual count five times as many men as women (it was about

1820) and wild young buckoes everywhere, drinking and gambling, raising the wind down in Wolf Row, headquarters of "wine and wassail," too friendly by half with the faro dealers who had come to bilk them.

But Mrs. Singleton had to face it alone, or at least with only her kinswoman, Miss Carter, and her son John, age seven, the Boy Escort. She took the waters for seventeen days, paid her bill of $101.64½ and departed for the Sweet. Hastening as fast as might be from Philadelphia, the Colonel did not meet her until she got to the Warm.

Such was the beginning of the Singleton regime, dictated by ill health and carried through with reluctance. But the results were good: Mrs. Singleton bettered her situation, the Colonel took to the life, they began making annual trips and before he knew it the Colonel was financially involved, having taken over a debt of $1,200 to relieve the hard-pressed Calwell, proprietor of the White. The ever obliging Colonel Singleton was running true to form. With that as a starter he next bought the first mortgage on the Springs for $22,000, which a Congressman by the name of Sheffey induced him to take over as a good investment. The Union Bank of Baltimore had been trying to unload it for years, with no takers.

Money was coming easy to the Singletons and their kind. In the year when he first became tempted by the $22,000 mortgage, his cotton was selling for from 16 to 17¾ cents a pound and a hundred bales at 300 pounds to the bale, which was the average bale in Carolina, would bring $5,000. Old John Singleton was dead now and Richard was the master, in whole or in part, of some 12,000 acres. He was counting his bales by the thousands these days and it came to a lot of money. The South Carolinians were the flush folks of the country. It was not easy for Congressman Sheffey to find tobacco people with $22,000 to put into mineral water, but the cotton people were the true seigneurs; they all had golden linings to their pockets.

A private cottage at the White Sulphur followed as the night the day; it was ready by 1825, the year he finished paying for the mortgage. It stood somewhat detached and aloof, between the ballroom building and the row that cut across the grounds and was henceforth to be called Carolina Row. The Singleton cottage was more sophisticated than its log-hut neighbors, "a neat little cabin at the foot of an old oak standing by itself most picturesquely," and it was specially pointed out to visitors. Latrobe thought it "the prettiest cottage in the place."

The planters were beginning to demand private cabins; run-of-luck was not their style. The arrangement with Mr. Calwell was simple. A planter would pay him a hundred or two hundred dollars, say, for the erection of a cottage, or he chose one of the section in the long range called the new Brick Row, later to be known as Paradise. When the owner was not at the Springs Mr. Calwell filled his cottage with whomever he pleased; when he was in residence Mr. Calwell charged him the same rate for board, room and water that he charged anyone else. It was fine for Mr. Calwell. But the owner had his satisfactions: no waiting at the gate but sailing through, bowed in by the minions; no Fly Row in his lot and no pallet on some draughty floor. He had a home in need.

So Colonel Singleton and his family occupied their new cottage under the oak for the first time in August, 1825.

There was quite a family, ten altogether counting the three servants. That June the Colonel had bought a new carriage and an almost new chariette ($470 and $455 respectively) and thus freshly equipped he had brought his crowd northward by way of the new western route, via Asheville and Abingdon. That way they got into the cool mountains a week or ten days sooner than by the old eastern road, and besides it was shorter.

Across the road was Virginia Row and there Mrs. Singleton's brother, Tucker Coles, had taken a cabin for the summer. Family and friends were rallying around the genial patron from Midway Plantation and his Virginia wife; the social ball was rolling. They all stayed at the White for a week then trekked over to the Sweet, where the food was better. A week later they were back at the White again, remaining until the middle of September when they moved on to the Warm, that pleasant neck of the Springs bottle where the clans were drawing in for the long farewell.

It was a different story now from what it had been in the beginning, particularly for Mrs. Singleton, the timid invalid of only five years before. Now she was a social pivot, wife of the man who had bought the first lien on the White Sulphur, mistress of the prettiest cottage there, charming center of a group that had succumbed to Springs fever. As long as the Singletons stayed on, so did the others, but once they mounted their carriages and drove up Warm Springs Mountain, the party was over.

"Your departure was the signal for breaking up," her brother John A. Coles wrote her; "by that time there was not more than 15 persons remaining. Poor Fry looked as melancholy as an owl."

In common with his contemporaries, the Colonel believed in a brilliant future for the Springs. He said that the White "must and will be sooner or later the Bath of America," and he could not but congratulate himself on his investment. The whole property stood pledged for his advances; he had a first lien, or thought he had. But then other debts began to bob up; people tried to sell their claims to him, $20,000 here, $2,500 there, assuming that he was a cotton-land Croesus with no better use for his money. His "first lien" was contested in court, and he was compelled to say, reluctantly, for it did not go well with his nature to bring charges against anyone, that old man Calwell had not communicated with him "as freely as he might" about the finances.

And there were other flaws in the pretty prospect too. In the late season, for instance, people wanted to know whether the place was run for the pigs or the guests? John Coles thought for the pigs. It was just after the Singleton party had left the Warm Springs for Albemarle in that pleasant autumn of 1825 and John Coles had returned to the White on his way west. There, he said, he found "the lawn occupied by hogs instead of company and the fare worse if possible than formerly. There is not a spot in the world where there is more filth or less attention paid to the comfort of a guest. With so many spare beds I was last night put upon the cords in too much pain to sleep. I go to Lewisburg as a matter of necessity."

That discouraging report of managerial *laissez faire* came to the Colonel's attention even before he left Virginia. He had $22,000 sunk there but it was not too late to put a halter on further generosity. With that way of running things, how could it ever become the Bath of America? If the beggars came to him for more money he would shut down on them, and sure enough, when they returned soon after to the golden fountain holding out their cups, he had the strength to say no.

Then came the happy year of 1827 when the Singleton horses won every race of importance at the Jockey Club, when the fame of Redgauntlet, Ariel and Nondescript rang in the ears of every horse breeder in the country, and other stables rushed to make engagements for their brood mares at the Singleton stud. Cotton, after a sharp slump and some bad luck with rot and caterpillar, was better. Money was easy, the times pretty fine. Up in Virginia Mrs. Singleton's kin were bright with reflected glory, and in June they all laid plans for a gala summer. They were preparing to meet in "great force," wrote John Coles, on the other side of the mountain when the time came and all go on to the Springs together.

It seemed to James Calwell a fine time to make another strike; gently, persuasively he explained to Colonel Singleton his latest financial predicament. Certain creditors were riding him hard, etc., etc. The Colonel, just as gently, said, "No," and went to the Sweet with the crowd. But William B. Calwell, son and emissary of the old man, appeared at the Sweet and detailed the situation: they really were in very great trouble and they did so need to make improvements to take care of the crowd. The Colonel could see himself what a press there was to get in; this popularity, the unequalled strength of the waters, were these not surety alone for any further investment? They would be $2,500 or $3,000 short of their engagements.

The amiable planter from South Carolina was not the

man to withstand such a siege. Times were good, he was the son of fortune, the mood was one of celebration and benevolence. Yes, he could let them have the $2,500. In fact, come to think of it, if they needed more for their improvements, he could just as easily let them have $4,000 by the first of the year. Just as easily as not. And soon he was adding another $2,500 to *that,* so that by 1830 his total advances were not much short of $30,000.

But of course the Springs were no great risk. Unlike an ordinary business or a bank (the Colonel had sold his Bank of the United States stock to make this investment) they had marvelous undiminishable powers; they were, in a way, divinely directed. Had not Thomas Jefferson himself said that the State should buy them, at least the White Sulphur, for the good of all? Were there not geologists testifying that their value was hardly less than the deposits of coal and iron? Was there not a growing demand throughout the whole South for bottled and barrelled water? Why, they were gold mines. What with nearly everyone liverish and crying for relief, how was it possible to overrate their value?

❦

John Coles of Albemarle was not the only hog-ridden guest to call upon the avenging gods. J. P. Kennedy of Baltimore, author-to-be of the popular *Swallow Barn,* arrived at the White on August 8, 1827. When, three days later, he got down to writing his friend Latrobe, he had worked himself into a literary lather over the indifference of the management to the suffering of its guests, and this is the way he headed his letter:

"White Sulphur Springs, in a hovel nine feet square—with four hogs stretched at length in black sulphur mud, immediately before my door, six o'clock in the evening —a hundred stupid people in view with their hands in their pockets."

Dear Lat., he went on, he hadn't had a moment to write and now he was doing so under many circumstances of privation and discomfort. By incessant travelling over shocking roads he had arrived at last in "what may be called preeminently and *par excellence* the most ingeniously uncomfortable spot on this continent. The waters here are invaluable and a conviction of that fact has rendered the owner of the estate the most reckless of human beings to everything that is essential to the accommodation of his guests. There are scarcely less than two hundred people with an immense train of horses and servants and I can honestly affirm that they are worse provided with lodging and food than a bivouac of a regiment of raw militia. We shall in consequence leave this refuge of the damned as soon as a moderate enjoyment of the waters will permit us—perhaps in a week —and cross over to the Sweet Springs, where everything stands in most inviting contrast with our present state of destitution."

Four years later the management was still putting its pigs on an equal footing with its guests. Mr. Alexander Wilson and his wife Sophia of Charleston, South Carolina, had just spent a delightful five days at the Red Sulphur, followed by a very pleasant fortnight at the Salt, and they arrived at the White about five o'clock on July 26, intending to remain a fortnight for the sake of Sophia's health. They had heard some tall tales of this place, but pooh, not half they heard could possibly be true.

Alas for such incredulity. "In point of filth, dirt, and every other bad quality," said Mr. Wilson, "we found it decidedly the meanest, most nasty place we ever visited. Such was our disgust we would have left it immediately but there being no house of entertainment near, we were reluctantly compelled to remain there the night, to be eaten up with fleas, annoyed by the hogs grunting under our house at night, and the incessant yell of 20 dogs, keeping time to the agility and activity of the fleas. We had consequently no sleep the whole night. My dear wife, from the shock she received from the horror of the place, was made quite sick with headache and vomiting."

Mr. James Calwell, the owner of the hogs, the dogs and the fleas, was a smallish gentleman of extremely pleasant bearing, his ruddy face wreathed in pleasant smiles and his white hair tied antiquely in a cue at the back, with a narrow black ribbon. Technically Mr. Calwell was a Colonial, having been born three years before the Declaration of Independence, and as a Colonial he was really entitled to his cue.

He had been a merchant of Baltimore and had married one-seventh of Bowyer's Sulphur Spring in the person of Polly Bowyer. After about twenty years and a dozen children, this pair decided that they could improve on the way the mountain resort was run. The first act of the Calwell regime was to borrow money; it was the second and the last acts too, for they were never finished with borrowing money. At any rate, eight Baltimore friends in 1817 signed notes to the amount of $20,000, and on these notes the

Union Bank advanced the money, which went for slaves, feather beds, buying out some of the other Bowyer heirs and the erection of that ark of a building to house the dining room, bar and receiving rooms.

The news spreading that Bowyer's Sulphur Spring had a "hotel" among the log cabins, people flocked to see. The summer of 1818 was a grand success. But 1819 was terrible. The country had bogged down in the worst panic ever known, the inevitable crash following the post-Waterloo boom; three out of four factory workers lost their jobs and shipping went bankrupt. The new proprietor of the Sulphur Spring could not pay the interest on his debt, so he signed a note for it, which was easier, and the Union Bank of Maryland, suddenly skeptical of mineral springs, began peddling the notes.

From that time on James Calwell got deeper and deeper into a morass of debt (what with half a dozen sons to bring up as princes of the spa it was little wonder), but you would never have known it by looking at his suave, pink and apparently carefree countenance, the face of a diplomat with an excellent wine cellar. He had such cheerful manners, said J. L. Petigru, and "a dash of the old school." Frank and agreeable with all who did not come to him with complaints, he won for himself a host of friends who agreed, first, that he was a very engaging old party and, second, that he had no business trying to run an inn.

Planters, statesmen, bankers, generals, admirals accepted him on their own footing, as a gentleman among gentlemen. To Henry Clay he might have been a beloved uncle. The Senator wrote him intimately through many years the family and political news; sent him distinguished guests,

Judge Gayarré of New Orleans, Colonel Perkins of Boston, Lord Morpeth, the Honorable Abbott Lawrence, "a man such as you and I can love"; presented him with his own portrait and made him a gift of blooded Durham cattle to improve his stock. While at the Springs, even Calwell's most prominent guests soon discovered that they did not distinguish him by their attentions, he distinguished them. If they were asked to his house for breakfast or a glass of wine, they knew they were among the elect; or if they did not know it they were told.

His friends were not only genuinely fond of him; they stood by him in his difficulties. When in 1842 he was in more than usual hot financial water, Colonel Hampton asked Singleton to get some legal acknowledgment of his cottage ownership, but by no means to upset the old man. "Whatever you do, pray avoid any measure calculated to injure the old gentleman's feelings. I would not add a feather to the weight he has to carry." Singleton would not hear of a suit that Abram van Buren wanted to bring against him for a long-overdue debt. Friends protected him while he was alive; they mourned him when he died. "How we shall miss him," exclaimed Andrew Stevenson, one-time Minister to England, "at least you will, for I am not able to go."

To James Calwell a kind and fatherly Providence sent men like Mr. Taggart of Baltimore and John Tabb of Norfolk and John Wilcox of Petersburg, each with $15,000 or more, and Richard Singleton of Midway Plantation with $30,000, and heavens knows how many more with lesser amounts. With all this money he built, little by little, row by row, the largest and most picturesque, the most popular and the most execrated of the Virginia Mineral Springs.

He never repaid any loans if he could possibly let them run on, preferring to spend substantial sums on houses for his numerous sons in the neighborhood. No other Springs was run as badly and with as little regard for the comfort of the guests, but Mr. Calwell kept a bland and pleasant countenance turned on the world and evolved a system for dealing with disgruntled visitors that was the envy of all the other proprietors. An aura of fame gathered round his person, and as time went on, men came hurrying to see "the man with the cue," survivor of another age, before death should take him off, which it was not to do for many a long year.

V

The Plague Lends a Hand

THE plague broke out in Norfolk and Portsmouth the end of July, 1832. From the port cities it spread up and down the coast, up bays and rivers inland, striking terror to Virginia and Maryland Tidewater. This was cholera making a decennial visit to the new Republic. It had been several years on the way from Asia, flowing river-like westward across Russia and Europe, crossing the Atlantic to America. But the Virginians and Marylanders did not know that; all they knew was, it rose from the earth with the miasma. All things noxious and lethal struck at them through the miasma.

In an effort to stem the invisible tide of death the cities cleaned up the accumulated filth from which the contagion wraithed into the air. Portsmouth was laid off in wards and citizens were formed into brigades to "purify" the streets. Norfolk and Richmond followed suit. Cellars, yards, offices were scoured, trash destroyed, sulphur burned in the houses. It didn't make any difference. The invisible fingers came on anyhow, to gripe the bowels and stop the heart.

The experts prescribed: Do not eat fresh fruit and vege-
tables; they are poison. Repent, oh ye gluttons, cried the
Richmond *Enquirer*, for you will be the first to die; cholera
loves debilitated organs. Advice from Baltimore: wear a
flannel shirt, flannel drawers and yarn stockings, impene-
trable armor against the foe. Advice from Dr. Cobbs of New
York, epidemic veteran: bleeding is best, bleeding through
the arm, "to restore the equilibrium of the circulation," to
be followed by opium and calomel.

None of it was any good, the creeping death came on
just the same. "To the cure of these maladies nor counsel of
physician nor virtue of any medicine appeared to avail or
profit aught," Boccaccio had said of another plague five
hundred years before. The toll was forty dead a day in Richmond, three quarters of them Negroes. Against the yellow
fever the Negro had a racial inoculation but the cholera
laid him down. Were these the *Enquirer's* gluttons, the high
livers who had dug their own graves? But that was it, everything was guess, experts and journalists alike shouted ignorance, bleeding was ignorance, flannel drawers were ignorance and the proof of it was, people kept right on dying.

There was only one recourse and that, for all who could,
was to fly. Boccaccio's Florentine ladies had known as much.
"Methinks it were excellently well done that we depart this
city and betake ourselves to the country and there take such
diversion, such delight and such pleasance as we may." Like
a great wind the plague swept men westward over the flat-
lands of Virginia to the mountains.

The Springs were jam-packed. It was the biggest and jol-
liest crowd that ever was. There was no plague there, they
were safe; the height, the cool air, the waters and the mint

juleps conspiring together to give them blessed immunity.

Mr. J. H. B. Latrobe, young Baltimore lawyer and son of Benjamin Latrobe, the architect, was late. Not too late in quitting Baltimore, for he was at least one jump ahead of the plague, but late in getting to the White. Major Anderson had no room to put a cat, as usual, and Mr. Latrobe was invited to remain outside the gates of this Fiesole with the rejected ones. But he was a Southerner and that made a difference, for with Southerners all hope was never lost. The Latrobes and Featherstonhaughs belonged to different races entirely.

A slave passed by, a slave who had served him often at the house of a friend. A quick eye, a call, glad greeting and a question, only these were needed and Mr. Latrobe and his baggage were on their way to the cottage where four of his Baltimore cronies were in providential possession of a ten by fourteen cubicle known as a chamber. Their hospitable manoeuvre was spontaneous: they moved over for a fifth. Bed? That made them laugh. How could anyone know who had got the last bed? But there was bribery still and out of it came, via one of the Calwell darkies, two benches, a miserable pallet, a pillow and a horse blanket.

A Featherstonhaugh would have stormed and cursed; a Southerner could take his luck where he found it. Latrobe was the object of universal congratulation for having procured such "admirable accommodation." Five hundred, they said, had recently been turned from the gate by the man in brown . . . By morning his body was scarified. The horse blanket was full of fleas.

Another plague vied with the cholera in filling the Springs with refugees. It was the Jackson Administration. These people of property, these mossbacks of inherited wealth, these intellectuals, these American "aristocrats," these statesmen and bankers of the Federalist stripe, even these Southern planters now repudiating Jeffersonian democracy and suspicious of any democracy, these were the new pariahs of government. Mr. Jackson had no use for them. The People should have its innings; the People had taken Washington and all these were outcasts. Wrapped in their gentility and nursing their fears, they met in rendezvous, here, by the temples over the waters, where the People, bless its bones, did not come and where Mr. Jackson did not come either.

Here at the White when Latrobe arrived was the champion of property, the sworn enemy of Jacksonism, the Moses of this outcast squirarchy, Henry Clay himself. He had written his friend James Calwell from Staunton: he was returning home with his family and he wished to stop at the White for a fortnight.

"The rumor is that you are overflowing and can take in no more. On the other hand our friend Judge Brooke . . . told me that you were reserving a cabbin for me. . . .

"P.S. Supposing you would like to know who I have with me. . . . Mrs. Clay, a little grandson and myself comprise the whole members of our party. Then, we have 4 servants, two carriages, six horses, a Jackass and a shepherds dog— a strange medley, is it not?" Four servants and six horses. The champion of the nabobs travelled like a nabob.

Mr. Clay was an old standby here, not only a favored guest but a sort of unofficial host, always the chief entertainer as long as he remained in residence, the ever-moving center of attraction. One morning a young lady from Louisa

Court House, Miss Ann Price, came to the breakfast table
and found there a stranger, a newcomer who seemed to be
dominating the proceedings. Everyone cocked his head to
hear what the stranger had to say, all deferred to him, everyone was under the spell of that beautiful voice, now high
and light as a breeze, now low and rich as an organ. There
was a swatch of unruly hair hanging down over his fore-
head, his mouth was excessively wide and heavy like a
boy's, there was an Irish tilt to his nose and rawbones was
his name. Little Miss Ann Price stared at him fascinated.
That day she entered in her diary, "Had a right good view
of Mr. Clay, who was no sight."

Indeed he was not but what were looks? Mr. Clay, particularly at the Springs, was a charmer of another sort, and
several days later Miss Ann was whistling a different tune.
The great man dropped in to call at her cottage, paying his
respects as he always did to everyone, large and small, with
that disarming friendliness of which he was a master, no
hint of *noblesse oblige*. Miss Ann capitulated. "Like him
very well," she said to her diary, "he seemed to be very
affable."

Latrobe was another who succumbed to the spell. He had
a long conversation with Mr. Clay on "several subjects"
that were agitating the citizens: Negro Colonization in Africa (Clay was Vice-President of the Colonization Society;
Latrobe was a member); the terrible Nat Turner Rebellion
of the previous summer in Southampton County; railroads
and internal improvements; the dying Madison and the eternally young Dolly, his wife, whom Latrobe had just visited;
crops, economics and what not, for there was no exhausting
this man Clay. Latrobe was enchanted. "He is certainly the

[71]

most pleasant man I ever was in company with, and I willingly confess myself indebted to him for much enjoyment."

And what was it they did *not* talk about? They did not talk about politics. People didn't talk politics at the Springs. Latrobe emphasized the point: their subjects, he said, were "unconnected with politics, of course." Of course. It was understood. "Politics," said another Baltimorean (Mr. Hoffman) in reporting the doings at the Springs, "was a forbidden topic." Southerners who knew each other beyond a doubt might get their heads together, but let an outsider, a Northerner perhaps, join the group and the taboo was on. Even though a man might be a candidate for the presidency, as Clay was in the summer of his talk with Latrobe, he saved his electioneering for other places, other audiences. The magic waters were not to be muddied with controversy. Wag lightly, oh silver tongue, of other things, let Southern punctilio put a check on your great talents. The governing principle of this company is gaiety; a sweet, unbroken dalliance rules the summer. Far from being a mere pretense, a pose, a pious wish, it is the code, and every gentleman is its guardian.

When his fortnight came to an end, Mr. Clay gathered his wife and grandchild, servants and horses, jackass and shepherd dog together and continued homeward, to Kentucky. The gentlemen of property and the pretty ladies bade him farewell, and their hopes and prayers went with him, champion of their security. How wonderful if he would knock Jackson out of the White House in November!

And yet he was but half a Southern hero after all. If he would only drop this colonization, emancipation, anti-slavery bug of his, if he would only stop calling slavery "the deepest stain upon the character of the country." For the slaveholding hierarchy had just made up its collective mind about slavery; from now on it was to be no longer a stain or a shame but their bright and guiding star, their unadulterated blessing. That was their stand and they would defend it to the last drop of blood if necessary. The meddling abolitionists and the wholesale murders of the Negro preacher, Nat Turner, had seen to that; hereafter no more humanitarian shilly-shally; keep the blood-lusting brutes within bounds.

But Nat Turner had not changed Mr. Clay, and the attacks of the abolitionists had not changed him either. Come right down to it, he was a sort of abolitionist himself. And many men in that crowd gathered to see him off to Kentucky shook their heads over him, won by his charm but damning him for only half a friend.

Latrobe stayed on to enjoy the company, to ride out in the pleasant afternoons in an open barouche, to be entertained by the delightful Mr. Stanard of Richmond and to fall head over heels in love. Love and pleasure were in the idyllic air, the plague was very far away. More than two hundred and fifty people at the White alone, to say nothing of the several thousand scattered about the other Springs, were gathering their rosebuds, having escaped the dreadful scythe. It had been the same with Boccaccio and his friends up in Fiesole, while below in Florence the Black Death raged like a fire.

On the lawn at the White Sulphur there was a continual *fête champêtre*. Here were fencers within the tight circle of their audience, foil hissing on foil, ringing against the bell guards. Over yonder quoits were flying through the air, clanging musically against the pin. A laughing party of equestrians careered by, returning from their evening ride, and wherever one looked riders were showing off their mounts. Servants rushed to and from the bar, the spring, taking horses to the stables, carrying baggage. From the tenpin alley down near the kennels came the rumble of balls and the clatter of pins.

The Year of the Cholera, as it was ever afterwards called, did for the Springs what prosperity was not yet ready to do: it sent them off to a flying start on the decade. Higher prices were hanging fire. A pound of cotton was worth about nine and one-half cents; it had been the same a year before. Tobacco was selling at about last year's levels; sugar had slid off a little. The boom was not in crops but in death and coffins, in burial clothes and in Springs. For when the first three drove a thriving business, so did the last; and Mr. Calwell wrote Colonel Singleton how necessary it was for him to keep putting up cottages.

"It appears I cannot do too much in that way as the company always overruns the room. I shall continue the improvements although I am not yet clear of my difficulties." Cholera and yellow fever * were doing what they could to make life cheerful for the old man and render him solvent. Pestilence and the doctors were working hand in hand to send people to the waters. So impressed were the doctors themselves with the fruitfulness of this partnership that two of them invested their all in springs of their own: Dr. Thomas Goode bought the Hot, and Dr. William Burke the Red Sulphur, both in this terrible year of the plague.

---

* New Orleans suffered an epidemic of yellow fever in the summer of 1832 as a prelude to the cholera, which did not strike there until October.

VI

Colonel Pope and the Belles and Beaux

YOUNG Robert DeVeaux did not go home to South Carolina for the summer of 1831. There was no sense in going down to Pineville in the most malarial months of the year, when everybody else was coming up to the Virginia Springs or Saratoga or Newport. So in the summer vacation young DeVeaux and some kindred spirits from the late Mr. Jefferson's college at Charlottesville went over the mountains to have themselves a time. DeVeaux kept a diary.

"July 26—Left college for the Warm Springs. . . .

"July 27—Arrived at the Warm Springs—little company—times very dull—proceeded on to the White Sulphur—found upwards of two hundred people there—several families from South Carolina. Met Mr. Claiborn and family.

"July 29—Still at the White Sulphur—times very dull—no dancing—women horribly ugly—in nearly one hundred only two or three passably pretty—and not more than six of them can dance. Times not what they were last summer. The only amusements now are drinking sulphur water—not getting to eat at meals—and looking at ugly women.

[75]

"July 31st—Just met an unsophisticated, sweet, lively girl from Petersburg—a red-haired lassie. She is the only pretty one in the place—except Mrs. Bentham.

"August 1st—Sunday—horribly dull.

"August 2nd—Most dead with the blues."

But there is to be a ball that night, Monday, and he will see the girl from Petersburg again.

"August 3rd—The ball was well attended, but I did not get acquainted with a single d—d soul—determined to do so to-night. Several elegant ladies lately arrived from Baltimore and Kentucky. . . ."

Four days later a great change had taken place.

"August 7th—Enjoying myself as much as possible—enraptured with my little French Emilie—she is the prettiest creature I ever saw. Had determined to leave this place but so spell bound as not to be able to move.

"August 8th—Rainy day and Sunday to boot. Suddenly taken with a fit of the blues. What ails me? Am I in love? No, by Faith! I see nothing I could love longer than a day and a night —I shall leave shortly for college.

"August 11th—Still raining. Times dull.

"August 12th—Fine fun going on—find it impossible to get away—already overstayed my time. Time passes pleasantly. Fallen in love with —— ——.

"August 17th—Met the charming Miss L. B., a pretty girl and a skilful coquette, I'm told."

Then he met another charmer, Colonel Singleton's daughter Marion, at the fresh and ravishing age of sixteen. Little French Emilie and the red-headed girl from Petersburg and the coquette L. B. were forgotten. When Marion left for one of the other Springs with her family, his heart sank.

"Farewell M—, may heaven prosper you wherever you roam, and may your voyage through life be as fortunate and favorable as your own estimable qualities entitle you to deserve.

"August 20th—Ye Gods! what a page does the journal of yesterday present! That's rather too sentimental—must quit—it's something of a squint at Cupid—must have as little to do with him as possible—took a long walk this evening with Miss A—n from South Carolina."

To put Miss Marion out of mind he took antidotes furiously, walks, dances, rides with one girl after the other, and so succeeded in entangling himself in the gay life that it was two weeks before he could tear himself away. And as for the diary, he was "too busy with the girls to write anything of consequence." But no more squints at Cupid.

The point about young DeVeaux was not that he made such headway with the ladies (one was not a South Carolinian for nothing); the point was he had such a hard time getting started. "Times dull." "Did not get acquainted with a single d—d soul." There was no one to give the boy a social push. Another and even sadder case of the same trouble was that of young William Battle from the University of North Carolina. There was this difference between undergraduates DeVeaux and Battle: the latter never did get going.

"There was a Ball every night," Battle wrote his friend Johnston Pettigrew, "and though the music was not first rate (only a band of five) yet the dance was graced by some of New Orleans loveliest daughters—That is from their appearance I should judge they were her loveliest—After all, I made not a female acquaintance! To mingle with the crowd of ladies was not necessary to my enjoyment. I preferred standing off and feasting my eyes on forms of loveliness to mingling in the crowd and breaking the charm thrown o'er the scene.—But this is all *stuff*. There was no one there in whom I felt any *interest,* is the truth of the matter. I left her in Carolina."

If Colonel Pope had been on hand such stalemates would have been unnecessary. The Colonel was not the man to let good romantic material stand helpless on the sidelines; it was his destiny to put it to work.

There was a great press of belles at the Springs now and hundreds of eager beaux after them, but no more order to the whole business than there was in a fox chase, not as much, not even a whip. The belles were being imposed upon by flashy exteriors, penniless fortune hunters, wastrels, even gamblers. On the other hand there were young men of good standing having to waste precious time getting themselves introduced. It was inefficient and wasteful.

As for the dancing, that was unorganized too; some of it was ludicrous. The country gents and their hearty girls made spectacles of themselves with their outlandish gyrations; the waltzing crowd from the cities wanted the floor to themselves. People of taste found this waltz disgusting anyhow; bodies came into actual contact. Cotillions pleased everybody, cotillions with their dignified evolutions and their square figures, but they needed men of imagination to plan them and men of grace to lead them, and both were lacking. What with one thing and another it was a situation made for Colonel Pope who, about 1832, saw how things were going and undertook to become master of ceremonies.

Colonel Pope came from Twickenham Town, Alabama. It was not called Twickenham Town on the maps (it was called Huntsville), but it was Twickenham Town to the Popes and the Clays and their like, and it always would be. This was the name bestowed upon it by Colonel LeRoy Pope in honor of the Thames-side town where Alexander Pope had lived and was buried. The Alabama Popes claimed kinship with the poet. But Huntsville triumphed. The hardy folk out there couldn't stomach Twickenham Town.

Colonel William was a short man with a modest embonpoint, gray hair and a face of beaming benevolence. Dangling from the pocket of his waistcoat was a fob of blue ribbon; on the end of the fob hung a locket, and in the locket was a strand of hair, sign and memento of the widower. "Kind, good old man," sighed one of his lady admirers. He might have been fifty.

Three years after he took charge of the ballroom his mastery was complete, his word was law, his judgments incontestable, his skill unchallenged. He enjoyed this state of affairs and so did everyone else. The dances were models of propriety and variety; the cotillions of his devising were delightful and he led them with an aptitude that no one else could touch. Devoted as he was to the cause, he would spend a part of each day devising cotillion evolutions, and each evening he would unfold them before the enchanted spectators.

Parents, aunts and chaperones in general were much in Colonel Pope's debt for his system of introduction. His aim being to protect young and innocent womanhood from impostors, he made up a list of respectable gentlemen from all parts of the country; any candidate for a lady's acquaintance must be known to at least one of the gentlemen on the list, else the Colonel regretfully denied his request. And that was an end of it. In the South, what with everybody cousin to everybody else, one had to be very strange indeed to be absolutely unknown.

But of all the Colonel's inventions and devices, the Billing, Wooing and Cooing Society was the best. This was the organization through and by which he became the Cupid of the Springs, for the purpose was to promote more and better marriages. The membership list of the Billing, Wooing and Cooing Society was written on a long roll of pink paper, said to have been manufactured especially for this purpose. There were seventeen hundred members. On the same pink roll, preceding the names of the initiates, were the articles of the Constitution. Colonel Pope kept it hanging on the wall of the ballroom where everybody could see it, weekdays and Sundays, and during service it was said to be as salutary as any sermon, reminding the young men whose eyes wandered to the wall that in that Constitution were set down the rules that must govern a gentleman pursuing a lady. For transgressors it was a silent, pink rebuke; no preacher was so eloquent.

Between dances of an evening the Colonel would be over by the wall explaining the Constitution, writing in the names of new members. Asked how he was getting on in August of '35, he cheerfully quoted figures. Ten matches had already been consummated and there were fifty bona fide courtships in current agitation. Out of the fifty the Colonel thought he could safely predict twenty happy unions, experience having taught him that the mortality rate of courtships was three out of five.

Colonel Pope was the Beau Nash of the Springs, though a very different Beau from the original, a genial and whim-

sical gentleman instead of a sarcastic tyrant. Both Richard
Nash and Colonel Pope had a passion for correct and decent behavior and an equal passion for drawing up rules.
Both were indefatigable masters of ceremonies, fascinated
by the machinery of society. Both were resourceful as social
engineers, but perhaps Colonel Pope had the edge there,
for in addition to skill he had humor. He was known, late in
the season when the young ladies had lost interest in dancing either from fatigue or surfeit, to place himself at the
head of the band and march around the grounds, up on the
left along Paradise Row, down on the right along Virginia
Row and across in front of Carolina, stopping at the cottage
of each laggard belle to serenade her. The weary butterflies
awoke with new life, fluttered out of their cabins and
marched to the ballroom behind the band. After that they
shirked no more but danced on to the end of the Colonel's
stay.

What better nursery for such a master than Twickenham
Town, where the ladies, beautifully gowned, vied with each
other in the streets as though this were Vanity Fair, where
there was a Thespian Society that gave a succession of plays
and cotillions each winter, where the Popes lived in a great
house on the bluff overlooking the town which they once
owned, lock, stock and barrel? Where could social graces
grow more fruitfully than in Southern land so rich that it
raised a bale of cotton to the acre? Ann Royall wriggled
herself into the Popes' house and was "amazed" at the taste
and elegance, "massy plate, cut glass, china ware, vases,
sofas and mahogany furniture of the newest fashion. To
those unaccustomed to the wealth of this new country, the
superb style of the inhabitants will appear incredible. There

is nothing like it in our country." Colonel Pope was not just an accident.

He was well rewarded. For six years he was the darling of the White; no lady writing in her journal would think of omitting his praises and his fame was spread in books and pamphlets, letters and newspapers. The authoress of *The Belles and Beaux of 1835* dedicated her little book to him, idolizing him for his "untiring zeal" in the promotion of enjoyment. They very nearly made a saint of him.

The climax of the adoration was a poem of fourteen stanzas written to him by the clever wife of Judge William Cabell, "anonymously." "To William Pope, Esq.," it was called, and in the first thirteen stanzas the authoress celebrated the features of the spa: the Marriage Market, the fortune hunters, the dining room, the belles and the balls and even the sulphur water. In the fourteenth and last quatrain she came to grips with the hero himself:

> Yet ere I conclude, lo! a paradox hear!
> Though protestants all, yet obey we a POPE,
> Whose mandates give pleasure whene'er they appear—
> That long he may reign most devoutly we hope!

This work stirred up such a fluttering in the dovecotes as never was, a nine days' wonder they called it, assiduously copying it one from the other, sending it to the magazines, dispatching it to the newspapers. One of Mrs. Cabell's adorers who worshipped her more than he did Pope wrote a poetic "Answer" full of her praises and sent it to a Richmond newspaper. An anonymous poem born of the charming Mrs. Cabell could stir up as much excitement as a royal baby born out of wedlock. But it was a small world and diversions were scarce.

In time Colonel Pope ceased to come; even in Twickenham Town responsibilities could tie a man down; even
there a second marriage and adversity could clip a skylark's
wings. The White lost its master of ceremonies to the accompaniment of bitter mourning, and things went rather to
pieces again. "Take him all in all," cried one of the mourn-
ers, "we shall ne'er behold his like again."

❦

The Billing, Wooing and Cooing Society was the recognition of a fact, and the fact was that no other places in the
whole South were the equal of the Springs for the making
of marriages. They were the common ground where a
widely scattered aristocracy foregathered to choose its
mates. The business of healing and the business of pairing
went on furiously side by side, old and young together, pell
mell, hit or miss. You took the waters or you took a mate or
you took both, and with both it was the same: there was no
knowing what the effect would be. There were doctors to
prescribe for the liverish and the gouty, how many glasses
they should drink and how long they should stay, but there
was no one to prescribe for the romantics until Colonel
Pope came along with his long roll of pink paper and his
Constitution.

Back in Bath, when that place was in its heyday, James
K. Paulding discovered that of all the diversions at that delightful place the chief was mate hunting. In this, as in the
other Springs arts, Bath lit the torch; and everyone took it
for granted now that Springs and Marriage Market should
be synonymous. The waters came to be regarded as love

potions, swift and fatal and often very embarrassing for those who thought they were drinking only to be rid of dyspepsia. It was the unsuspecting who might be the hardest hit. A New Englander by the name of Mackie saw how devilish it was. "It will happen that a man who, on coming to these Springs had no more thought in his head of entering on the state of matrimony than he had of making a fortune, finds, before he has drunk and bathed a week, that he is in the most imminent danger of making proposals."

In the play on the White Sulphur that was written by one John Selden, plot and action hinged on the magic of the water. It had become the special agent of Eros. Stanhope, one of the characters, states the thesis: "It's all in this sulphur water!" he cries. "I'm never in love. I never flirt. No paint, powders, ribbons or ruffles are wasted on me. Mothers encourage my innocent attentions, fathers promote my safe acquaintance. I never drink the water! It is the most insidious, amatory, provocative, demoralizing liquid on earth. One goblet would cause a cardinal turn Turk."

Young DeVeaux of Pineville tried desperately to escape it, to shake off Cupid by throwing up a dust of light flirtation, but it was no use. He had drunk the potion and in a year or two was leading sweet Marion Singleton to the altar. On the recalcitrants and the hard to please it worked when all else failed. There was the case of Sally Dix of Natchez who when at home did nothing but entertain her beaux and when taken to New Orleans in the winter went to all the parties and all the balls, but who was obstinately proof against love and matrimony until she went to the White Sulphur. There the thing happened, inevitably.

But the classic victim of water-witchery was J. H. B. La-

At Botetourt Springs

Bare comfort inside the Claibornes' cottage.

From a water color after the original by J. H. B. Latrobe

trobe, the young Baltimore lawyer who came up in the Year of the Cholera and was so charmed with Clay. Latrobe was a widower and a disconsolate one; his beloved wife had died only the year before and when he came to the Springs he was a bereaved and grieving gentleman.

The crowd was exceedingly attractive: Reverdy Johnson and Mrs. Johnson, with a barouche; Miss Anna May, "a beautiful girl from Petersburg," and Cora Livingston, the belle of belles from New Orleans. The Claibornes were there from Natchez, and so was the famous international dandy, Arthur Middleton of Charleston, in a screaming check suit and a velvet shirt that had stunned New York and a full set of whiskers and mustachios; also Robert Stanard of Richmond, almost as entertaining as Clay and far handsomer, and Miss Carlton and Miss Barbour and Miss Randolph and so on and so forth, "all good, clever and agreeable people."

Latrobe met Miss Virginia Claiborne on August 10. She was seventeen, the daughter of an English lady named Hutchens and the late General Ferdinand Leigh Claiborne. His widower's eye, losing its jaundice, perceived that she had "a pretty face and figure." Soon his listless widower's hand was able to write that she was "the fair Miss Claiborne" and to note for his friend Hopkins in Baltimore that she was "very pretty, very sensible and very unsophisticated," and finally he wrote that she was "the handsomest woman at the Springs and the most admired."

This little tree of love was less than two weeks sprouting and putting forth leaves at the White. Then the Claibornes moved south to Botetourt Springs on the first leg of their overland journey to Natchez, and widower Latrobe went tearing after. Near that small resort, in a graveyard, the bereaved man and the unsophisticated Miss Claiborne plighted their troth. Time: exactly two weeks and four days from the day of their meeting. Latrobe's own version claims it was not so long. He said the courtship proper was *all* at Botetourt and that it required "less than a week." Anyway it was short.

If the waters unassisted did not bring these affairs speedily to a head, the chase did. As a mating device Eros never had anything better than the Springs Tour: the belles entraining with their families for the next resort, the beaux tumbling after, breathless in pursuit, fearful of losing them forever in that wide domain that was the South. Another Baltimore lawyer, one David Hoffman, recorded the ups and downs of four assorted affairs which he followed all the way from Capon Springs in eastern Virginia through the whirligig around the big Springs, the Warm, the White, the Salt and the Sweet, in that order. One more Spring, one step nearer the altar. By the time the eight of them, widow, widower, belles and beaux together finally reached the Sweet, they were ready for the grand showdown. As the score came out, there were two matings, one stalemate and one complete bust-up, a fair average. That was the way: at the Sweet or the Warm where everybody jumped off for home, the scramble must end, it was now or never.

A two-weeks' chase would do more for a girl than a year of sitting at home; flight was the thing to break a man down, flight and pursuit. Any belle who returned home from the Springs without at least one bona fide engagement per season was renegade to a great tradition and no credit to the family, to say nothing of her own feelings in the matter.

But it was sad about the belles just the same and anyone who knew how the system worked in Virginia could pity them, for the more successful they were the sooner came an end to their gay careers. Everything conspired to get them husbands, Colonel Pope, competition, their soft beauty and not least, their own eager, romantic little hearts. But once whisked into matrimony, they were belles no longer, they were wallflowers and discards. Up at Saratoga it was different, there the matrons still starred in the ballrooms, leading the cotillions; there they could have their wedding cake and eat it too. At the Virginia Springs marriage brought an end to belledom in all but the most exceptional cases, like those of Octavia Walton and Sally Ward. Men's eyes turned from the wedded ones to the fresh crop of debutantes. Dozens of yesteryear's stars, alas, too successful, sat demurely on the sidelines, "nailed," as one of them said, "to the hated wall."

"Oh! piteous to behold, that sad class of beings, young married ladies; like dethroned Princesses they witness triumphs that once were theirs; there they waste their sweetness on the indolent beaux that are too lazy to dance, or some antiquated hero of the old school who compassionates their lonely and deserted state."

Belledom was sweet but the flame of love could singe its wings forever.

The marriage market was overrun with fortune hunters. Any complete catalogue of personnel must include them prominently, as Mrs. Cabell realized when she wrote her Popeiad.

But others there are, the base sordid elves!
Who sigh not for these—their object is *money!*
Ye favored of fortune, take care of yourselves!
Ah! list not their love-tales, though melting as honey.

A young lady from Richmond was shocked one morning to hear from her maid that a very attentive beau had been inquiring about the extent of her papa's worldly goods. However, not all the hunters wore breeches; one had to beware of the skirted schemers as well. J. J. Pettigrew's young cousin Frederick was being pursued by a Miss Randolph, said Mr. P., and he thought it proper to warn the family; if Miss Randolph's aunt was not a "calculating, scheming woman," who had her eye on Frederick as a young man of property, then he was much deceived. In that foursome of lawyer Hoffman's there was a desperate widow who had brought her daughter on the tour for the express purpose of trapping her a husband; it was Hoffman's idea that the old girl had sold one of her slaves to finance this *putsch,* and he chuckled when the daughter drew a gambling wastrel from Prince George County. Served her right and mama too.

The simple truth was that there were more and more fortune hunters because there were more and more fortunes. Southern papas had been growing too rich for the safety of their daughters. In this first half of the Flush Thirties every kind of planter had prospered: cotton, rice, tobacco and sugar. In 1832 the tobacco grower had received an average of four cents a pound for the weed; by 1835 he was getting eight cents. The dollar value of his exports soared in almost the same proportion; now in '35 he was shipping out over eight million dollars' worth, whereas three years before it had been about five millions.

Down in the sugar bowl, in the twenty or so rich parishes around New Orleans that could produce a matured cane, the Mannings and Sorrels, the Aimés, Hendersons and Bringiers were actually receiving about a cent less per pound in '35 than in '30, but they had increased their production about fifty per cent. Strangers gasped at the rate of enrichment to which the sugar bowl planters were accustomed; for all that they were turning out a sticky, tawny, experimental mass of sweetening, no other class of men in the United States could accumulate wealth so fast. Many a man who bought those fabulous arpents by the river proved it by paying for his land with one lucky crop.

Rice and sea-island cotton kept the South Carolina and Georgia coast in a state of chronic prosperity, but the true Midas of all the crops was upland cotton: it gave the magic touch to more pocketbooks over a wider area than sugar or rice or tobacco or all of these together. For the first three years of this decade cotton had brought our friends of the Mid and Deep South something over nine cents a pound; now it was bringing seventeen to nineteen cents, depending on the grade. Double. The export value of the crop in 1831 was twenty-five million dollars; in 1835 it was sixty-four million. More than double. Next year it would be seventy-one million, almost triple. The Singletons, Hamptons, Taylors, Chesnuts, Mannings of South Carolina, the Waltons of Georgia, Claibornes of Mississippi, Rouths and Perkinses of the Louisiana cotton country were able to live in more princely style, buy handsomer plate, build finer mansions, go oftener to the Springs and make a grander show than ever they had or their fathers before them. And all because the world had gone mad about the cheap cotton goods made by the new machines in Liverpool and the cheap cotton laces made by the even newer machines in Lyons.

Take a bale of cotton down Natchez way, what would it do now for an ambitious young lady who longed for the Virginia Springs? What would it do, for instance, that it would not have done in 1830? Perhaps the young lady is Miss Matilda Jane Routh, daughter of John Routh and granddaughter of old Job Routh who was such a magnificent specimen of a man and had accumulated such a sight of land over on the Louisiana side around Lake St. Joseph, an old bend of the river.

The bale of cotton that is to start Miss Matilda on her way to the Springs will weigh, say, 475 pounds. The cotton presses of the Mississippi Valley are more powerful than the Carolina presses; were she depending on a bale of Mr. Singleton's cotton, she would be handicapped at the very beginning, for it would weigh only 325 pounds and probably less. However, 475 pounds at 18½ cents a pound (granting Mr. Routh at least a cent premium for "fine Louisiana" grade) would come to around $87 gross. If we knock off $7 for handling and commissions, Miss Matilda's bale will net her $80.

Clothes aside (she is not buying clothes with this bale), the first thing to come out of her $80 is her cabin passage from Natchez up to Louisville, Kentucky, which she probably calls Shippingport. That will be about $30 and we will allow her $5 for extras and gratuities during the ten days, making $35 in all to Louisville. Arrived at that port, which is just below the Falls of the Ohio, she must debark with the others who are bound up-river and transfer to another steamer that waits above the Falls and will carry her first to Cincinnati, then on to Guyandotte, Virginia, where she must take the stage.

The last leg of her river passage costs her in the neighborhood of $8, including provisions, and raises her expenditure so far to $43. We have brought Miss Matilda by river on the assumption that she is a girl of stamina and firm joints, that she prefers eleven days and nights of the most violent shaking the human frame was ever called upon to support, assuming that she prefers this to the overland journey which would have taken her about twice as long and given her a good shaking of its own kind.

Landed at Guyandotte she has a little less than half of her bale left, that is to say, she has $37, and out of this she will pay $11 to the stage contractor for the journey to the White Sulphur, which is east and a little south from Guyandotte one hundred and seventy miles. Add $3 for the innkeepers along the route and that will bring her total outlay to $57, set down and delivered at Mr. Calwell's receiving rooms, with $23 in her pocket.

That gentleman will charge her $8 a week (or $1.50 by the day) whether she occupies a private cottage or not. Also, Miss Matilda will have to bribe the slaves at this place to get proper service (bribing slaves will give a young lady from the Deep South something of a jolt) and tipping will set her back, say, $3.50 a week, though there were those who figured it twice as much. Board and tips, then, will come to $11.50 a week, on condition that she stays away from the store, resists the itinerant jewellers and the travelling museums and does not patronize the cake man who comes around about noon when her stomach will be intolerably empty. (A great deal is being asked of Miss Matilda.) As she arrived with $23 of her bale left, she will, by a remarkable coincidence, be able to stay at Mr. Calwell's place exactly two weeks, to the minute and to the penny. Which is to say, she has had her trip and a fortnight at the waters out of one bale.

And what would the same bale have done for her in 1830, five years before? Obviously, as her father did not realize much over $40 for it, it would have gotten her as far as Guyandotte and there it would have left her high and dry on the landing. Mr. Routh would have had to throw in the greater part of another bale to get his daughter on to the White and give her a fortnight there.

Not that Miss Matilda would have been hung up very long on the Guyandotte landing. After all, any man who owned fifteen miles of the richest alluvial land in the world on an old Mississippi cut-off, who annually set three to four thousand bales of cotton onto the levee and who was able to furnish his house with marble mantels edged with sterling silver bands would not have stuck at throwing in that extra bale to get her on, as well as another couple of bales to get her back again. But when it came to '35 and he found that the whole business, round trip and all, *and* an extra two weeks at the Sweet could be got out of only two bales when it would have taken twice as many before, he could not have helped being impressed with his good fortune. This was prosperity. This was the vindication of the slavery system. This put the seal of God's approval on their handiwork and made it possible for everybody to go to the Virginia Springs, Newport, Saratoga and Europe.

Or take a fine buck nigger in Virginia, a "prime field

hand," what can he do for the family that he couldn't have done a few years before? Say he is a Gloucester County nigger and his folks have decided to let him go. The family has just sold some more land and can no longer support so many blacks, or the bank is pressing for repayment of the loan it made some years ago for the purchase of a new carriage, or the children are frightened of him; at any rate he is to be sold. In '28 he would have brought perhaps $500, now he fetches $1,200. The price is the top, but he is top too, a brute of a man.

Well, after the old carriage loan is paid off, there is $700 over and above what they would have gotten a few years back, $700 velvet as clean as a whistle. All sorts of possibilities suggest themselves: a new outdoor kitchen, repairs to the east chimney, repairs to the crumbling Negro quarters, a wing to the main house, buying a new cook. Everything about the place is falling to pieces and the cook is tottering on her ancient shanks. But the folk in Gloucester County have never taken kindly to repairs and upkeep; life there has always been regarded as a skylark, their fame is firmly founded in *dolce far niente*, every day in Gloucester is a holiday. So instead of buying a new cook they decide to give the old one a rest, let the repairs wait till some providential tomorrow, go to the Springs with their $700 and come back refreshed for the autumn festivities.

The Sweet and the Salt are their favorites, the White puts on too many airs, and they expect to spend a few days at the good old Warm going and coming. It is quite a party: five adults including father and mother, son, daughter and Aunt Sally. There are three children, a black nurse, the coachman and an extra "boy." There are four horses, two for the carriage and two for father and son, who will go in the saddle.

The five-day journey from Gloucester County to the Warm costs them very little; almost every night they stay with friends and kin on the way; $30 should cover it. At all the Springs they will be charged the same: $1.50 a day or $8 a week for adults, half price or $4 a week for slaves, horses and children. They spend two days with their old friend Colonel Fry at the Warm ($15 for the lot, by the day) and two weeks at the Sweet ($80 a week or $160) and they are about to hop off for the Salt when it occurs to them that after all it might be foolish to pass up the White. People have been arriving with news of the exhilarating doings at that place, how everybody in the world is there, even celebrities from Europe, and how important it all seems compared to the other Springs. And a friend of father's has promised to let them have half of his cottage if they will come, which settles it. The grown-ups, with the exception of Aunt Sally, go to the White, four of them with two horses and two servants, leaving the children, the nurse, two horses and auntie as aforesaid at the Sweet.

One delirious if undernourished week at the White costs father about $60, counting tips for the dining room darkies, champagne and segars for their host. It might have ended there fairly and squarely if father hadn't been put into the notion of buying a private cottage himself. The notion had been driven home by the combined efforts of Warren, his son, and Mary Frances, his daughter, neither of whom, after tasting the joys of Colonel Pope's Billing, Wooing and Cooing Society, could contemplate existence without the certainty of returning next summer. And how, they asked, could they be sure of that unless they had a private cottage? Look at the swarms of unfortunates who were turned away each day at the gate. Father bought one of Mr. Calwell's new cottages in Virginia Row. It cost him $350.

Out of the $700 velvet from the black he sold, father has spent about $600. On returning to the Sweet he finds that the bill for the children, horses, Aunt Sally and nurse comes to $36, including doctor's fees and medicine for summer complaint. Further, it is apparent that the horses have been on thin rations for their $4 a week; feedings of extra grain for the return journey take another $8, and what with this and that they start back home with not much more than $40 in pocket.

Money makes the marriage market. Many a Virginia, Kentucky and Maryland belle who might have been kept steaming at home (and would have been were this five years earlier) was now, in the middle Thirties, able to go on her dream-adventure because the field hands her father sold South were bringing historically high prices. Likewise, many a Mississippi or Alabama or South Carolina young miss came in greater style and an irresistible brilliance of gems because the cotton moving to Liverpool was netting father between fifteen and twenty cents a pound. Naturally, male aspirants of every degree of eligibility and perfidy crowded after them, and what with one circumstance leading to another, Colonel Pope was busy as a bee in a tar bucket keeping things on a properly Southern, or chivalrous, level.

VII

Boom in Cottage Rows

THE upsurge of prosperity touched off a building boom at the Springs and one of the maddest of all the builders was Dr. Burke down at the Red Sulphur. The Red Sulphur was in a narrow little valley, "a wild and unpromising gorge," in the words of its new owner, so deep that it lost the sun about four-thirty in the afternoon, even in summer, surely an unlikely place to sink a fortune. "It would be difficult to conceive a spot better calculated to discourage an attempt at improvement," said the doctor and, blandly undismayed, he began at once to demolish the log huts (it had been a primitive spa for years) and build his pretty cottage rows.

The good doctor was convinced that he had found the one water in the world for the cure of phthisis pulmonalis in its milder manifestations, and since phthisis pulmonalis was far and away the most desperate scourge of the country, any reasonable person could understand that a cure for it would pack any gorge, no matter how deep, right to the top with consumptives. In the end, the little village that the doctor prepared for them was as trig as any you could hope to see anywhere, all shining with white paint and interlaced with walks, which he bordered with neat white railings.

The big surprise at the Red Sulphur was the Social Hall. It stood, or hung, on a terrace cut into the steep hillside, poised precariously above Bachelors' Row. It was eighty feet long, forty-two feet wide and had a frontage of nine Ionic columns twenty-five feet high. Who else had a Social Hall? Nobody else, nobody at all. The White didn't even have a drawing room, nor the smug Sweet either, and the affair that Fry called a drawing room in his hotel wasn't big enough to turn a goat cart in. The Social Hall was a measure of the doctor's superiority as a proprietor and a builder.

He was mad about piazzas. He could never get enough piazzas and he could never get them long enough. Ranged along the foot of the hill on one side of his ravine were three cottage rows in the Virginia manner, that is, long narrow ranges under a single roof divided up into compartments euphemistically called cottages: first Carolina House, then after an interval Bachelors' Row (with cabins, said Buckingham, "hardly larger than those on an American packet") and after another interval Philadelphia Row, the abode of families since it boasted two rooms per section. Each of these ranges had its piazza but that wasn't enough for Dr. Burke; there were gaps between them and he didn't like gaps. By filling in between Carolina House and Bachelors' Row with a receiving room and by running a covered way between Bachelors' and Philadelphia Row, he got what he wanted, which, in his own proud words, was "a continuous piazza from the extreme end of Philadelphia Row to that of Carolina House, four hundred and seventy-five feet in length."

On the other side, along the foot of the opposite hill, the piazza display was quite as proud, prouder, what with a two-story portico in front of the Hotel proper and three hundred feet of covered way in front of Alabama Row. The doctor wanted his patients to be able to take their constitutionals, rain or shine. Besides his endless porches he had other little ways of giving pleasure to his guests: good ventilation in the ballroom, a musicians' gallery above the dancers, ice cream on the menu every day and a carpet on the floor of the drawing room.

"In the extent of accommodations," he could say finally, "this Spring ranks next to the White Sulphur." In a way, he was overmodest. The White had so little ventilation in the ballroom that people complained of the "effluvium," and it certainly had no carpet anywhere, not to speak of a Social Hall and four hundred and seventy-five feet of piazza.

James Silk Buckingham, one of the incoming mob of British journalists, happened along about the time the doctor had reared his most magnificent gallery, and Mr. Buckingham declared flatly that as between this place and Saratoga, the pride of the North, there was just no choice. The Red Sulphur could give Saratoga its powerful medicated water and still win, hands down. At Saratoga there was, said Mr. Buckingham, a hot, sandy, dusty town, hardly higher than the heat-stricken cities around it; there were five or six hotels under different managements, "all crowded to excess," and at all of them there was a mad and disorderly rush for seats in the dining room.

Here at Dr. Burke's there was no hot, sandy town, indeed no town at all, but a cool green valley and one commodious establishment with room for everybody. In the dining room there were only two hundred people in a space designed for three hundred; you were blessed with attentive waiters, place cards and, wonderful to behold, a series of those broad Southern fly fans hanging from the ceiling over the long tables, all connected together so that one darky at the ropes could swing the lot of them at once. No such delights were to be found at Saratoga, he said. Some of them, dear Mr. Buckingham, were not to be met with at the other Virginia Springs either. What about ice cream every day in the week?

So the dining room was only two-thirds full. Dr. Burke could not have been so pleased with that as was Buckingham. He had spent about $100,000 on the place, much of it borrowed, and he would have preferred at least some genteel crowding. People should have been rushing to this water. Not only could it take phthisis pulmonalis in its stride, it had a remarkable efficacy for allaying the rapid pulse and putting over-excited folk to sleep, so that the place came to be known as "Sleepy Hollow."

As if that wasn't enough, the doctor discovered that it was splendid for sterility, the kind that came from menorrhagia, a disease of the uterus. You couldn't beat the Red Sulphur water at that, not even the Sweet Spring could hold a candle to it. In fact the Red Sulphur was the only water known that could cure sterility from menorrhagia, said Dr. Burke, cornering the market. Charming women, he said, whose hopes of fruitfulness had been blighted, would, if they followed his directions faithfully, present their lords

with new and improved editions of themselves or per-
chance of their lords. The doctor welcomed the barren,
sped the pregnant guest. He had proof, he could point to
many striking instances of the kind. Dr. Lewis at the Sweet
was not the only one who could blow the sterility trumpet.

Somehow social life at the Red Sulphur never quite
emerged from under the pall of invalidism. For example,
there was a great deal of spitting that wasn't just the cus-
tomary tobacco juice, and while they had music and balls
like the other Springs and pretended it was gay and carefree, the music stopped early so the invalids could get to
bed at a decent hour; and that gave the show away. Also,
Burke would not allow the musicians to play the new and
popular operatic gem, "Home, Sweet Home," because it
made the mothers homesick for their children and obstructed the cure.

If the hale and hearty objected to these things and went
away, the doctor had confidence that double the number
of the afflicted would take their places. He and the Richmond *Whig* were in perfect accord on the prospects. "The
high prices of cotton and tobacco in the South," said the
paper, "and the superabundant capital in the North, will
bring multitudes to the mountains who have never before
experienced the incalculable value of these fountains of
health." And the doctor built on furiously, optimistic for
the future.

❦

Dr. Goode at the Hot was also making brick and mortar
fly, not with the exuberance of a Burke, to be sure, but

The Salt Sulphur

Where the South Carolinian nabobs reigned and nothing was ever amiss.

From a drawing by J. R. Butts, Esq.

enough to give the old place a brighter and broader expression. A sitting room was added to the already ancient hotel, the dining room was enlarged and the new brick cottages that began appearing about the grounds attested the character of Dr. Goode, who was a living examplar of his name, with a dash of hauteur added for stiffening.

But the grandest building of the whole boom was raised at the Salt Sulphur, grander than anything anywhere else, solidest and most imposing affair in the mountains. The Erskine Building, named for one of the proprietors, was of native limestone, blue-gray with touches of brown. It stood up on the side of the hill facing the old hotel, rising three full stories on top of a basement, looking as though its builders had gazed with envy upon those fine mills that the textile barons had been erecting in Rhode Island and Massachusetts, proud in their length and their solidity.

The Erskine was substantial in the same way but it was different too, and the difference was in the adornment: it was fancified with a triple-tiered portico the whole length and height of the façade. There were sixty-eight lodging rooms in the three upper stories (the basement was for the servants), each and every one of them with its own fireplace. The parlor on the main floor boasted four fireplaces. At regular intervals seven huge limestone chimneys pierced the roof.

This impressive pile was built, in large part, on rice and cotton money from South Carolina, for it was the South Carolinians, even the lordly rice-coasters, who had found what they wanted in the Salt and put upon it the seal of their patronage. What they wanted was decent comfort, a management that did not nod and good food, particularly hominy grits for breakfast. All these things being furnished in good measure by the obliging, the intelligent, the ever-attentive, the endlessly accommodating Erskine and Caruthers, the South Carolinians, those most travelled and cosmopolitan of all Southerners, more or less staked the place off for their own.

Erskine and Caruthers could display a streak of diplomacy as well as good management. Not only did they furnish the best table in the mountains, the best indeed anywhere west of Barnum's Hotel in Baltimore, not only had they had both a ladies' and a gentlemen's parlor for years, they knew where a neatly placed compliment would do the most good. When it came to naming that trim row of cottages they had built the year before, they dubbed it Nullification Row, honoring the affair of '32 when their prize guests had shaken their muskets at a Congress and a Union that displeased them. What could make a fiery Charlestonian feel more at home than to live in Nullification Row, what except hominy grits for breakfast?

At two of the Springs the boom of the mid-Thirties had not caught in fertile ground; they were the Sweet and the Warm. Dr. Lewis hadn't put up a new cottage at the Sweet in a dog's age, and when there were crowds, as there always were the last week in August and the first week in September, the overflow still had to sleep in the old stone Court House and the schoolhouse, which was rapidly decaying. Let the suffocating customers hold their patience; Dr. Lewis was saving his bricks and would lay them in his own good time.

The Warm Springs, that other ancient, had some time since been built up and was already running down. The numerous small cabins scattered about were considered, with the hotel, to be sufficient to the needs of the place and no expansion had been undertaken of late. Some of the opinions of his little village could not have made Colonel Fry blush with pride. Peregrine Prolix, the bookman of Philadelphia, dismissed the cabins as mere "huts," and Count Arese of Italy, a very good-natured young man, warned that the rooms were small and dirty.

The sporting equipment was in keeping: "a bagatelle table entirely used up and a ten pin alley with three wooden balls of different sizes, not round." Nobody had a good word for the pillows; they were so thin and meager that one time on a bet a Kentuckian was said to have stuffed eleven of them in his greatcoat pockets. The one and only original drawing room in the mountains was now the "ladies' parlor" and cramped enough, but the bedrooms above in the main hotel had always been thought amply large and airy. And if one must have improvements there was the new and lofty portico that had just been completed, so wide (fifteen feet) that the loungers could stretch their legs to the uttermost inch and still be short of tripping up the promenaders. Everybody was enthusiastic about the portico.

"The Warm Springs are free and easy—the White Sulphur for Etiquette," exclaimed Latrobe. People loved the Warm as they did the companionship of an old friend, for its very homeliness, for the luxury of the pool, for the food and particularly for Colonel John Fry. As long as that short-legged, fat, joking, jumping-jack of a man was on hand, the huts and the mean pillows and the lopsided tenpin balls could be overlooked. He was the greatest boniface of them all, so great that even the chronic croakers fell under his spell. Even Harry Humbug and Featherstonhaugh, for whom everything was too hard or too soft, too hot or too cold, too old or too new, found handsome things to say of Fry: Humbug that he was "one of the most polite, accommodating and facetious landlords that ever lived," and Featherstonhaugh that he was an obliging host and a worthy fellow, praise from Sir Hubert, praise indeed.

Coachfuls of arrivals drawing up in front of the hotel were greeted by no underling, no aid-de-camp but by Fry himself, calling out, "A merry welcome to you, gentlemen!" like a landlord in a book and handing the ladies out of the coach with elaborate gestures, giving them an arm up the steps and into the ladies' parlor while the gentlemen went straight into the office in the basement story, or as straight as possible with the bar right there. At departure time the Colonel was out front to hand the ladies in again and to crack his jest about their going to all the other Springs, then coming back here to be *Fryed.*

Dr. Burke had never seen anyone with Fry's facility in accommodating himself to the varied dispositions of his guests. He was not only a pal to the bar-flies, he was a brother to the invalids; indeed, he always found time to call on the sick either in the hotel or in the cabins. It was a New Englander who rendered him the finest tribute. "When my health was feeble," said he, "and my step slow and tottering, I have leaned on the arm of a Virginian, as on that of a brother. He has visited and comforted me in days of sickness and given me sweet counsel in moments of trial." The Virginian was Fry. He told them funny stories, of which he collected so many that he finally had to keep a list in his pocket, which he was forced to consult when his memory failed him. Burke's prescription for dyspeptics was to spend a week with Fry and either laugh themselves to death or back to health.

But his best parts were played in the dining room and the ballroom. Mealtimes, with his chunky body enveloped in a blue-and-white checked pinafore, he stationed himself at the side table with a great knife and carved the roasts: ham, venison and mutton. He skipped back and forth between the side table and the main table, bringing the ladies their helpings, changing their plates. Whenever a lady arose from the table to leave the room, "he was instantly at her side, armed with the carving knife in his right hand, and presenting his left arm in his most insinuating manner to conduct her to the door." * Some ladies got up and left the room when there was no call for them to do so, just for the fun of the thing. Kentucky ladies.

The ballroom was circled by wooden benches. At one end sat the music, a lone Negro fiddler who not only played his scant repertoire at night but scratched around the place like a ubiquitous katydid in the daytime. Colonel Fry had a son, George, who assisted in the management, and shortly after the business of eating was over for the day, both father and son posted themselves in the ballroom. Every lady as she entered was "whipped up by one of them" and taken over to a bench, often a little bewildered. As soon as there were enough guests on hand for a quadrille the masters of ceremonies arranged the sets; when it came to making up their own they pounced, as a matter of policy, on stiff, newly-arrived females who needed shaking down.

* Featherstonhaugh.

The Frys were enthusiastic dancers. They performed meticulously every curtsy, every turn, every toe-pointing, the back and forth movements, the wheels right and left and then added something of their very own. The embroidery that the elder man got in with his short legs was remarkable. Though he was in his middle fifties he was still the better man of the two at leg-work. This he admitted; his son, he said, was no match for him in the old dances, though he acknowledged the boy's superiority in the modern evolutions. Every evening before the ball closed the Colonel performed the *pas seul* for which he was famous: he cut the pigeon-wing.

That leg-work looked pretty comical, particularly as it came from a professional funny man, but a guest might easily be fooled that way. Minuets and quadrilles were not funny with him, they were serious business and a frivolous partner soon found it out. Let her try to pass a few remarks over her shoulder or let her slight her own leg-work and the Colonel would bounce to her side and set up such a clapping close to her ears that she soon enough got down to business. He could play the clown in the bar or in the parlor but in the dance he was a martinet and he enforced a proper respect for his art. By the time they came to the place for the grand whirl his partners were so disciplined that they were set and ready for anything, which was just as well, for the Colonel nearly whirled their skirts off.

It was a warming hospitality, it shook some of the stiffness out of the strangers, particularly the New Englanders and the Britishers. Right away, at the very first resort they came to, they were treated to a dancing landlord who was also, it appeared, something of a gentleman and of good

Revolutionary stock. It was very disarming. It was said the ladies soon discarded the heavy armor in which they arrived, unlaced and let down. By their second day Fry's gallantries had taken the starch out of them.

Also, there was the pool. There rigidity and tension melted away. It was a large hexagonal affair, covered with a hexagonal bathhouse; it was forty feet across and five feet deep, with a gravelly bottom through which the water welled up continuously in vast volume, bringing with it little bubbles of gas. It was perfectly clear and just as warm as the human heart. Beginning at five o'clock in the morning the ladies and gentlemen bathed at alternate periods, two hours per sex.

The initiates trumpeted this luxury to the world, mincing no words and groping for more. It was, one said, a reservoir of champagne, a pool of perfect delight, "the most luxurious bath in the world." It was so soft, said another, "that the roughest hide will seem smooth, as if anointed with myrrh and frankincense." It was "enchantingly pellucid." No sybaritic eastern monarch had ever commanded anything so transcendent as this. The bubbles, "creeping up your body, produce a titillation the most exquisite, surely, ever felt." And did not Lord Morpeth himself say it beat anything in Europe?

Between Colonel Fry and his pool a guest was certain to be relaxed, unbent, soothed, humored, softened, tickled and enchanted. A taste of that and it didn't matter that things were down at heel and improvements slow, or that in a period of prosperity the owners were inclined to pocket such a rare thing as profits and let their famous lessee get on the best he could.

But after all, the flower and the glory of the building boom was at the White Sulphur. Here was none of Erskine's substantial masonry, none of Burke's tremendous piazzas but in the multiplicity of design, in the breakaway from old forms and in the prodigious amount of activity there was nothing elsewhere to equal this.

Almost every complexion of guest was getting new lodgings. The young bucks, the hunting, drinking, gambling young squires were given some additions to Wolf Row, their abode on the lower bluff away from everybody, where they could whoop and halloo without disturbing the rest of the company and yet be close enough to the stables and kennels to smell them and feel at home. The Baltimoreans were being complimented with a beautiful row of unconnected cottages at the upper end of the grounds, each one a little Greek temple to itself, designed by the talented J. H. B. Latrobe who, with the beautiful young wife he had courted here, was on hand to oversee their construction.

On the opposite side of the lawn the Virginians could swell and blow over the "six noble tenements" that had gone up along Virginia Row since the previous season, several of them a story and a half with Gothic windows and dormers. Gothic and Greek faced each other across the lawn. Or, the South faced itself, the South that fancied itself Greece reborn, Greece of the golden age of slavery, looking across to the mediaeval South, sired by the one and only Sir Walter Scott. With cotton at eighteen cents Mr. Calwell could build in the image of his people, growing daily more classical, and his people could afford to invest in their own images. Joseph Patterson bought one of the Gothic, Jerome Bonaparte one of the Greek.

Mr. Calwell had got round to honoring Louisiana with a row too, in the early simple style, which was proper in the place it was, between old Alabama and older Paradise. But the thing that was creating all the excitement was the building that reared itself in the middle of Louisiana Row and divided it in two. This was Mr. Henderson's house, and partly because it was so grand and partly because of Mr. Henderson himself, it was a sensation.

It stood on a bluff looking down on the dining room, two proud stories on top of a tall basement and it was obvious to anyone that from its upper gallery Mr. Henderson could see all that went on, could see everyone who arrived or departed and, as it looked from below where the people got out of their coaches, could touch the sky with his umbrella.

Mr. Henderson was a Scotchman from New Orleans, a sober-sided gentleman with a rebellious sixty-year-old liver. He went around in the largest, baggiest pair of tropical pantaloons that anyone had ever seen, and the joke around the White was that when he was finished with these flapping garments he used them to bale his cotton in. Possibly. As a matter of fact the Henderson cotton press on the levee could have used most of the pantaloons in Louisiana, and the Henderson plantations up river could have furnished a lot of the filling.

The story of Mr. Henderson's life was the American success story at its most romantic and astonishing. Arriving in America a penniless boy from Scotland, where his father was one of the Dunblane drunks, Henderson had found his way to Louisiana before the United States bought it and had so used his native talents that he was now reckoned one of the richest men in the State, along with his countryman, Alexander Milne. At the age of fifty he had married a Creole heiress of twenty-five, Mlle. Eléonore Zélia Destrehan, granddaughter of one of the French King's Colonial Treasurers, a rich man. Mr. Henderson bought the great Destrehan sugar estate from Zélie's brothers and sisters for $176,000. Five years after their marriage his young wife died in New York City, strangely alone. By the simplest of wills she left all her possessions to her elderly husband.

There had been an estrangement, her sister said, but however that may have been, Mr. Henderson was the inconsolable widower. Erecting a splendid tomb over her grave at Destrehan did not lay his lamentations, and he took them with him, season after season, to the Springs. There in 1833 he found a sympathetic listener in Miss Catharine Sedgwick, the novelist from Stockbridge. He gave her Zélie's miniature and she slept with it under her pillow. Was the widower's grief bridging the way to a new romance? Was the literary lioness softening to sentiment? Miss Sedgwick herself gave the answer. No longer a spring chicken, she thought her pretty niece would be more "suitable" to the gentleman's taste, and there it seems to have ended.

Several years later his new house was finished, by far the finest at the Virginia Springs. As he stood on the topmost gallery he could look down on the splendid coaches under the trees and around the stables, most of them from far plantations in Georgia, Florida, Alabama, Mississippi, Louisiana. From his perch he could watch their owners, men of proud circumstance, parading the walks with their wives, sitting on their piazzas or on the benches under the oaks, riding out in open calashes, wandering in and out of the springhouse just below, and here and there groups of "ladies in pink, blue and white standing on the green grass, shading their delicate faces and gay headdresses under parasols." *

Turning left he could see Colonel Singleton's little cottage above the ballroom. He had a greater estate than Singleton though not so much fame; he must have been nearly as rich as Singleton's friend Hampton, regarded as the richest man in the South. The thing was, he was a part of all this, a nabob among nabobs. These others respected his abilities, they were his friends, they consulted him about the cultivation of sugar, the buying of sugar lands, and when they were passengers on the steamboats up or down the river, they crowded the rails to see the beauty and orderliness of Destrehan Plantation, one of the famous sights of the lower Mississippi. He had come a long way, the penniless boy from Dunblane, son of a shiftless and drunken father. This was the land where such things could happen, this was America.

For still another thing was Mr. Henderson celebrated hereabouts: Hygeia, the statue atop the springhouse dome, was his gift to the Springs. She was carved from a solid block of wood, probably cypress, and painted a gleaming white, a conspicuous and beloved figure from the time when she was mounted on her pedestal in 1835. Dozens felt called upon to describe her, seriously or humorously. Lord Morpeth wrote a poem to honor her and in after years she inspired the naming of a great hotel.

Hygeia's pretty shoulders and breasts were naked to the elements and below her waist her draperies were whipped

* Martineau.

around her legs by an eternal breeze. As to the employment of her hands the wags could never quite agree. According to one she held "in her right hand a cup as filled with water, and in her left hand a vegetable or herb"; according to another, "she holds a scorpion or spring lizard in one hand, to lash on those who grow weary or heavy laden with much eating or drinking and a bowl or platter in the other which is turned upside down." Peregrine Prolix said that "her left arm is folded in the coils of a serpent, which she has just poisoned with a draught of sulphur water." Gazing upon her charms, all men became wits or poets. They could agree, at any rate, that she stood on a base resembling a huge Stilton cheese and that on the cheese was engraved in gold letters, "Presented by S. Henderson, Esq." He had had her copied from a marble statue brought from Rome by his friend James Dick, a cotton factor of New Orleans.

Hygeia and the tall house served notice on the world of the Springs that the White Sulphur had acquired another rich patron, notice to the Virginians and South Carolinians that they could no longer enjoy their old leadership unchallenged, that cotton and tobacco must share the stage with sugar. Louisiana had at last been heard from, the land where money was so plentiful that, as Colonel LeGrand said, it was easier to borrow thirty thousand dollars in New Orleans on the security of a word "than it would be to get five thousand on the best property in Maryland from the cold-hearted Marylanders"; Louisiana where it was more trouble to save money than to make it and where the popular saying was, "Economy is the greatest thief of time."

Mr. Henderson's house was the first of the private cottages on the grand scale, the first to throw out its chest and raise its head and crow loudly of great riches. It was like a challenge, and Colonels Singleton and Hampton promptly took it to themselves. Cotton could take up any gage that sugar could throw down.

VIII

Fête for the Van Burens

ANGELICA SINGLETON and Kit Hampton went up together to see the fine new cottages their fathers were building at the head of the little valley. Masons and carpenters were still busy, would be, in fact, until next season. "They will be two stories high," wrote Angelica to her sister Marion, "each with two rooms and a passage between," which was to say, four rooms each.

There were three of these new summer domiciles in a row up there, of identical design, facing down the valley toward Hygeia and the springhouse. On the same, topmost level were Hampton's and Singleton's; a little below them stood a third for family and friends of the overlords. Each one had a double portico supported by six soaring masonry columns. The effect was imposing, eighteen pillars in one long file, capturing some of the grandeur that was Greece, some of the splendor that was Rome.

To Angelica the prospect was delightful. "We are to have our kitchens and stables there," she said, "and live like princes." The social effect was as dazzling as the architectural. People were saying that the Singletons and Hamptons were becoming exclusive with their new houses, so palatial and set apart, and Mrs. Bayly even told Angelica that if they moved up there the Springs would be "broken up."

The Richmond *Enquirer* was impressed, too, but on the pessimistic side. "The rich are beginning to vie with each other in these summer establishments," it said, deploring the new rivalry that Mr. Henderson had set going. They considered it vulgar. But not Angelica. No misgivings and no regrets assailed her. Being rich and exclusive and able to live like a princess in one of the noblest cottages of all was immensely satisfying.

It was a day in August, 1837, that Angelica went up there with Kit Hampton. She was twenty-one now. As long as she could remember she had been coming to the Springs in the summers with her family. Since she had first started going to Mme. Greland's in Philadelphia years ago, this was the time she saw her parents most; she was seldom at Sumter. Her mother had cried out in rebellion against the long separation; with Marion married and living at Pineville it was lonesome and she wanted the Colonel to bring Angelica home, but he had set his heavy chin. There had been a tremendous row and she had been defeated. Angelica, he said, must have the finest education and after that the finest society in Washington; every advantage must be hers. You will see, he had told her, it will work out for the best in the end.

Angelica had come from her second social season in Washington. Senator Preston and his wife were her immediate sponsors; Dolly Madison was friend and counsellor and often chaperone. She knew everybody, had acquired poise and sophistication. Her clothes came from New York and she had just received a consignment of dresses and hats, a camel's hair challis for evening, a brown linen riding cap with cord and tassels, a sweet bonnet. Perhaps she wore the bonnet that day with Kit; it was white crepe with a wreath of artificial flowers around the crown and three full-blown roses underneath. She would have been very fetching, white crepe and roses against the rich dark ringlets hanging down and framing her face, a face perfectly oval and perfectly amiable. Like her father she had a warm complaisance and like him too, a broad Irish upper lip, but her nature and expression were sunnier than his. That name Angelica had borne the right fruit.

By the following summer they were installed in their new house, Angelica in one of the upper rooms, her father and mother in the other. Any morning across the hall she could hear her mother reading while the Colonel went through his two-hour ritual of preparing himself for the day. It gave plenty of time for Rebecca to read him the papers, the letters (he never read or wrote a letter if he could avoid it), the magazines, the Bible, a message from John Rutherfoord of Richmond to say that he had arranged for the *Whig* and the *Enquirer* to be sent them, another from James Chesnut saying he was on his way, nearing the Salt Sulphur, and that he was bringing some mail and Mrs. Singleton's umbrella. He even proposed spending a week at the White, "if so humble an individual as I am will be permitted to occupy a Cabin there." The Singletons would be laughing at "humble individual." The great tall master of Mulberry was something of a wag; this self-imposed lowli-

Bath Americanus

Spring-going started here with mannerisms imported from Bath, England. Later they changed the name to Berkeley and built this hotel.

From Moorman, The Virginia Springs

The Red Sweet

"Amorous" water and good food made it famous. The ladies
bathed in the smaller bathhouse, lower left.

From Moorman, The Virginia Springs

ness was simply his way of throwing off on the pretensions of some of the empty Spring-going swells.

As Angelica looked out through the pillars she could see their old vine-covered cottage down in the swag of the lawn, once the wonder of the place but looking very insignificant now. Still farther down she might catch a flicker of Hygeia's whiteness through the trees. Up on the right bank Mr. Henderson's lofty house stood out beyond all the other cottages on that line, but it was masterless now. Angelica knew, as did everybody, that the Scot of the baggy pantaloons would never return. That year, in March, they had laid him away in the burial ground of the Red Church at Destrehan, beside the body of Zélie, his young wife, whose tomb gleamed whitely in the sun. Mr. Henderson would not be back to see how the South Carolina cotton planters had outbuilt his own magnificence; the New Orleans doctors had leeched him to death.

The Springs was abuzz with talk of the will he had left. Had anyone, even Catharine Sedgwick, on whom he was said to have been more than a little "soft," suspected that the loosely clad figure that had walked these paths so recently was even then planning his sensational bequests that were raising a stir in the papers of England and Scotland? His slaves were to be freed and sent back to Africa, if they chose; a manufactory for making cheap shoes and cloth was to be established at Destrehan and the residue of his million and a half was to go to relatives, the charity hospital at New Orleans, the churches, the asylums. Down there they were saying that he had been a peculiar man in life but that the peculiarities of his will were too much. How were his vast plantations to be run if the Negroes were to be freed or put to work in the factories? Impractical Scot, humanitarian dreamer. Wills as chuckle-headed as this one were made to be broken; the heirs and the Courts did a good job.

The season promised unexampled brilliance. Over on Angelica's right hand, in the topmost Colonnade cottage, were Colonel Hampton and his pretty daughters, the Hamptons whose name and wealth were already legendary in the South. In the other Colonnade on her left were none other than His Excellency, Martin Van Buren, President of the United States, and Abram, his son and secretary. If neighbors meant anything, they were certainly living like princes. Had she not said they would?

Their own style, too, was bearing out the prophecy. Her father and mother had come up from Sumter with a retinue of six horses and five servants, their largest ever. New furniture to match their elegant quarters had come on from Philadelphia: a sideboard, new matting for the floors, another bedstead, more andirons, fenders, shovels and tongs. With their own kitchen and their own cook from Home they could entertain with lunches, dinners and teas to their hearts' content, escaping Mr. Calwell's eternal potpourri. And if by any chance all these things were insufficient to make them royal, there was this: Angelica was being pursued with the most honorable intentions by Abram, the President's son. In truth, it was probably due to her that the President was here at all.

Since April Angelica had known that the Van Burens were scheduled for the Springs, a fact that did not become common knowledge until several months later. Among Washington society she had acquired the reputation of having "great influence at the White House," and society was making no mistake, she assured her mother. When the Springs plan did come out in Washington, it was laid to her influence.

Or, put it this way. Abram was in love with her and his suit wasn't prospering, since Angelica seemed to have eyes only for a handsome young Englishman named Vivian in Lord Gosford's entourage. So Abram seized upon the idea of a campaign in the romantic, if sulphurous, air of the Springs, with no Vivian around. His father would find the Springs salubrious after his tussle with the 1837 panic and would have the Singletons to look after his comfort. Altogether a charming scheme that might kill more than one bird.

🏵

Angelica had come on early, even preceding her parents, and by the time the presidential party arrived on August 4th everything was in readiness to receive them at the Colonnades. Late, about dusk, word came that the Van Burens were on their way over the mountains from Callaghan's. At once gentlemen ordered out their carriages as though they must rush to repel an attack, and about a score of them swept out of the gate and headed eastward to pick up their guest at the foot of the mountain. It was the custom. The bigger the celebrity, the larger the cavalcade to bring him in.

For weeks now there had been no rain. The roads were deep in dust. People refused to leave the Springs, preferring to sit tight where they were, whatever the cost, to death by choking. When the reception committee returned, bearing proudly in its midst the President and his son and some of their political satellites, the horses snorted miserably in the dust and vast clouds of it rolled into the grounds.

Ever since the President left Washington, reports had been coming in of the extraordinary simplicity of his travelling outfit, and the curious hundreds who now gathered round could see for themselves how true it was. Yes, sir, there was the "plain, half-worn coach" and the single extra horse, the old white driver and the lone Negro servant. There was the baggage strapped onto the boot in the manner of ordinary folk, no extra baggage wagon in planter's style. The social sounding board of the Springs began to throw out praises for such exemplary lack of pomp, such plain republican manners, and it never left off during the whole of the President's stay.

Suddenly aware that it was the summer capital, the Springs buckled down to its duties, plunging into a train of festivity the like of which the mountains had never seen before. First off there was the reception ball, in which the cotillions were put in the shade by some showy Spanish dances staged by the Floridians. After this opening salvo fête walked on the heels of fête: a great barbecue at the Greenbrier River, picnics with orchestra playing in the bushes, a dress ball every night and deer hunts led by the two veterans, Richard Singleton and Wade Hampton II. After nearly every chase Hampton sported the deerslayer's feather in his hat. He was rated the best bird shot in America too.

The gentlemen of the Colonnades were, of course, the recognized hosts-in-chief, with Singleton and his lady taking their responsibilities rather more seriously than their friend, though with an admirable absence of push. They appeared, said the renowned Charleston lawyer, J. L. Petigru, "in the character of persons giving tone to society. She is not ambitious but conscious of her duty to Society and fulfilling it well. Mr. Singleton is here a different man entirely from what he is at home. There he is an indefatigable planter and inveterate turfman. Here he is the politest man of the age, scrupulously attentive to his dress and marked in his civility to the ladies."

Their *politesse* guaranteed the other leaders a hand in the entertaining. One of them was the Honorable John Barney of Baltimore, a lively gentleman in his late fifties who had acquired the title of Beau Brummell of America. Mr. Barney dressed in the "tip of the ton," the *Whig* said, and he was "up to snuff" in a ballroom. That made him a worthy successor to Colonel Pope and something of a rival to Colonel Fry at the Warm, for Barney could cut a pigeonwing with the best and what was more, would be cutting it for many a long year to come.

The Floridians, entrepreneurs of the Spanish dances that opened the festival, and apparently charged with a social seltzer that never stopped fizzing, consisted of Colonel Downing of the Congress, General Hernandez, Judges Allen and Randall and, most important of all, Madame LeVert, whose marriage to a Creole doctor and removal to Mobile made little or no difference to the Floridians. To them she was still the "Florida Rose," and they re-possessed her on every possible occasion.

Octavia Walton she had been, born in Georgia and raised in Florida and, with Cora Livingston, one of the country's nationally famous belles. Better known at Newport and

Saratoga than in the Southern resorts, she had been a favorite of Henry Clay and Washington Irving. Marriage had put no check on her career; she was still a belle and that, at the Virginia Springs, took genius. Later, Sally Ward would be of that stripe and later still, Minnie Allen. Like all geniuses, rules were not for them, and the old one in Virginia that belledom was reserved for the virgins was not so much as a straw in their paths.

In a way Madame LeVert was more extraordinary than the others because she was not beautiful. Professor Frederick Porcher of the College of Charleston, seeing the famous lady at the Sweet Springs for the first time, remarked at once that her figure was under middle stature and wasn't good either; her face "owed more to a good humored expression than to any power of beauty for its charms."

Still more puzzling were her actions. She was "perpetually in motion and continuously noisy," two traits that offended the Professor. At the Sweet he saw her walking down the "street" between the cabin rows and stopping in front of each door to call out to the occupants, "and in a voice so loud that it could be distinctly heard all over the grounds."

But to see her in the ballroom at the White was to understand and forgive. Her animation was infectious. Beaux crowded around her, pleading for dances. Unable to reward them all, she turned her cast-offs into partners for her mother, Mrs. Walton.

"Oh!" she would say, "I am so sorry, I am engaged. But there's Ma without a partner."

This information was delivered with such ineffable sweetness that no beau could refuse. Ma was whisked onto the floor like any belle. Octavia might have been noisy and always unwinding, she might have had a touch of vulgarity that one didn't find in perfectly bred ladies like Mrs. Porcher, but her ultimate charm lay in the warmth and cordiality of her manner. This was irresistible and the Professor admitted, like the gentleman he was, that it finally overcame all his captiousness.

Neither Madame LeVert nor any other female was asked to the President's barbecue at the Greenbrier River, five miles from the Springs. It was exclusively a stag party to eat stag. At long tables under a rhododendron arbor a hundred gentlemen of moment, some of fame, sat down to a feast of three courses. For palate ticklers there were squirrels, pheasants, trout, chicken and turkey. The main dish was venison, in three forms: roast, steak and stew. Those who stayed the course could have pie, apple and cherry, quite lean. Behind the arbor a large band played continuously. The music was shot through with the incessant popping of champagne corks.

"Beau" Barney got to the barbecue late. His handsome stock was askew and his tip-of-the-ton clothes were covered with dust. It seems that a squad of ladies, wreaking their vengeance for having been excluded from the jamboree, had pounced on the Beau and shut him up in a room in Paradise Row, from which he had just made his escape. He was led into the arbor by Colonel Downing to deafening cheers and pounding on the tables. He was the hero of the day. Behind the arbor the band played, "Barney, Let the Girls Alone."

Even grander was the President's hunt. Colonels Hampton and Singleton had gallantly invited the ladies. The gentler sex and their non-hunting escorts were to follow in carriages and on such nags as they could find, as far as Mrs. Bedford's great meadow and there, grouped around His Excellency, they were to await the divertissement. The hounds, if they did what was expected of them, were to run the stag out of the deep hollows and onto the stage.

Young James Calwell (one of the nine Calwell princelings whose financial requirements turned the old man's pockets inside out) was master of the pack. As always on a hunt morning, he rode up alone from the kennels below the springhouse. Not until he reached the center of the lawn did he sound his horn, whereat the Negroes opened the kennel gates and thirty couple of famished hounds came tearing up into the grounds, where everybody could see their frantic excitement and catch it too.

It was the signal for mounting. The ladies who had been waiting on the cottage porches around the sylvan amphitheatre fluttered down the steps into their carriages. The huntsmen moved off westward with the pack and a large and colorful cavalcade scrambled after. There were cabriolets and hacks, landaus and berlins and even coaches, filled with human bouquets of mingled pink and blue and white, in embroidered muslins, organdies, lawns and filmy woolen challis. Fluffy and puffy and coy were still the predominant notes in dress, very large sleeves and blown-up skirts, but some were there in the slinkier new style, tight sleeves down to the wrist, gowns that looked infinitely longer and more graceful because they were not bouffant with petticoat filling. From under bonnets, tied with long veils, elaborate side curls escaped. Tiny, lace-trimmed parasols waved aloft, shading faces of delicate, rose-tinted pallor.

The elements were propitious. "A slight rain the evening previous," said Mark Pencil, "had laid the dust somewhat and the ground was thought to be in good order. We went forth in gallant style, and only wanted the hawkers to have imagined ourselves in the reign of Queen Elizabeth on a Holyrood day." Gallant style, indeed. Sixty hounds made a noble sight shimmering along the roadbed. Some of the hunters wore the red broadcloth called "pink," others were in velvet coats and caps, still others in linen and some in white corduroy breeches. There was more style to hunting nowadays than there had been.

"In the reign of Queen Elizabeth on a Holyrood day," summed it up. They were transformed into Elizabethans and theirs was the elegance and panoply of a royal court bound for the tourney. In imagination they were winding through Great Windsor Forest on a holiday, with gaping yeomanry bowing on either side. Or better still, they were Walter Scott's lords and ladies on a journey from one castle to another, but in any case they had been transported into the times of their dreams, wafted back into an age of chivalry they adored and emulated, a time of hawkers and jesses, of long capes and stags at eve. As a matter of fact, those new flowing styles the more modish ladies were wearing, with conscious mediaevalism in bodice and sleeve and skirt, made the archaic mood not only easier to achieve but to understand.

Deployed in Mrs. Bedford's meadow, through the long wait for the hunters' return, what were their recorded amusements? For one, the recollection of Sir Walter's poetry of the hunt, for another, Greek mythology. The young man who melodiously declaimed "The Lady of the Lake" was matched by the other young man who retold the story of Actaeon, the hunter, how as a penalty for having gazed upon the naked Diana bathing he had been turned into a stag and torn to pieces by his own hounds. Very beautiful, very apt.

The carriages turned and wheeled from point to point, drawn by false rumors of the approaching hunt, but at last it came as the master huntsman had promised, the stag bounding into full view, the hounds sweeping across stream and meadow after him, finally running him back into the fold of the mountain again. The kill was off-stage, as though in deference to the sighs and cries of the tenderhearted creatures in the carriages who called for mercy and hid their curl-framed faces. It might have been rehearsed, so neat was the performance.

Throughout the festivities of the season Major Abram Van Buren courted Angelica, hoping to drive the picture of the beautiful Vivian from her memory. No others were more observed than they, unless it was the President himself. That gentleman was affable and ingratiating, mixed with the crowds, breakfasted, dined and supped at the public table, exchanged calls with the ladies and gentlemen. "He graces the ballroom," said one, "mingles in our rides, walks and daily amusements as one of the humblest individuals of the Republic." He was not just a guest of certain toplofty families from South Carolina, he was a democrat.

Politically conscientious, he made side trips to all the Springs, even the Blue, the Red and the Gray Sulphurs, missing none. He made the popular excursion to Colonel

Crow's tavern for breakfast and was courteous to all who introduced themselves. At the Salt he was given a Grand Ball and an illumination, "two thousand candles simultaneously bursting on the eye." Everywhere it was the same, he garnered "golden opinions."

Best of all, he observed the taboo, the truce of the waters: no politics. At the sulphur fountain, it was maintained, men were purged of their political virus and Mr. Van Buren was purged like all the rest. It was remarked that all had been sweet harmony at the barbecue among the disparate political elements, Van Buren men, Whigs and Conservatives. The arts of gentility had completely possessed them. What was base and sordid had been driven from the gates as the genteel themselves had been driven from Washington by the Jackson hordes. If that was to be the capital of rowdyism, this would be the capital of good manners, and indeed it was.

They were entranced by a handiwork that was part their own, part God's. God had furnished a pellucid, mirroring pool which, when one looked into it, gave back reflections that were only noble, if male, and only angelic, if female. For their part, they had built, through the years, a social atmosphere that any man need only breathe to have his baser metal turn to gold.

As though by divine direction, the choice fell upon Beau Barney to express how they felt about this. He wrote that there were, surrounding His Excellency, descendants of Pocahontas, Patrick Henry, the Harrisons, Brooms, Tallmages, Hamptons, Singletons and Carrolls, "with many others equally talented and respectable, composing a society where sprightly and intellectual conversation, joyous with refined politeness, and invariable good humor, give an unfading gem to the swift flight of time. Pleased with ourselves, we are delighted with each other, calumny is unknown, and scandal is not even breathed in faint whispers."

❧

This enchantment, this idyll, seems to have been genuine and not just a case of auto-intoxication. It worked almost as well on the New Englanders and the Old Englanders as it did on the Southerners themselves. It worked so well on that old sea dog, Captain Marryat, that he went away convinced that the spas in Europe could not hold an aristocratic candle to this one.

To begin with, Captain Marryat was lucky in his host, none other than Beau Barney himself. This gentleman had grabbed off the literary lion and installed him in his cottage at the upper end of Baltimore Row, from the piazza of which one could easily toss a pebble onto the hallowed verandahs of Wade Hampton and Richard Singleton. A little more heft would put one right up to the front door of the President of the United States. On his right hand, an even shorter throw away, the Captain had Lady Stafford and Lady Carmarthen, two of Baltimore's daughters (and granddaughters of Charles Carroll) who had married English titles. Any British commoner was bound to be impressed, if not by the President, then certainly by their Ladyships.

The sophisticated Maryland crowd saw that the Captain got around and tasted all the pleasures. He went to the balls and danced not only with the belles but with the "pretty and wealthy widows" who seemed so plentiful. His admirers took him to the phrenologists, who were holding session in the ballroom and were all the rage. It was hoped that the professors of the cranium would reveal how the author of *Midshipman Easy* turned out his works at such phenomenal speed, but all they got was: "Idealism very large, Humor large, Wit very little, Modesty and Diffidence very large." Stupid stuff, at one dollar a head.

He went to the *soirées musicales,* which were, of course, the old informal gatherings of the ballroom removed to the private cottages, socially brushed up and lubricated with tea. There he heard the exceptional musical talents that had converged on this place from the wide South, including Mrs. Blank-Blank of Nashville singing "The Banks of the Ganges" accompanied by Mr. So-and-So with *both* violin and voice; and among numerous other lights there was Madame LeVert, strumming her own guitar and singing the Spanish airs of Florida.

They took him to a party in Wolf Row, overlooking the stables, and there he met the young huntsmen, the bucks. Their drinking was prodigious, their singing, too. "Hock! Give us Hock, sparkling Hock from the Rhine." There was a large mint julep in the middle of the table, in a bowl hoary with frost. It was called a Hail Storm, he learned.

After that they went to hear the serenaders and follow them on their rounds. That would be about midnight. The ball would have been over at eleven and the little village retired to its rest, the lights out and quiet settled down. Then softly out of the night there would come music, a flute playing, a man's voice singing. What could enthrall the foreigner more than this frank romance, what could speak so eloquently of the soft graces of Southern culture and give him to believe that he walked in a sweet, strange Provençal night as in a dream, with troubadours?

Serenading had its code. Incognito was the word. The night that hid identity must never be drawn aside, the songster give no warning of his coming and leave no token. Behind drawn blinds the lady trembling in her bed must betray no sign of recognition, never shake the curtains or show a pale hand. But one thing they and everybody else knew: this was the song of farewell. Tomorrow morning, lover or lady would be gone.

No lad sang alone. The support of a companion voice or of a flute or a guitar was always there with him in the shadow, or the more substantial support of Murray's entire band, as happened most often nowadays with money so plentiful. The buckoes who could neither sing nor play got Mr. Murray and his musicians out almost every night now. Under one window after the other they played softly for the silent lovesick Cyranos who followed on, huddled together in the misty darkness.

Visitors from a bleaker North were enchanted. One of the New Englanders told of being awakened on a midnight "by a strain of sweet music, breaking in upon the stillness of the night," an interruption to sleep that he was never to forget.

"Soon a voice came stealing, in unison with the strain, upon my ear. It was breathed from the lips of some youth beneath a lady's window in Paradise Row, and it was with singular appropriateness of selection that the serenader, in a mirthful and arch style of execution, commenced with 'We're All a Noddin',' following this introduction with 'Oft in the Stilly Night,' and closing his performance with 'Farewell, But Whenever You Welcome the Hour.' Soon all was hushed, the tinkling of the guitar, the breathing of the flute, the warbling of the clarionet, the swell of the mellow horn, and the accents of the serenader, all died away, and the fair objects of this graceful compliment were left to dream of the sounds to which they had been listening, just as the evening star was also pillowing itself upon the clear mountain top."

With such a course of treatment—the eminent neighbors, the wealthy widows at the balls, the *soirées musicales,* the Hail Storm in Wolf Row, the serenades—it was little wonder that the rumored gruffness of Captain Marryat melted away. Every day more proofs of aristocracy came to his attention. Angelica, that pretty, dark haired girl of the Singletons, was destined, they said, to be mistress of the White House if she accepted the Major, for Papa Van Buren was a widower and the first house in the land was without a hostess. That urbane and handsome gentleman across in Virginia Row (which he preferred to "the hill") was Andrew Stevenson, Minister to England and uncle to Angelica. That tremendous fellow, his companion, was Governor Barbour of Virginia, called The Thunderer. Their Ladyships down the Row were even more impressive when one learned they were the sisters of Mary, Lady Wellesley, sister-in-law to the Duke of Wellington. Press all these people and circumstances through the Captain's literary head and some glowing opinions were bound to come out.

Even Spa, he said, in its palmiest days, when the princes had to sleep in their carriages at the doors of the hotels, was not more in vogue with the elite than these White Sulphur Springs. Of all the places in America, here and here only could one meet with really select society, far superior to that "great mixture" in Washington, the capital.

❦

After the final serenade all was quiet again, but there were still several lights burning, breaking the darkness at the lower end of the grounds. One was a lamp hanging under the dome of the springhouse, dropping a feeble glow onto the dark pool. Occasionally a muffled-up invalid would appear in its circle, hoping to speed his cure by this nocturnal drinking. The other lights were in two cottages off to the right of the springhouse, backed against the hill and surrounded by a white paling fence, which the Calwells rented to the gamblers for their faro banks. There, after all else was silent and asleep, life at the Springs went on.

The rooms were low-ceilinged and hot, thick with segar smoke and the smell of horsey men and oil lamps and the strong cutting odor of whisky and cognac brandy. At one side of the room was the table with the drinks, a Negro in attendance filling the gentlemen's glasses. A large table in the center would be the "bank" with the faro layout spread over it and the keeper moving about it, making change, selling counters to the players, standing watch over the game. The dealer, always a man of resplendent though not notably clean garments, sat in the middle of the table's long side, in front of the layout, sliding the cards from Captain Bailey's patent box and calling the play.

"The six loses, the Jack wins." Turn by turn (two cards were a turn) he slipped them out of the box. "The Queen loses, the ten wins." Between turns he settled the bets, first

Rockbridge Alum

For a long time it was second in size only to the White Sulphur. Scene of Cabell's *Jurgen*.

From Moorman, The Virginia Springs

Bath Alum

Over-optimism in the 1850's built the charming group at
the Bath Alum beside a spring that often went dry.

From Moorman, The Virginia Springs

picking up the counters on the losing cards, then paying the bets on the cards that won. Resuming again, the voice would drone out, "The four loses, the ace wins," and then on an average of three times in every two deals, provided the cards had been honestly dealt, there would come a split: "The five loses, the five wins," and on the splits he would take half of whatever was bet, whether it was bet to win or to lose.

The betting could be complicated and the dealing could be tricky, but essentially faro was a simple game in which suits were without meaning and only denominations mattered; the Queen of hearts and the ten of diamonds, for example, were merely a Queen and a ten, and the players bet them that way to win or to lose. It was as intriguing as it was simple; few men played anything else. "Its fascinations over other games will ever beget it votaries," Captain Bailey had said and that was still true long after it had whipped him.

Pharaon it was called in France and it had entered America by way of New Orleans. The equipment was rudimentary: a deck of cards, some counters or checks, some markers (oblong ivories) and a layout, which was a green baize cloth with a complete set of thirteen spades painted on its surface and spaced far enough apart to permit the placing of the chips without crowding.

When a player was betting on a card to win he simply placed his counters on it, but if he was playing it to lose he topped his counters with a checker or button and that was called coppering the bet. With automatic regularity the dealer drew in the counters the players lost and paid out the bank's losses, but out of all he paid he took the bank's two-and-a-half per cent, that fatal percentage of which Bailey knew the consequences. "And let all things be managed however fair, the bank will beat you." The gaming gentry had been warned, by an authority.

Lose-win, lose-win, the dealer's voice swung up and down interminably, far into the morning hours, while the gentlemen of the South wagered everything from hard crop money to the horses and Negro servants they had brought with them to the Springs. Others might cry out against Calwell for permitting this "blot on the fair face" of the establishment, but they, never. This was what they came for.

One midsummer night in the Van Buren season there were two men in that low, odorous gaming room who were to make some trouble for themselves, for their friends and for two gentlemen of consequence in the Colonnades. The first was a young man up in the front rank around the bank, in the thick of the play, placing his bets on the layout, tense and anxious, for this was the breakdown of his resolutions against gambling. Here in this carefree and reckless company of the Springs his resistance had melted away and for the first time in months he was bucking the Tiger. He was young J. W. Stevenson, son of the popular Minister to England and own nephew to Mrs. Richard Singleton. Luck was against him. The counters raked in by the dealer far outnumbered those that came back to him.

The other was an older man, Powell McRa, nephew of Colonel Singleton. He was not in the play, just chin-wagging, looking on. One never quite knew what to expect from Powell, an erratic gentleman who had married a Northern lady and lived in New York, but then one never knew what to expect from Mary, his mother, either, a pathetic woman who wandered hither and yon trying to shake off the furies that clutched at her skirts and who finally fetched up in a Philadelphia asylum.

The early-to-bed crowd never knew what happened in the faro room that night. In the morning the word flashed round that one of those fierce, periodic gambling storms had broken and that one of the bucks had fled on the early coach for Lexington. It was young Stevenson. He had been seen cheating at cards, they said. Who had seen him? That was the mystery. Powell McRa had passed the charge, acting, he said, for a friend of his whose identity he would not reveal. He denied that he himself had witnessed the lapse.

It was a peculiar and delicate situation and everyone was walking on eggs. But already the case had gone to its judges, Colonels Hampton and Singleton, as a matter of course. In all breaches of the code they were the court of arbitration, nobody questioned their authority or their leadership.

Young Stevenson wrote from Lexington to Colonel Singleton protesting his innocence. "It is a foul slander!" he cried. He had not cheated and he had a right to know who his accuser was. Why should Powell McRa be allowed to disgrace him in the eyes of the whole Springs and refuse to bring out his accuser? "Surely," he pointed out, "the keeper of the table and the dealer of the cards with their accustomed keen-sightedness ought at least to counterbalance the suspicions of a man who will not come forth."

The arbiters took their time; the thing was serious, it could mean death on the field of honor. The dilemma was a cruel one for Colonel Singleton: his wife's nephew against his own. But when he had finally resolved his doubts, he wrote to Powell in New York. Stevenson's innocence had been publicly proclaimed by his friends and if sustained, "you will stand charged with an unfounded slander, with being the vile calumniator." Hard words. You must come here, he said, and fight or admit your error. The stern judge ruled the uncle, kinship was a thing aside. This was the South; slurs on a man's gaming table manners were payable in blood.

Mysteriously that letter was never sent and the duel never fought. Could the Colonel then have suspected the truth? The full force of it did not hit him until several years later when he was summoned to the asylum at Charlestown, Massachusetts. There, in solitary confinement, was his nephew Powell, a hopeless lunatic. At last, that strange business of the gambling room was liquidated. Powell's explanation that he was "acting for a friend" had plainly been a step forward into madness, and so young Stevenson was absolved. For Richard Singleton, aghast before this new evidence of dementia in the blood, it was a heavy blow.

But that was still in the future, where the furies waited. Now, in '38, in the Van Buren season at the Springs, Richard Singleton was the social leader, "marked in his civility to the ladies," patron of the White Sulphur, rich, a famous racing man and horse breeder, friend of the President, happily installed in his splendid Colonnade cottage and regarded with envy by the multitude.

❦

In their last walk together under the eyes of Hygeia, Angelica and Abram Van Buren looked into a future suffused with *couleur de rose* and made their final plans. Abram's pursuit was over. Angelica had put all hopes of Vivian (whom in April she was calling "the handsomest, most lovable man I know") out of her mind. She and the President's son fixed their marriage for the 27th of November at Home, in Sumter.

So the climax of the season of '38, the greatest the Springs had ever known, took place off-stage, in those high square rooms overlooking Richard Singleton's private race course. There were gathered the President, Cabinet members, Senators, Congressmen, great family names of Virginia and Carolina, Richardsons, Prestons, FitzSimonses, Hamptons, Coleses to give their blessing to the sweet, dark-ringleted Angelica and to gaze admiringly down those radiating trees as down the spokes of a fabulous wheel to the rose-bordered Camden road.

It was a triumph for Richard Singleton. By keeping Angelica at Mme. Greland's in Philadelphia, giving her two seasons in Washington and maintaining her all her life as a little princess of the Springs, he had put her into the White House. Did not Rebecca his wife see how right he had been? Why, no daughter of the haughty rice coast had gone so far as that.

Angelica and her husband set out from Home on the journey to Washington in a coach drawn by some of her father's proudest horses. She was on her way to be mistress of the White House. She would be in the center of a great stage. So entranced was she by this glittering prospect that she did not stop by to see her sister Marion at Pineville as she had promised she would.

IX

Mr. Calwell Had a System

IN A managerial way things were better at the White Sulphur than formerly. Some effort was made to live up to this broadening fame, to these renowned guests and the rising level of cosmopolitanism which they brought with them.

The hogs were now confined in other pastures, no longer permitted to root under the cabins where beauty or dyspepsia fought for sleep. At the receiving rooms the new Mr. King was a great improvement on the old Major Anderson. "His obliging attentions and courtesy are acknowledged by all who know him," quoth Boston's Colonel Perkins. Alabama's Dr. Burke said he was "uniformly civil and obliging, trained for his calling."

The deer hunts were better organized and the pack increased from thirty to thirty-five couple of hounds. The culinary department could take on even the largest picnics without breaking down. Which is to say, there had been some advance since the day a decade before when J. P. Kennedy had pronounced it *"par excellence the most in-*

geniously uncomfortable spot on this continent." It was something but it wasn't enough. Voices of complaint rose from hundreds of throats and hundreds of pens dripped with the bitter ink of protest.

For example, Mr. James Silk Buckingham of London was shocked at the almost total indifference to bedroom furniture on the part of the management. Francis Scott Key complained of the dirt and the noise and the fleas in rhymed stanzas of four lines (a long time after "The Star Spangled Banner"), advising a friend poetically to stay away. Professor Porcher revealed that even in the Van Buren season the dining room was the same old madhouse it had always been.

"In the service of the meals the wildest disorder prevailed," he said. "One was scarcely secure of the dish which lay before him." Here the human race sank to its lowest level, ate like animals and brandished forks at waiters who snatched up the pie. It was here that Miss Ann Price had seen a man "who so far forgot himself as to walk across the table for something he wanted." The tipping system still flourished, with the silent consent of the Calwells, and there were those who calculated that in order to eat at all one had nearly to double his board bill with bribes.

It was said that all meats were cooked together in one huge cauldron. They were perhaps given a touch of individual roasting afterwards, which did not, as Professor Porcher remembered, prevent the mutton from tasting like ham and the ham from tasting like mutton. When President Fillmore became deathly ill at the White it was given out that a combination of mutton and corn had done it, but those who were familiar of old with the practices of that kitchen thought they could understand it without the corn. "As everything is cooked together there," Mary Watson, age fifteen, set down in her journal, "it is very unwholesome."

The chorus of grumbling was occasionally punctured by a hosanna from someone who said the food was good and abundant and that all were satisfied, though on examination such tributes were usually found to have been inspired in June before the rush began or in September after it was over. Peregrine Prolix said that all that was needed was patience; if you could sit still long enough you would be well fed. But the few banzais were drowned out by the caterwauling.

Such lack of appreciation could be vastly annoying to a proprietor who had admittedly built up the greatest, the most picturesque and the most popular Springs in the South, who could point with pride to the crowds clamoring at the gate. Patently the kickers were ingrates and deserved what they got. What they got was the Calwell System.

It was a good system because there was no answer to it. When a guest came to the be-cued Calwell with the usual tale of woe about not getting anything to eat or not having his room changed, the suave old gentleman very politely suggested that the guest must surely be laboring under a misapprehension. He was not being charged anything for his food or for his room either.

"You are paying me $9 a week for the use of the water; I am giving you your food and lodging free." He was sorry if the guest didn't like the food or thought the quarters unfit for habitation, but after all when he was getting them for nothing what had he to complain about?

Blue Sulphur Springs

Where many a rejected guest went when he couldn't get
in at the White Sulphur. Others preferred it.

Water color by J. H. B. Latrobe

As the master found this dodge successful, so did the servants. When Harry Humbug objected to the cubbyhole he was given over the orchestra, his porter set him straight at once. "Mars Calwell don' charge fo'pence ha'penny fo' eatin and sleepin," said the darky. "He charge nine dollars a week fo' de use ob de water."

That was the Calwell System for quieting the pesky guest, and it remained in active service as long as its inventor lived, bringing him peace of mind and fame as well. Long after he was dead, even after the War Between the States, people liked to recall how at the White one always paid $9 or $10 or $12 or even $18 (end of the Fifties) for the use of the water and had his bed and board thrown in.

Not that he was always so devious. Pushed too far he could hit straight from the shoulder. The story was going round in the late Thirties that he had informed one troublesome stranger, "Sir, I did not send for you to come to my house and when you desire you can leave it as freely as you came." He was known to order a servant to saddle the horse of a malcontent, take it around to his cabin door and deliver him a message that the space he occupied would be required for another guest immediately.

It was the stranger, not the Southerner, who ran afoul of the Calwell System, the stranger who was under the mistaken notion that he should be getting his money's worth and went to headquarters for redress. The Southerner did not put his neck into that noose at any rate, knowing as he did that the only difference between a private host and a public one in Virginia was that the latter had to take money for entertaining you. You didn't outrage his dignity by running to him with complaints about the roast and the linen any more than you ran to your private host. Buckingham remarked, not without surprise, that the Southerners contented themselves by breathing their complaints, if they complained at all, *sotto voce* among themselves but not in public, innkeepers being gentlemen. He was amazed that many of the richest guests not only did without the furniture of civilized man but did so "quietly and contentedly."

The Calwell System of charging for the water and throwing in everything else helped to bring prosperity to many of the surrounding resorts. Those who took umbrage at the system or couldn't stand having their comforts curtailed took refuge at the Sweet, the Red Sweet, the Salt, the Blue Sulphur, the Warm, the Red Sulphur, the Rockbridge Alum, the Healing, the Fauquier White, the Hot (if they were ill) and many others which were springing from the earth. And Southerners, however long they were on patience and forbearance, could mount for other points as quickly as the aliens.

But now something else arose at the White which turned many a Southern face toward other waters. The miasma of social change rose into the air. When the Virginian in particular sniffed this contagion he was truly disturbed, saying things were no longer what they were. A correspondent sent the dolorous news to the Richmond *Enquirer* and that journal spread it down a column for all to ponder.

"I regret to say that I find an evident change in the social character of this famous watering place. The different elements of society do not seem to mingle in that harmony that used to characterize the place. The Northerners seem to keep together—the Southerners, with a few exceptions, form their own party. Instead of there being one great family, all contributing to each other's pleasure, there are distinct castes that move in their particular orbits.

"One fatal error seems to me to be the fact, that a number of wealthy gentlemen have built elegant establishments on the skirts of the Springs, have furnished them luxuriously and keep up separate and distinct ménages. This at once breaks up the original and simple plan upon which things were once conducted here. I am sorry to see this striking evidence of change. I am afraid that it will destroy the great charm of this mountain retreat. One thing I am sure, that the Virginians are not to blame." (The Virginians did not have the money.)

The Virginian liked to think of himself as a plain and homespun appearing gentleman with a noble pedigree, which naturally put him above airs and snobbery and fine clothes and turnouts. Spying these low-down affectations at the White he was inclined to pack his portmanteau. Editor Syme, for example, of the Petersburg *Intelligencer,* was altogether out of sorts with the place for its "exclusiveness, coterie-ism, cliqueism, swell-headism and every other antisocialism." Off he flew to the Blue Sulphur where, he claimed, there were fewer but more agreeable people.

One malcontent who subscribed himself merely "Harry" announced that he was tired of the pomp and circumstance there (besides being tired of an empty stomach) and that he was going to the Red Sweet. A Richmond gentleman looked into the ballroom and saw much that was finnikin in manners, he said. The easy dignity that once had characterized the society there was no more. He congratulated himself; he was off to the Salt on the morrow. So it went. Some rebelled at the System, some shied off from social change. The great pin wheel that was the White Sulphur whirled and sparkled and popped, shooting off its disgruntled guests like angry sparks in all directions.

⁂

Those who fled to the Salt and into the arms of Messrs. Erskine and Caruthers found waiting for them one pleasure after the other, beginning with the hearty welcome. As the coach rolled over Indian Creek and into the yard, there were Colonel Erskine and his partner, Mr. Caruthers, on the porch of the office. They hired no minion to greet their guests, they were always on deck themselves. It was a fine thing to hear Colonel Erskine's loud whistle summoning Ryall and the other servants to take down the baggage. Mr. Caruthers didn't whistle. He had a harelip and left all the whistling to Erskine, though he made up for it later by his assiduous attentions to his guests, being fond of making himself useful to the ladies, who might, Professor Porcher thought, have cheerfully dispensed with his services.

The harelip of poor Mr. Caruthers stands out more prominently than it should because it was against a background of practical perfection. Nobody could find anything of ill report there, everything was always marvelous from first to last, "the table better, the rooms neater, and the company more select than anywhere else." Only two things were ever said of the Salt that could by any possible chance be construed in its disfavor. One was that there was "a *smaller proportion* of low characters than was to be found, perhaps, at any other of the Springs," and the other was that the proprietors regularly, after everyone was abed, threw muriate of soda, a strong purgative, into the water. But Professor Rogers, who made a comprehensive analysis of all the Springs, proved this to be a canard. There was enough Glauber salt of its very own in this water to satisfy anybody.

One did well to arrive there on a Saturday, for a Salt Sulphur Sunday was soothing as a benediction after the tumult of that other spa. The folk down here, many of them pew holders in St. Michael's on Charleston's Meeting Street, believed thoroughly in God and in the praise of his name, which they did not intermit simply because they were in the mountains on a holiday. They had services on Sunday and they had vespers on weekdays when vespers could be got. The Reverend John Johns of Baltimore and some fellow divines, when they heard of such godly people at the Salt, came down from the White Sulphur to be with them and conduct services, though it seems they had heard about the good food too.

The time came when there was a pretty stone chapel erected across the road, paid for by the contributions of the guests themselves, and there every Sunday one might find the consolation of two Christian services, church in the morning and meeting in the afternoon. It was an important distinction; church was Episcopalian, meeting was Presbyterian. At church the divine in vestments gave a discourse, which was tasteful and properly circumscribed; at meeting the divine in the frock coat preached a sermon which was more than likely to be constructed according to Blair, with introduction, divisions and conclusion, and which was certain to be too long. Both the Episcopalian and the Presbyterian were paying for their board, the conduct of service being the only charge rendered the gentlemen of the cloth by the Springs landlords.

Another thing that was consoling about the Salt, one always found lots of South Carolinians. They gave it a high tone; they ranked, in the opinion of most people, with the superior food and the Glauber-salted water. "It was always their place," said Dr. Mütter, one-time resident physician. They outnumbered the Virginians three or four to one; by actual count one summer there were 136 South Carolinians to 40 Virginians, 12 from Maryland, 11 from North Carolina, 10 from Louisiana and so on down the list. It was said in after years in *The Nation* that their "exclusiveness and somewhat arrogant demeanor" drove lesser folk out of this Eden but the truth was, the fame of their cultured and agreeable company brought more people running there to see them than their haughtiness chased away.

Even an occasional Virginian (such was the benign influence of the waters) thought the South Carolinians were the cream. Go to the Salt, said Mr. Cowardin, and experience the pleasure of talking politics with pure Southerners, not party heelers. Go to the Salt, said a Mr. B, and see genuine refined manners from the Palmetto State, look upon people in the ballroom who know what it is to dance decently, "leaving your polkas and schottisches for other more fashionable and more vulgar watering places."

But the most pleased of all were the South Carolinians themselves, pleased with each other, with their comfortable quarters in the great stone Erskine Building, with the neat cottages and with the skillful managerial touches of the Messrs. Erskine and Caruthers. Such an apparently small thing as hominy-and-gravy for supper could be cause for

ecstasy. Caroline Pettigrew (Mrs. Charles) arrived one
Sunday evening from the Red Sweet, bringing with her a
large appetite and an upset child, travel sick. "And what,"
she asked the folks at home, "do you think they gave us at
tea? The *nicest hominy* and butter, with batter cakes that
were homelike. It was like many a supper we have had at
Badwell arriving from a journey. Think what a pleasant
feeling it gave us! Charley after refusing any dinner eat
his native dish with great satisfaction."

What had delighted Professor Porcher was the unex-
pected meeting with so many of his native kind: Judge
Huger and Dr. Benjamin Huger and Mr. Bacot and John
Harleston and the Poinsetts and scores more from Charleston or the Carolina rice coast. It was neighborly. For all of
them, native company on top of native dishes made a day-
long feast.

But to see the place through the enthusiasm of one of the
great planters is to see it at its best. The more important
the man the more impressive the tribute. Nobody took the
Springs more seriously than the grandees themselves, nor
found more diversion in them, nor placed them higher in
the Southern scheme. The nabobs were the inveterate ones
who rallied annually to the waters and who, between making their enormous crops, were fascinated as boys with the
pleasant trifles of life around the pavilions.

Colonel James Chesnut cast his eye over the assemblage
on the piazza one morning in the summer of 1843 and
found it heterogeneous but good. There was, he said, "an
agreeable mixture of all kinds of people (except the haughty
and presuming) of these there are none, tho' many Carolinians and Mr. Jerome Napoleon Bonaparte and family as-

semble at the table and mingle with the folks in their walks." No haughty ones, *tho'* many Carolinians, etc.; the lord of Mulberry had a sly humor.

Mr. Bonaparte pleased him. One could have expected that the half-regal son of Betsy Patterson of Baltimore would throw out his chest and be mighty careful who was touched by the skirts of his coat; but no, he was behaving himself with true democratic feeling, smoking his cigar on the piazza amidst the "dandys, the Tobacco planters and Cotton growers of the South like a plain sociable gentleman," said Colonel Chesnut, nothing airy about him at all.

As for the Colonel himself, he had been known as the Young Prince at Princeton and had subsequently justified the title by stretching his Mulberry inheritance into a kingdom five miles square and ruling it with a strong but benevolent hand. On this land there were two residences which he built himself: Mulberry, the main house, solid and substantial and without pretentiousness, and Sandy Hill, on high land, for summer. Sandy Hill was three miles from Mulberry and connected with it by a smooth, bee-line boulevard through the pines.

He was a martinet with a hundred crochets: he hated red and forbade red dresses to all his womenfolk; cabbage and onions he couldn't abide and he banned them from the house, agreeing in return to do his smoking outside; he didn't like closed doors, preferring draughts. And he had very little use for the White Sulphur. There was too much show and racket there for him and he liked to twit his good friend Singleton about the grandeur of it all. On one occasion he said that he didn't expect to stay more than a day or two under Mr. Calwell's roof, "unless he found better company than he expected." But as for the Salt he could blow its horn with a will.

They were comfortably fixed, he wrote his daughter Sally, in excellent quarters. The hosts were most attentive and the servants exceptionally good. And though he had been for the past quarter century one of Colonel Fry's most loyal guests at the Warm, he was forced to admit that at the Salt "we have the best table I ever sat down to in the mountains."

And besides, the water was strong, well suited to Colonel Chesnut's interior economy which demanded its daily dose of "Panacea" (bottled Saratoga water) at Mulberry; the kitchens and the dairy were models of cleanliness and order; the pool had a fine Parian marble lining. Everything appetizing, everything shipshape. Lords of great estate, tyrants in their own domain like Chesnut, could appreciate the Salt for its sterling worth even more than those who put on the dog.

Of all the refuges, the Sweet was the favorite, not alone because it was nearest the White but because of its charm, its society and, on rare occasions, because of its food. Mr. Buckingham of London wondered why everybody didn't go there. "The mutton," he said, "was equal to the finest in England; and all the food good, clean and nicely dressed, while the attentions of the proprietor and his servants was quite as great as that shown by landlords to their guests at English hotels, the only instance in which we could truly say this, during all our travels."

What the old-timer could say to you, Mr. Buckingham, was that it had not always been thus, what with the vagaries of the lessee system. Much that had recently happened was due to Dr. Lewis's taking the reins himself. The story had been briefly told by an advertisement that he had inserted in the Richmond papers.

"These Springs so long and so advantageously known, having passed into the hands of the proprietor, are now in complete repair for the reception of visitors. The old buildings have all been refitted in a neat and comfortable manner, and other extensive improvements are being put up."

The "other extensive improvements," when finished, gave Mr. Buckingham the surprise of his life: a beautiful long brick building with three Greek porticoes spaced along its façade, standing in a grove of what was still backwoods America! It might have surprised anybody, even an American. The building was of red brick, three stories high, the lower story close on the ground and arcaded in the familiar manner of Southern houses. On top of this arcade ran the long piazza, unroofed except for the three high porticoes that crossed it. It looked for all the world as though three typical be-pillared mansions from the lower James had been moved to this upland valley and put together on a common front, with the additional feature of a fine bar behind the basement arcade.

Inside were an enormous dining room, two drawing rooms and thirty-nine bedrooms, so spacious and airy that the managers of the United States and Congress Hotels at Saratoga, where the chambers were no larger than mortuary vaults, should have blushed with shame to hear of them. This affair cost $60,000, just sixty times the amount that

Colonels Singleton and Hampton had paid for their Colonnades.

Everyone sighed over these splendors, over the Greek porticoes and the tasteful Greek cornices and the three black-walnut flights of steps and the $60,000. Colonel Perkins of Boston opined that it was superior in architecture, beauty and accommodation to anything in the United States which he had seen; Burke, the busy builder of the Red Sulphur, handsomely admitted that there was nothing to equal it, even at his own Spring; and Mr. Buckingham ranked it with anything he had seen in America, both as a thing of beauty and as "a complete establishment." These gentlemen did well to praise it, for the plans were closely related to designs of the great Jefferson himself, architect of the University of Virginia. The Sweet may have been the last of the Springs to fall in with the building boom of the 1830's but it brought up the rear in triumph.

In 1839 guests were swarming through the new and spacious chambers of this caravansary, lost in admiration but not so completely lost that they failed to note that many finishing touches were yet to be made owing to the sudden drying up of the golden stream. Four years later it was still unfinished and people were wondering when Dr. Lewis would get around to plastering the dining room, where the walls were still of bare, open laths, but by then (1843) they were right in the middle of hard times. Prosperity and plastering were just around the corner.

"This depression," said one of the Sweet Springs guests, "is trifling; the fame of the springs is extending, and at no distant day their celebrity will not be bounded by the Continent." The water at the Sweet had always been stimulating to the imagination as well as to the body. As it turned out, the guests would still be eating in a dining hall of unplastered laths as late as 1850.

❦

In general, the Calwell cast-offs knew better than to seek consolation at the Hot unless they were sore afflicted. It did not minister to purely figurative pains in the neck. The case of the Hot was covered by a brief dialogue of Mark Pencil's. "I will get out here," says the invalid. "I will leave this place as soon as possible," says the man of pleasure. It was the mecca of the afflicted and it looked the part.

But for his bad shoulder, Johnston Pettigrew's friend Battle would never have traded it for the White. "From the White Sulphur I came over to this place," he wrote, "thinking I'd try the benefit of the Hot Baths. The difference in the two places I can scarcely pretend to describe. There it is all bustle, fashion, gaiety—here there is a crowd of invalids of every description.

"Here moves before you, with slow and measured pace, he whom age is hurrying to his last rest, thinking to prolong yet awhile his worthless life by bathing in these health restoring waters; there limps along on stick and crutch the miserable rheumatic—yonder hobbles one whose limbs have been racked with pain and whose feet swollen by use of old wine and feasting on good dinners—he has the gout—anon the gaunt dyspeptic comes in view, and he whose face is saffron's color, whose skin is, or looks to be, thick enough for sole leather. I am not jesting—there are some miserable looking objects at this establishment."

But there were others like himself with some of the Old Nick left in them; they vented their high spirits with games of chess and backgammon. These two were the "raging amusements" of the place.

President Van Buren had not even stayed for breakfast. He took a look in his gracious, unaffected Republican manner at the Boiler and Spout baths, mounted his plain coach and rode on to a tavern called Paris's. Customarily, the westward coaches left the Warm Springs in the early morning, covered the five miles to the Hot in less than an hour, discharged their cripples, if they had any, and pushed on to another tavern before seven o'clock and breakfast. Those without cripples did not even stop. All that the poor stove-up creatures on the hotel piazza could do was cuss the coaches as they went by, "out of all patience," as Ann Price said, "with the White Sulphur and the Warm Springs, because all of the company staied at them two."

Pity the poor soul who called himself "Dash" and who had just come over from Mr. Calwell's establishment, where there was a German band, in '43 when times were dark. Dash had admired the German band. There were a lot of complainers, he said, who professed to prefer the plain music of home performers, but he felt differently. "There is so much feeling and expression in the German pieces—such rapturous flights of melody, that the imagination bears us up to the seventh heaven."

When Dash got to the Hot there was no band at all, nothing but a banjo picked upon by a suffering rheumatic in the cool of the evening. In place of fine German music there were morning and evening prayers in the parlor. The banjo and the intoning voice of the Reverend Dr. T. sounded very melancholy in Dash's ears after the "rapturous flights of melody" he had left behind.

Unfortunately, the Hot was always suffering at the hands of people who compared it with Springs where the guests skipped about like pixies and enjoyed rude health. That was hardly fair. Dr. Goode did not pretend to furnish anything but good food, good quarters, his own rather superior manner (unintentional) and salvation for physical wrecks. He saw his several springs for what they were, outpourings of God's mercy at a nicely calculated temperature for the relief of rheumatic and other congestions, and he set no snares for the frivolous. What he wanted was sufferers, and to that end he plastered the country with testimonials, frank revelations from patients who had come to him in a most shocking state and gone away laughing.

Mr. Williams Carter of Hanover County submitted that a ten-year-old dyspepsia had sent him to the edge of the grave, that the White Sulphur and Salt Sulphur had only made him worse, but that the Spout Bath at the Hot had cured him completely. . . . There was Mr. Morgan A. Price, whose bilious intermittent fever had bloated his liver and spleen and indeed his whole physique. He had been leached, cupped, blistered and salivated. He had tried Saratoga without effect; tried the White Sulphur plus the blue pill, also without effect. Then to the Hot, and after bathing for three days he experienced the most remarkable deflation in liver and spleen. He was well on the road to health. . . . Mr. Elliot Gray's bilious fever developed ulcers on both his ankles, rheumatism, lumps on his legs the size of hickory nuts, and piles. He went to the Hot on crutches. For the first ten days his troubles increased, if anything. Then his liver began to make copious discharges of bile, and from that moment there came an improvement in the ulcers, the rheumatism, the piles and the hickory nuts. . . . Dozens gladly set down their catalogue of horrors, and Dr. Goode scattered their testimonials like scar tissue across the land.

Since he chose to throw all his weight on disease (just about any disease at all, said Dr. Goode optimistically) the newspapers were pleased to help him along. "The company," as Charlestonians could read in the *Courier*, "consists chiefly of invalids, the tottering paralytic, the crippled rheumatic, the emaciated consumptive." On the very front page of the Richmond *Dispatch* were pictured in grim detail some cases of spinal curvature and bent necks. The *Whig* passed on the happier picture of cripples throwing away their crutches.

So the butterflies had sufficient warning, but an occasional one got in and was not content until it had fluttered out again. Miss Mary Watson of Charlottesville, as charming a piece as ever came out of Virginia, alighted there on her way to the Red Sweet from the Rockbridge Alum, and although it was quite full of people and they even managed to get up a dance, she pronounced it "decidedly the dullest place she was ever at." She was looking for fun and departed in haste for the Sweet Springs valley.

❁

If it happened that any of Calwell's defeated guests were headed back East, they would find some mighty pleasant havens on the way, but none pleasanter than the Fauquier White Sulphur near Warrenton. Like Berkeley Springs it was handy for Washington and Alexandria people, but unlike Berkeley it was on a rising and not a falling tide.

Long ago the great Jefferson had given it a puff, but despite that it remained for many decades an insignificant property known as Lee's Sulphur, and Mr. Lee had not even bothered to put windows in his cabins. Then almost overnight it acquired a company of financiers, a four-story hotel with two three-story wings, a great many cottages thrown out on either side in a wide semicircle, a lawn with green grass and, of all things, flower beds. Add to these a kennel of fox hounds, a race course and training stable, a ball every night and those indispensable adjuncts, bowls and quoits. "Bowls and quoits," said the management in its advertisement "invite the rougher sex to more athletic exercise."

The Fauquier White was situated in a rolling country far eastward of the mountain group, only fifty-odd miles west of Washington. It had become very popular with the citizens of the national capital (coach fare only $4.50) as well as with Alexandrians, and it had blown itself up frogwise until it boasted a capacity equal to that of the Greenbrier White Sulphur itself.

Definitely the Fauquier people were set to out-do the Queen of the Springs, though when it came to the water, fame put a spell on them and made them servile. "Of the water," they said meekly, "it is only necessary to say that it resembles in nearly every respect and is perhaps very little if at all inferior to the celebrated White Sulphur in Greenbrier."

But for those who might be escaping from a place where the management did very little for them but charge for the water, there was no doubt that the Fauquier offered an asylum where the staff nearly broke its collective neck in offering a variety of amusement, cultivating a pleasant, if dropsical, company and setting a table supervised by one of Washington's most eminent caterers, Mr. Bronaugh himself, of Gadsby's. And then there were the tournaments, with lances bright and ladyes faire. The hunting horns tooted and the hounds gave voice, the racers pounded around the track and the quoits rang against the pin, but in the end the tournaments made the most noise and drew the greatest crowds. The tournament became the specialty of the Fauquier, its very crown and glory.

The latter part of every season was filled with tournaments, one right after the other. The Knights rode at a ring instead of each other and they wore bright silks instead of shining armor, but otherwise they were as close as possible to their mediaeval models. Each had his title, either of romantic fancy or of his homeplace: Knight of the Red Rose, Knight of the Everglades, Knight of the Black Lance, Knight of the Rappahannock.

The ideals of the tournament age were burnished anew and held high for Southern youth to shoot at. Filling the judges' stand were gentlemen of the highest positions in State and Nation. Young ladies of pale, translucent loveliness were crowned Queens of Love and Beauty. For those who stood aloof and wagged the finger of fun at the tournament, one of the devotees at the Fauquier penned an eloquent rebuke, killing, surely, all further thought of ridiculing this ennobling sport.

"Let them imagine," he said, "sixteen handsome, well-built men, mounted on proud, fiery steeds, drawn up in array. Excited by the thrilling strains of music and the smiles of beauty, they successively urge their impetuous chargers over a distance of several hundred yards, towards a cord sweeping across the vast area; from this cord is suspended a ring, no bigger than the Faery Queen's girdle [which must, then, have been about twice the size of a silver dollar] which with their lances couched it is their province to pierce and carry off in triumph.

"Each knight has three trials; he who bears off the ring the greatest number of times is declared victor, and has the high privilege of choosing out of the bright parterre of flowers the Queen who is to grace the evening ball. Let them imagine all this and the severest cynic could not fail to enter into all the spirit and beauty of the knightly struggle. Never were seen more elegant and skillful riders, or more gallant cavaliers. Their aim is not a paltry prize of gold or silver, but the noble guerdon of woman's love; delicately poised on their lances is the balance which is to decide their lot, whether of happiness or despair."

Come and join us, cried the happy guests of Fauquier, and the Richmond *Enquirer* passed on the invitation to the public. We had a tournament yesterday, we shall have another tomorrow, a Grand Tournament winding up with a Fancy Ball. The excitement is showing itself "on the face of every fair lady and gallant knight." Twenty knights will ride and every effort will be made to "assimulate it closely in dresses and arrangements to those Tournaments that Ivanhoe witnessed and Sir Walter has celebrated." There he was again. There was Sir Walter behind the tournament business as he had been behind the great hunt at the White Sulphur, behind the excited maidens kindling to manly valor and most particularly behind the Gentleman Judge who delivered the charge.

True to his shadowy prompter, President Dew of William and Mary when he charged the knights bade them remember that the Institution in which they were enlisted grew out of that dark age when the rights of womanhood were denied, that it was "to arrest the downward progress of civilization"; that all true knights must be honorable, courteous, liberal, clement, loyal, devoted to woman, to arms and to religion. When Judge Beverley Tucker addressed the lancers he was moved to do so in blank verse, quite a stretch of blank verse, with this at the last,

> Then forward to the lists. Bright eyes are on you,
> And love's warm breath shall lend its rich perfume
> To the applause that waits upon your triumph.

If the words weren't supplied by Sir Walter, everything else was. He was the master of ceremonies.

The greatest of the knights who rode in the lists at this and other Springs was Turner Ashby of Rose Bank, Fauquier County, black of mustache and swarthy as an Indian. The titles he rode under were Knight of the Black Prince or Knight Hiawatha, both of which matched his complexion. He was the outstanding horseman of that country and so perfectly mounted that they compelled him to ride without saddle or bridle. But even so he had soon pierced more little rings with his lance and crowned more tremulous queens than any man alive.

Turner Ashby was the pure and parfit knight, cut to President Dew's specifications. It was fitting that he should have been the invincible one for he was matched in every way for the heroic-romantic role. He never touched strong drink and was never known to curse or to use tobacco, keeping his shield of character spotless against the day when Destiny would finally call him into the real and bloody tournament of the War Between the States.

There it was that Death found him, mounted as he should have been, on a pure white stallion, with his great beard coal black against his shining uniform and his boots black against the snowy flanks of his horse. When Death unhorsed him then he was grand and Moor-like, exalted by his cause, dashing and in the full flower of manhood. He was the archetype of all the knights who had ridden on the tournament fields of the Springs, crowned the Queens of Love and Beauty and listened fruitfully to the ideals of chivalry as expounded by the scholars, the judges and the divines of the day.

With the tournament for buckler and lance it turned out that the Fauquier White was better armed than its rivals when the old Black Knight, Depression, came riding into the summer crowds, thinning them out by the thousand. Take 1845, the exact middle of the lean decade. At the other Springs things were dull, but at Fauquier in August and September the tournament season was humming. About August 20 there were reported five hundred guests. Ten days later: "We have an immense crowd, such as I never saw at this place, perhaps not less than 1,000 at dinner." And the ballroom on the evening of a tilting day could not hold them all.

Out in the mountains, at the Greenbrier White, they were trying to rout ill fortune without cavalry and without lances. Tournaments had never caught on there, even though the

Ashby brothers and their spirited sister tried planting the seed one summer, so they put their faith in other and seemingly more solid tactics.

They procured a new factotum in the person of a Mr. Edwin Porter. They spread the news that the place was under "a new and very superior management." People were actually welcomed at the gate; once inside they were given inducements to remain. Mr. Porter brought in French cooks to replace the darkies in the kitchen. Food was suddenly of "the best quality and served up with elegance." He imported a band of musicians from Philadelphia. They built a theatre, a "commodious building," and installed a troup of actors. (Shades of Bath and starved comedians.) In short, Mr. Calwell's famous System went into eclipse.

But they should have tried tournaments. They did a better job. At the Fauquier in mid-August of '45, knighthood and Queens of Love and Beauty were drawing a full house, whereas at the White Sulphur there were a scant four hundred for the French cooks to feed and the troup of actors to entertain. Mr. Porter's campaign got them nowhere and it wasn't long before French cooks, theatre and actors all passed into limbo.

X

The Singleton Dynasty Fades Out

SUDDENLY and ominously, cotton dropped below nine cents a pound in 1840. Two years later prices the world over went crashing and the South went with them. Somehow the economic vaccine that had worked in the 1837 panic had worn off. A slave aristocracy could be as sick as the rest of the world.

One day in January, 1845, Richard Singleton's Charleston agents wrote him that the best they could get for his latest hundred-bale shipment was four and a half cents a pound. He cried out like a man struck in the dark. Four and a half cents! Worse than bankruptcy, it was insulting. Even so, he was doing better than his two Broun nephews in Alabama. The Mobile market hit the sickening low of three and a fourth cents. Liverpool went to three. Nothing like it had ever happened before.

Debt, an occasional visitor in the best of Southern households, now became a constant bedfellow and travelling companion. But this unhappy state of affairs was never certain, of itself, to solve the question of whether or not to go to the Springs, come July. After all, it was pleasanter to go to the Springs on a little more borrowed money than to sit glumly at home on a little less borrowed money. A Southerner could arrive at that conclusion by a shorter route than other men. And so it turned out that there were now observed around the fountains a large number of "gentlemen of delicate constitution who find it oppressive to be too near a sheriff." In the ballrooms men were pointing out their debtors tripping it ever so lightly, gayer by a long shot than they themselves who held the notes.

A North Carolinian, after a taste of sulphur water and society, wrote home enthusiastically that more people should be at the Springs recuperating, fortifying themselves with health and good cheer. "Do tell your folks to come," he urged. "It won't cost much and if they haven't the money, why jest let 'em push the credit system a leetle farther." Pushing the credit system a leetle farther was a fine old Southern custom. When the bank informed one that it had been pushed too far, another Negro moved off the place to the nearest auction block.

One of the gentlemen who got to the Springs on a little more pushing at the credit system was the eminent Charleston lawyer, Mr. James Louis Petigru. Mr. Petigru's debts were nearly five times his assets, the result of a plunge in Mississippi lands where, like so many other Southern speculators, he had become thoroughly mired. The collapse of the Ossawichee (or Oswitchie) Company had already stripped him of his Savannah River rice plantation, fifty Negroes and the family coach and horses. He was now struggling to save his beloved up-country estate, Badwell.

But he got to the Springs, though not for pleasure. Caroline, the daughter who had married a Mr. Carson, was ill. Charleston doctors, at the end of their short string, had given her up and were passing her on to their "last resorts," the Springs. It was either that or the next world. Since the duties of escort and bill-footer fell inevitably upon her bankrupt father, he rose to the occasion nobly, turning his back on clients, fat fees and St. Michael's Alley, where his office was, and mounted the Wilmington boat at the Charleston Battery. With Caroline, her child and the nurse, they made a party of four.

Mr. Petigru was an arresting figure. He looked like an over-indulgent actor, possibly Roman. His face was becoming pudgy and the flesh was closing in on the eyes. His hair was of theatrical length, resting on his shoulders. People at the Springs accused him of wearing a wig and he had it cut to prove that he wasn't. As a matter of fact, he was an actor, one of the best in the legal profession, so sure-fire in bringing tears to the eyes of judge and jury that he commanded the best fees in Charleston.

His Gallic mother had endowed him with a mercurial disposition. Now he was most punctilious, like a Cavalier (which he wasn't), and again he was as impulsive and prankish as a boy. One of his youthful impulses was to change the spelling of his name from Pettigrew to Petigru, as more French, in honor of his mother. This was made easier by the consistent failure of his father to amount to anything. He became, when the national issues were drawn, a stanch unionist and a figure generally reviled in Charleston, but that of course was later.

He got the lovely, dark-haired Caroline to the Warm

The Blue Sulphur in 1854

As it was twenty years after Latrobe's water color.

From Moorman, The Virginia Springs

Warm Springs

The old favorite had grown into a neat village before
the Civil War.

Lithograph from Beyer's Album of Virginia

Springs, more dead than alive. This was the upshot of being too tender of his creditors, economizing on transportation, bringing her from the Charlottesville terminus in a public stage instead of hiring an "extra." That taught him a lesson. When Caroline was sufficiently revived, he saw to it that they travelled to the White Sulphur in a roomy carriage of their own, in two easy stages. It was the beginning of felicity.

Mr. Petigru's arrival is notable, in striking contrast to that of the poor devils who struggled to get in and then had to fight their way up. At the gate he had only to breathe his name and he was passed through with obeisances. "The chief superintendent received us at the door and learning who we were, directed the driver to drive us into the enclosure, to the door of the cottage assigned us." Since the year is 1845, this obliging gentleman would be the new factotum, Mr. Porter, he of the French cooks and the actors.

They were given the cottage of Jerome Napoleon Bonaparte, still surcharged with royal aroma since the owner had departed only that morning. Mrs. Mat Singleton, the Colonel's daughter-in-law, was on the steps to welcome them. Even before Caroline was well abed, two of the great ladies of the Springs came to call, Mrs. Singleton and Mrs. Bull Pringle. They had engaged a maid for Caroline. Servants had been assigned to bring her meals. Not satisfied that she would have anything delicate enough for dinner, Mrs. Singleton "sent her a pheasant very nicely dressed by her own cook."

Every day, Mr. Petigru (and Caroline when she was able) had breakfast and tea at the Singletons' private table in the dining room. Mr. Calwell put the mark of "distinguished guests" upon them by having them in for a glass of wine and he sent Caroline more pheasants for breakfast. Little wonder the White became, as Mr. Petigru said, "quite natural" to them.

So congenial and amusing and brilliant was the crowd that he soon began to soar above his troubles. There were Henry Clay, Andrew Stevenson and Governor Barbour, as usual; Dr. Mercer of Mississippi, millionaire planter and close friend of Clay; Judge Cabell of Virginia and his remarkable wife and daughter; the Richard Singletons; Mrs. Wickham of Richmond, rich dowager and society leader; Judge Brooke, eighty-three, patriarch of the Bench; Mrs. Governor Gilmer, Mrs. Dupont and Dr. North of South Carolina; and hundreds more but these on the topmost layer. And of course the John Tylers.

The Tylers gave Mr. Petigru no little amusement. He thought the ex-President was not looking so chipper. In fact, forlorn described him. On the other hand, his bride, the former Julia Gardiner of New York, was flush and blooming, fashionable and irrepressible, as befitted a young lady of twenty-five, thirty years younger than her distinguished husband. The implications were apt to tickle a good Whig like Mr. Petigru; he even turned compassionate and felt that he had "more than half forgiven" Tyler for betraying the Whigs.

It looked as though the ebullient Julia was a little too much for the Captain, as they called him. Marrying him only eight months before his term was out, she had reigned in the White House not only as its mistress but as queen. At receptions she wore three royal plumes in her hair and received her subjects seated; when she drove abroad it was behind four horses even finer than those of the Russian Minister, which took some doing. And now that the White House reign was at an end she was leading him a dance on a Springs tour and calling him "Mr. President." The Whigs gave him nothing better than "Captain." He and Clay steered clear of each other, for fear of mayhem, and it wasn't long before the Tyler "dynasty" (Mr. Petigru's word) wisely withdrew to the Old Sweet.

The Cabell cottage was the rendezvous for these witty and distinguished people. Mr. Andrew Stevenson was at his brilliant best, making conversation, Mr. Petigru said, "as for the stage." Mr. Stevenson was in turn fascinated by Mr. Petigru, no mean talker himself. Mrs. Cabell, the clever poetess of the Popeiad of beloved memory, and her husband, the President Judge of Virginia, were a fit couple to conduct the salon, but the most amazing person of the lot, in Mr. Petigru's eyes, was their daughter Elizabeth. To all appearances she was a sedate, imperturbable young lady without beauty and without fortune, more interested in her sewing box and ancient war horses like Mr. Clay than in any beaux, yet the beaux simply besieged her and were driven to despair by her indifference. At thirty-four she was still unmarried and still a belle, flouting all the rules. Mr. Petigru was fascinated by this charming enigma.

A watermelon arrived for Mr. Clay from some distant admirer (statues and watermelons but never the presidency, which he had just missed for the fourth time) and he donated it for a final ice cream and watermelon party at the Cabell cottage. Everybody was headed for the Sweet, the Tylers and Singletons had already gone, and this was the last of those delightful gatherings that lifted Mr. Petigru quite out of himself. Only at departure was he reminded of what dire straits he and the world were in.

He had engaged an extra to take his little party to the Sweet in comfort, paying double fare. When word got round that the opulent Mr. Petigru had engaged a carriage with plenty of room in it, there was a rush for seats. Free places to the Sweet! What a boon in these mendicant times. There were Mrs. Wickham, the rich dowager of Richmond, her large boy and her colored maid; fifteen-year-old Mary McDuffie and a gentleman who begged a ride because he was a college mate of Mr. Petigru's cousin. That pretty well filled the inside, and the flush Mr. Petigru, who could afford to hire extras, was compelled to ride outside with the driver, where he could ruminate on the caprices of fortune, as Mr. Featherstonhaugh had done years before over much the same kettle of fish.

※

The hardest hit was the biggest frog in the puddle, Colonel Singleton. The man who had once sent his agent to buy thoroughbreds at the King's Sale in England was now so pressed for cash that the carpenter who made the verandah couches had to dun him for eighty dollars. Once he had maintained a great stud and swept the field at the Charleston Races; now he had to keep small tradesmen waiting for their money. Bashan, the animal moulder of New York, clamored loudly to be paid for the concrete lions that crouched so imposingly at the top of the Colonel's steps. Once when his son Matthew bought so many horses in London that his credit ran out, it had been an easy matter to ship a hundred bales to square it. Now his name was on so many notes for himself and others that he could not always meet the interest.

The Northerners whom marriage had brought into the family were, in his own words, "harassing him to death." Julia McRa, Powell's widow, was suing for her share of the Negroes. Nobody sold slaves in a market so suicidally low, but that made no difference to her; she wanted her pounds of flesh. Abram Van Buren was threatening to drag Singleton's dear old friend Calwell into the courts for non-payment of a $12,000 note which the Colonel had given Angelica. He needed it to go into business with, the Major said. These were the acts of mercenary, uncomprehending people. In the South one didn't do such things.

Another twist on the screw was the case of Matthew, whom Dr. Buckner ordered to the Red Sulphur for the summer. That meant consumption; Mary, his first-born, had died of it. Writing his nephew in Alabama, the Colonel cried, "I have known nothing but sorrow and affliction in the past 12 months. My cares, duties and labours are almost insupportable."

In terms of fortune it was a far cry back to the day of the great wedding at Home when Angelica married the President's son and the Colonel so easily flicked $3,000 into the Major's pocket for a European Grand Tour. By the calendar it was seven years.

So the Singletons preceded the Petigrus to the Old Sweet. Mrs. Singleton was anxious to take the baths there, setting great store by them. The "tonic" action was helping her, she thought. For himself, the Colonel would have nothing to do with mineral water, outside or in, ill as his troubles made him. Hadn't this very Sweet Springs nearly killed his poor father back in 1818?

This time, Mrs. Singleton's "situation" was beyond repair. For several summers more she resorted to the Sweet, but in the Spring of 1849 she breathed her last, at Home. This was the worst blow of all. He wanted to die; he agonized in loneliness. Angelica urged him not to go to the Springs that summer. "Do not go back over that old familiar road—it would only be one long agony which would drive you to despair, every house, tree, turn in the road would speak of her." She wanted him to come to them at Hastings, where they had such nice rooms in Mrs. Elliott's house and everything would be done for his comfort.

The long habit was not to be broken. He went to the Springs. It was best for him there, where he could be with his old friends, Clay, Calwell, the Rutherfoords, the Coleses, the Cabells, with Reverdy Johnson and, above all, the man nearest his heart, Andrew Stevenson. Summer after summer for thirty years he had gone to the waters for the healing companionship he found there. He had watched the Springs grow, seen practically the whole South swarming in and out of the little mountain villages, all the wealth and wit, the beauty and fame of his country. There he had met notable men of the North, Abbott Lawrence, Colonel Thomas Perkins, Rufus Choate, Daniel Webster, President Pierce, and European celebrities always coming and going. There where the world knew and kow-towed to him as the great patron of the great spa, he was sure of a heart-warming welcome. There was his other home.

To have gone to the Van Burens at Hastings would only

have reminded him that Angelica, after all, had married a man who was still living on prospects, and poorly. They were boarding, did not even have their own house, and one horse was the extent of the Major's stable. The brilliant marriage had flickered down to a mere memory of high position. Hastings was no place for a despondent father.

Without a break in the three years following the death of Mrs. Singleton he went back over that "old familiar road," and in 1852 we find him in his Colonnades cottage for the last time. It is September. Except for his servants he is alone in the house and ill, confined to his room. His friends call morning and afternoon, trying to cheer the lonely man with the small, weary eyes.

The Petigrus come in every day. Mr. Petigru brings the newspapers, loaned him by a prominent North Carolinian, Mr. Johnston of Hayes. Petigru, too, is finding time heavy on his hands, with "nothing to do but entertain my friend, Mr. Singleton." The distinguished lawyer has taken on more flesh since we last saw him seven years ago and looks more than ever like an actor who has lived too well, his face puffed up until his eyes are nearly closed, his straight hair long again, falling onto his shoulders. He is on the sick list, too, his arm in a sling. Betrayed again by his own impulsiveness, he had tried to recapture his youth by jumping out the coach window before the door was opened. He had achieved only a painful dislocation at the elbow.

With Petigru, it was the same as last time. He had not wanted to come, he was still slaving at that mountain of debt. But another daughter, Sue, was desperate to try the White Sulphur water and he hadn't the heart to refuse. This time, Mrs. Petigru had decided that she would have a

[*171*]

fling at the waters for those various and sundry disorders that kept her captive in her bedchamber. There were those who thought Mr. Petigru would have preferred leaving her in Charleston.

They are trying to persuade Singleton to see a doctor. What about Moorman, the resident physician? True, he does go around rubbing the backs of people's hands and smelling them to see if they have absorbed enough sulphur, but on the other hand he has made a great success with his book on mineral waters, he is well educated, he might know something else besides rubbing the back of your hand.

Singleton will have none of their doctors. All his life he has watched his loved ones die and the doctors helpless. If you are still alive their last prescription is, "Try the Springs." Well, his father tried the Springs, and Rebecca tried them. He asks them, have they heard the story about John Randolph and the overseer? When Randolph lost a valuable overseer, he said he must resign himself to the man's death; he had had a fair chance because no doctor had been near him. When people plead with him to have a doctor he tells them about Randolph's overseer.

His interest in life is at low ebb, so many of the men who have made the Springs a joy to him are gone. Only two months before, Henry Clay died in Washington and would come no more for his regular fortnight. All the old Springs landlords are dead or bankrupt or both. Colonel Fry and his jolly jokes are under ground and the Warm seems an empty place. Dr. Lewis of the Sweet is dead and his establishment taken over by the Chancery Court. That beautiful hotel with its three Greek porticoes was more than Dr. Lewis could swing.

Dr. Burke had been sold out of the Red Sulphur by the sheriff. Even consumption, the national scourge, could not pay for so many long piazzas. Saddest of all, only the year before, they had carried James Calwell, his cue neatly tied for the last time, up the hill to the burying ground. What a grim harvest the decade had reaped. So many cheerful, witty friends are gone, and for an old man like himself, seventy-six now, there will be nobody, ever, to take their places.

Mrs. Petigru, veteran of the sick room, persuades him to take one of her blue pills, and he rallies sufficiently to start for Sumter. On the road he is met by the only thing that life has left to give him, sad news. John, his eldest son, is dead.

His life, as Angelica truly said, was an "utter wreck of happiness," and fate was kind at last. Several months later they laid him in his grave in the family plot on the slope below his grandfather Matthew's first house in that country, not, strangely enough, crushed down by his grief but by an accident. There had been heavy rains, the roadbed of the railroad washed out, and the car in which he was riding rolled down an embankment.

Two years later Matthew died, the last remaining son. With the exception of Marion and Angelica a great Springs family had faded out. Since the children were babies they had all been faithful to the mineral Springs where Nature, the inscrutable pharmacist, gave out her elixirs for long life from the great internal drugstore; every summer nearly they had come up to Virginia, where there was every gradation and variety of curative water, where an all-wise Providence had arranged them in their proper order: first the minerals to soak the organs, then the thermals to boil them out.

"There are medical waters among the mountains adapted to the amelioration of almost every complexion of disease that human nature is subject to," boasted William Pettigrew in his Southerner's pride. But in spite of it, most of the Singletons were gone, even the young branches dead before their time, just as though these wonderworks of God had not existed.

XI

More Money, More Springs

MRS. CHARLES PETTIGREW considered the whole affair simply preposterous. She would have nothing to do with it. If Jane and Lou wished to go to the meeting in the parlor, just for fun and out of curiosity, there was no harm in that but frankly she wouldn't care to see sisters of hers in any tableaux gotten up by that Jew, Levin. What business had he to appoint himself master of ceremonies anyhow? In Charleston he would never have dared to push himself into any social activities whatever; just because this was the Springs and the crowd was mixed he had the brass to make himself impresario of the tableaux for the Grand Ball, to form a committee and to post a notice in the parlor requesting the ladies to attend a meeting for the consideration of scenes and parts. The man's nerve was colossal and called for a good snubbing.

Nevertheless Jane and Lou North, with Julius Porcher, went off to the parlor, down the long walk that fronted the cottages to the main hotel, just out of curiosity. Their departure left Charles Pettigrew and Caroline, his wife, and little Charley, the baby, and Mother Pettigrew and Cousin Marian to consider further the case of the Jew, Levin, and his irrepressible activities.

First of all there were those ridiculous long dispatches he had been sending home to the Charleston *Courier* over the pseudonym "Nat," in which he undertook to describe for folk less travelled than he the latest doings at the Springs: what notables he had seen at the White Sulphur, what cripples he had seen at the Hot, news of the Grand Fancy Ball at the Salt Sulphur, a budget of joy from the Red Sweet. It was to the Red Sweet that he had devoted his latest effusion, and if you wanted to know what Caroline Pettigrew thought of it, she thought it was "the most preposterous inflated rigmarole" she had ever read.

It was all about Mr. Bias, proprietor of the Red Sweet, and how, though an orphan, he had prospered until he was able to purchase this establishment in 1850 for $40,000 and how he had transformed it into a "blooming Paradise," and how Levin wanted nothing more than to turn his eyes every year toward this Mecca and its healing waters with the true faith of a "Moslem." Levin had outdone himself.

Not that Caroline begrudged Mr. Bias any praise. She would have been among the first to admit that he deserved it, she was eminently fair-minded, and after all didn't she and Charles prefer the Red Sweet and weren't they discriminating people? They knew a good Springs when they found one; they had taken the waters at Baden-Baden. No, it was not Mr. Bias who stuck in Caroline's craw, it was Levin the Jew, the spouter of hypocritical praise. His beating the drum for the Red Sweet was only a means of bringing himself into notice, like the man who yells loudest at the circus. He was a pusher, he had been pushing himself onto every Charlestonian who had "ever transacted the smallest business with him." At the Springs people were easy-going and suffered fools easily; it was a social churn, everyone was thrown together willy-nilly. But Charles and Caroline could console themselves. Once back in Charleston Mr. Levin would be put in his place.

The Red Sweet was just a mile below the Old Sweet in the same valley, and under its new proprietor it was idyllic, a new Elysium, combining all the advantages of civilized comfort and the most remarkable of mineral waters. Mr. Bias had the knack. He was both efficient and generous; he knew what people liked in the way of food and accommodation.

"Everything," David Hoffman said, "is fresh and new and cozy; a neat white frame hotel, and tasteful cottages. At the old Sweet things are on a more grand and pretending scale, but very rusty withall." Mary Watson of Charlottesville, who had found the Hot so dull, was fired with youthful favoritism. The Red Sweet was "much the sweetest and most agreeable place"; she didn't see how anyone could possibly prefer the Sweet. Mr. Bias had the most luscious food and he also provided his guests with a reading room, stocked with newspapers, the only one of its kind in the mountains. It was becoming very difficult to get in; people slept on the parlor floor and in the chairs to be on hand when someone gave up a room.

It was generally admitted that Mr. Bias had one of the finest of bathing establishments, a pool for the ladies and another for the gentlemen, the water continually fresh from two copious discharges under the cliff. Medically this water had the best of testimonials: both doctors Moorman and Burke used it for their own ailments. Even more important, it had become the *ne plus ultra* for sterility; the ladies were deserting the Old Sweet and the Red Sulphur and nobody knew how many matrons were bathing themselves into a happy state of fecundity.

Like his cousin J. L. Petigru of Charleston, Charles Pettigrew was doing the Springs on borrowed money; his plantation, Cherry Hill, was in quod for $70,000, an item which, when it came to the ears of his brothers, shocked them no end. But creditors or no creditors one had to get out of the heat and go to the Springs; debts or no debts one had to go to New York for one reason or another. After the Springs season was over, Charles and Caroline were planning to go to New York chiefly, they said, to hear the new opera, *Rachel*. And when the need arose, they could go up for dental work and medical treatment as well as art.

Jane and Lou North came back to the Pettigrew cottage in a burble of excitement. What did they think Levin and his committee had proposed? They wanted Lou to pose in a tableau as Queen Eleanor with dagger and bowl while some pale damsel not yet selected was to supplicate at her feet as Fair Rosamond. (That would be Eleanor of Aquitaine administering the fatal cup to her husband's mistress, a scene conjured by the minnesingers of the thirteenth century out of the thin air of the twelfth and their imaginations.) And what had Lou said to that? Lou had balked at Queen Eleanor and her poison and withdrawn from the room. But you couldn't say she had severed relations with the committee, not quite that.

Enter then Julius Porcher with the latest tidings from the parlor. The committee, sensitive of Miss North's opposition to the murderous Queen, had cast her in a new role, that of Virginia, the popular heroine of Sheridan Knowles, who was done to death by her father, Virginius, to save her honor. In other words, if Miss Lou did not care to be on the administering end of murder, she might like to be on the receiving end. Levin himself was to be the Virginius and do the stabbing; Julius Porcher was to look on as the startled Appius, her lover.

That, Caroline decided, was the final straw; it finished the folly. Have Lou swooning helpless on the arm of the "dark brown horror Levin" and he to be stabbing her? No, said Caroline, never, it was becoming more preposterous by the minute. She would not permit it. Whereupon Julius Porcher lost his taste for Appius and the withdrawal was complete. The younger ones did point out that the committee would certainly be angry with them and think them snobs but Caroline said they must do as they pleased. Levin, of all people!

The Grand Fancy Mask Ball was set for the fifth of September, in the same week with the Old Sweet's Grand Fancy Mask Ball. These two Springs acted together in friendly concert and took in each other's balls almost en masse. Levin, deprived of the assistance of the Pettigrew camp, turned his attention elsewhere; and the Pettigrew camp had time for other things before the fifth of September.

One of the great advantages of the Red Sweet was its proximity to the White. No other Springs was nearer, sixteen miles, and there was a continual shuttling back and forth, departure of those who were panting to see the great names and great doings, arrival of those who sighed for rest and good food, disgusted with the follies of the fashionable world. Caroline went over twice and agreed with her friend the Reverend Mr. Alexander who said that the White reminded him of a line in Heber's missionary hymn, "where every prospect pleases and only man is vile." Miss Lou had her fill of the place when she attended one of the Grand Balls; she was compelled to spend the night on the floor.

Their friend Mr. Johnston of Hayes, one of the big guns at the White now, rode over several times to see them and that, in a way, was even better than going over there, for they had none of the discomfort and yet got all the gossip; Mr. Johnston might be an old man in his seventies but he was keen, nothing escaped him.

The great affair lately, he told them, was the reception for President Pierce, all in the approved White Sulphur style. An august committee had been formed, with ex-President Tyler at its head, and had ridden out to the foot of the mountain and brought the guest of honor back in an open barouche drawn by four white horses. Ex-President Tyler had made the welcoming speech, quite long, all about how there was no politics at the Springs and President Pierce had made answer, also about no politics at the Springs and had been led off to a collation in the Heath cottage. Mrs. Pierce was in mourning for her little boy and she was given a separate reception by the ladies.

Julia Gardiner Tyler had a fascination for Mr. Johnston just as, ten years before, she had for Mr. Petigru. "Mrs. ex-Presidentess," as Mr. Johnston called her, was very much

Shannondale Springs

Situated at the Northern end of the tranquil Valley of
Virginia.

Drawn by C. Burton

Hot Springs, 1857, Dr. Goode's Pride

The rheumatics grumbled because it was not gay, but they got better.

Lithograph from Beyer's Album of Virginia

in evidence, "in full swing of skirts, showing an immense mouthful of artificial teeth and cheeks painted up to the eyes," according to him. She was still speaking of her husband as "The President" and wearing a tiara. Some said it was a tiara and some said it wasn't, and Mrs. Smedes of Mississippi was one of those who said it was, that it was of diamonds, "curiously suggestive of a queen's crown." She (Mrs. Smedes) had seen the ex-Presidentess descending from the dusty stagecoach at the Warm and wearing this fancy affair, dust or no dust. Some people said she never appeared in company without it, travelled with it and everything. "Neither useful nor becoming," was Mrs. Smedes' opinion.

Another lady who caught Mr. Johnston's eye was Miss Ella Eaton. The Pettigrews knew about Miss Ella of course, daughter of old Billy Eaton, one of the richest panjandrums of North Carolina. She had just returned from an extended trip to Europe as full of airs as a barrel organ, showing off her new Paris gowns, a new version of the Italian language (her own, very rapid) and a new religion, having just taken on the Catholic in exchange for the Episcopalian.

The finest sight at the White just now was Miss Ella and her stylish carriage, the handsomest outfit in the place, bar none. It was drawn by four spanking bay horses and it was "covered with plate." Every afternoon the lady would drive through the grounds, lolling on the back seat and looking most languishing. She sometimes took Mrs. Pierce with her and that was a study for you, Miss Ella with all her fashionable la-de-da and Mrs. Pierce subdued and sorrowing for the boy that had died in the White House.

The evening of September fifth came at last. Miss Lou

put the final touches to her "Autumn" costume which Caroline declared to be stunning. Mr. Bias was downstairs in the pantry before the Ball opened, superintending the most sumptuous supper ever served gratis at the Red Sweet or perhaps anywhere. Mr. Bias was in the best of humor, having lately become a father. (Everyone had been treated to champagne on that occasion.) Levin the Jew was busy rounding up his performers and adjusting their costumes behind closed doors, putting the final touches to his big surprise.

Levin's surprise was a Menagerie. When the doors opened his beasts appeared in the frame one by one and posed while he recited their histories: an elephant, a monkey, a tiger, a giraffe, a cow and so on. The recitations were his own concoctions, with ingredients from Fontaine, Aesop and the ferment in his own brain. Everybody was convulsed, the beasts were so comical; shouts of laughter brought them on, storms of applause sent them off. Levin's show was a great success.

One of the first to grant that it was a success was Caroline Pettigrew. His officiousness forgotten, Caroline declared his histories quite wonderful; he was smart, she said, and had unbounded assurance, and some of his hits were capital. Mark up a victory for Levin the Jew, Levin the indefatigable who took a hand in everything. In the great gallimaufry around the waters he had seized the chance of a lifetime, tasted the fruits of social triumph as he never could at home in Charleston. The Springs were full of Levins, not all Jews.

And mark up a victory for Mr. Bias, too, who produced a sumptuous supper downstairs at eleven, "delicate game, salads, choice meat, cake, bon-bons, jelly," and for washing these things down, gallons of wine, not just ordinary wine but "wine of the best brands." It would have done credit to a private entertainment, said Caroline Pettigrew. With such liberality Mr. Bias had brought the Red Sweet up from an old rattletrap into the first rank. It showed what could be done with energy, taste, a big heart and money, money most of all. Mr. Bias and his confreres were in luck. Money was in flow again, the South was out of the financial dumps.

❦

The return of prosperity after 1850 had brought with it a fresh access of Springs fever, such a wild epidemic as had never been seen before. People crowded into the old resorts and rushed to the new ones, seeking the magical cure-all that was just around the corner. Out of obscurity new Springs came into sudden fame, leaping from the earth as though a Moses had lately stumbled over Virginia smiting rocks with his staff.

Whoever had heard of Yellow Sulphur, Grayson's Sulphur, the Alleghany Springs, the Bath Alum and the Montgomery White? Or the Rockbridge Baths or Cotoosa Springs, the *soi-disant* "Saratoga of the South?" Not one in a hundred had known before of Jordan's White Sulphur, Capon, Orkney and Shannondale, all in the Valley of Virginia, or farther east, of Amelia and Huguenot and Buffalo Lithia. A little while ago they had been holes in the ground on isolated farms. Now they were full blown establishments with bandstands, resident physicians, fabulous powers for healing Southern diseases and incorporation papers filed in Richmond. It was a poor Springs that did not incorporate for $100,000.

With reckless optimism a company of gentlemen had sunk $150,000 in building up the Montgomery White Sulphur, down on the southern rim of the region, transforming it in a few short years into a Grand Spa, with such refined touches as a ladies' parlor, pronounced to be "a jewel of a place," and round tables in the dining room in place of the old long ones. So impressed were the visitors that they spoke of having been to the "renowned Montgomery White," unmindful that it was a prosperity upstart.

A gentleman named John Frazier spent a fortune and his life grooming the Rockbridge Alum as a rival of the White Sulphur, and after he died his brother William carried on. Between them they built accommodations for seven hundred guests, on a squeeze, and gave the Queen of the Springs a run for her money. Alum was the new craze, sulphur was having to hustle. Alum was the "cure" for the endemic scrofula, that half-brother to tuberculosis that gave its victims a leaden or a sunset complexion according to its whim. There was a nice point of economy about running the Rockbridge Alum, since much of the colored service came for nothing. Scrofulous slaves were farmed out there for the summer by their masters, to work and take the cure simultaneously, and were returned by the management in the autumn clear as bells. Pretty clear, anyhow.

Buildings of great elegance broke through the rural landscape. The tasteful array of brick at the Bath Alum, another Frazier project just over the mountain from the old Warm, was fine enough to be mistaken for an insane asylum. The pride of Capon Springs was a hotel on the same style as the

Saratoga caravansaries but more in the classic mold and handsomer, with columns thirty-five feet high and three feet through at the base.

If anyone still doubted that prosperity had returned he could find out at the gate of the White Sulphur. There they were brusque again, even rude; the affable greeting of the lean Forties had vanished in this more golden air. It was a sure sign. "What party is this?" they wanted to know as the coaches drove up. The old refrains were revived. "Better go to Lewisburg." "Better go to the Blue Sulphur." And a new one. "Why not try the Red Sweet?"

Despite enlargements the place was continually packed. The last time people had heard those curt invitations to go away from here, the suffocation point was five hundred guests. In the interim, little by little, it had been expanded to a thousand and there was no more room to swing a cat than before.

"At night," said Mr. Mackie, down from New England on his honeymoon, "the floors of drawing rooms and parlors [tacked onto the ballroom] are strewn with mattresses. Trunks are piled up ceiling high, in the halls and passages; so that, excepting the fortunate inmates of the pretty private cottages, the thousand and one visitors at the White Sulphur are, of all men, the most uncomfortable." The discomfort was now costing $2.50 a day, two or more in a room, bare floor, straw beds, unbleached sheets and pillow cases.

Just in the mid-Fifties it was exceptionally gay, a summer-long carnival: the plague had broken loose again. It always turned out like that; the greater the scourge in the lowlands the bigger the fun in the mountains. Nobody planned it or wanted it so, it was a matter of circumstance.

Mr. Bias's reading room was full of people with anxious faces when the newspapers were brought in. Always it was the same question: what news from Norfolk and Portsmouth? The plague ports of Virginia were full of death again, not cholera death but yellow fever, death of the black vomit. The "black" was blood from internal hemorrhage. It was awful, the Year of the Cholera could not touch it. Quarantine had been lifted for the brig Ben Franklin from the West Indies that she might make repairs and hell had cut loose. Now there was no stopping it. Nurses and doctors volunteered from everywhere; many of them died. Hundreds were taken up by the death carts. By September first half the population of Norfolk was stricken, half the white population. That was all that mattered. The Negroes did not die.

Everyone was heartsick at the daily budget of sad news from the lowlands; everyone contributed gladly to the collections at all the Springs ($500 at the Red Sweet, $600 at the Old Sweet, $2,500 at the White); and everyone had the time of his life. Mary Watson had no sooner put her dollar into the box at the Red Sweet than she was off with Grandma and her young friends to the Grand Masquerade Ball at the White. Everybody else in western Virginia seemed to have had the same idea and so great was the crush of revellers that Mary and her little friends had to dress and sleep in one tiny room containing four beds. There was one small mirror. There were two candles.

XII

Heralds of Disaster

A PROPHETIC thing happened at the Grand Masquerade of '55. About ten o'clock when the party was at its height, with the old ballroom so packed that a person could hardly move and the ladies standing on chairs to see the maskers, the floor caved in. There was a great crash at one end of the room followed by sudden panic and furious jumping up and down on the part of the ladies and such an embracing of the gentlemen as Mr. Johnston had never seen. The old sleepers underneath the floor had broken down after so many years of jouncing, carrying part of the musicians' stand with them. A little later the band reassembled on firmer ground and the revels took up where they left off, but it wasn't quite the same after that, not with the crack of doom still ringing in their ears.

Two years later the White was sold, on May 1, 1857. Negotiations had been started five years before, shortly after the old man died, and every year a new crop of rumors had sprouted: it had been sold to a Northern company, to an

English syndicate and so on. Finally the ownership was kept at home with Virginia money, the eight gentlemen who made up the purchasing company being Jeremiah Morton, Commodore Matthew Fontaine Maury, his brother R. H. Maury, Allen T. Caperton, Alexander K. Phillips, A. F. D. Gifford, James Hunter and J. Warren Slaughter.

The price was $600,000 but the only money that changed hands was $200,000, which went to the ten Calwell and Bowyer heirs. Divided so many ways, it must have been as disappointing as the morning-after tissue of a carnival dream; they had always expected such a lot of money. Still, they were the lucky ones. The true children of misfortune were the creditors, as usual. They got no cash at all, only a new set of promissory notes.

The notes aggregated $400,000. That was the grand total of the debt that had rolled up during the forty years or so of Calwell management. That is to say, in every year of the forty the most popular and renowned, the most esteemed, powerful, odoriferous and successful of the Virginia Mineral Springs, the Queen of them all, the Almack's of watering places, had gone another $10,000 in the hole.

Everyone was jubilant about the sale. For years and decades this is what they had wanted, that the White should be taken out of this inefficient family management, should be bought by a stock company that would run it as a business and not as a milch cow for the benefit of six (nine, at one time) princely Calwell sons. Let some Yankees get hold of it, they had cried, let this monopoly be broken up and the place parcelled out to different owners who would perforce exert themselves under the spur of competition. They didn't get that, it wasn't broken up to be run competitively like Saratoga, but it had been bought by a stock company. That dream at least was a reality.

"This establishment has been much improved by the change of ownership," wrote William S. Pettigrew on the eighth of July, 1857. "No one could wish a better dinner than there was today." The omens were good, the new broom was doing fine. Everyone was thrilled by the energy of the new owners, by their ambitious plans. They were to break ground at once for a mammoth hotel, four hundred feet long and one hundred feet wide. At one end was to be a parlor and at the other end a ballroom and between the two a dining room that would seat twelve hundred diners with plenty of elbow room. A huge place. The parlor would have the distinction of being "half again as large as the celebrated East Room" in the White House.

Already they were building four cottages, the new South Carolina Row, modelled on Latrobe's Baltimore. Plans included a new bowling alley and new bathhouses. Before they were through they planned to spend $400,000 on improvements and additions, bringing their total investment to a round million dollars. Such liberality delighted the clients; they considered the place was at last getting the treatment it deserved. Because their stomachs had been so long abused by the old regime, they were inclined to forget that old man Calwell and his son William, for all their shortcomings, had built the White up to a spa of the first rank and kept it there.

It was at the beginning of the second week in July that William Pettigrew had written his sister about the good dinner and tendered his compliments to the new company. By August everything had gone to pieces again: the food, the clerks, the servants, all were indescribably bad. People were leaving the place in shoals, particularly the old-timers.

"It has been the most disagreeable here that I have ever known," said Mr. Johnston of Hayes, "and made every person very restless and dissatisfied the crowd is immense and a constant pressure from the outside to get inside and then grumbling and complaining and desire to get out again. I have never seen anything like it since I have been attending this place." In over three weeks he had not eaten in the old dining room more than three times, but even that was too much. Mr. Johnston fled to the Healing where, during the entire month of June, the old gentleman had stayed to gather strength for the rigors of the White Sulphur season. It had not been enough. Here he was back at the Healing so soon again, a wreck.

"Many," he declared, "will not return to the White Sulphur, being much disgusted by the way it is managed." It was the more disheartening when one considered that all the White had needed for so long was to get the Calwells out and get a stock company in.

It didn't matter about the old-timers. They might swear never to return but they did (Mr. Johnston himself was back at the White two weeks after he left it), and even if they hadn't it wouldn't have made any difference. More powerful and fateful forces were at work to fill the vacancies, to fill to overflowing the new hotel at the White and all the other arks around the water holes. They had always prospered on pestilence; now they began to grow fat on national calamity.

"Stay at home," cried the editors to the Southerners who had been spending their summers at Northern resorts. "You are only insulted up there, you only pour your money into the pockets of the abolitionists who have sworn to destroy you," which was true enough. "You are more and more embroiled in fights with impertinent Northern niggers whose brains have been fired with dreams of equality and vengeance," which was also true.

The fights had gotten to be frequent and notorious; Southern men were bashing "fresh" Negroes over the head with chairs, hot-headedly pulling knives and pistols to defend their honor and the honor of Southern womanhood and writing letters to the home papers about their troubles, until the Richmond *Dispatch* grew weary of an indignation for which there was so obvious a remedy. "If people will go among abolitionists and free negroes, they must be prepared for the consequences." Why don't they stay at home? We have resorts in abundance on this side the Potomac, far more delightful than all your Cape Mays and Rockaways, Newports and Saratogas rolled into one.

And another thing, chorused the editors, the company is better. Where in the United States can you find the equal of that "frank, elegant and high-toned society" that gathers at the Springs, a writer in the *Southern Quarterly Review* wanted to know? With some mighty small exceptions, only in the South, he answered. Mr. DeBow, the gifted editor of New Orleans, looked out of his window in Paradise Row and reflected on the pleasures of being among such a society as filled the spa. Its polish of manner, its courtesy, its cleverness, its propriety of demeanor (all anti-political graces) set it apart, contrasted it "very favorably with the resorts of other sections." And that, also, was true.

"Stay at home!" became the daily slogan of the press.

The people who went North the editors called Soft-Heads. They cried "humbug" at honeymooners who preferred Cape May to Sullivan's Island or the Springs. They flung "traitors" at the spenders of Southern money above Mason and Dixon's Line. Professor Silliman of Yale had given it as his opinion that the mountain ranges and waters of Virginia were better adapted to the Southerner and his ailments than the highlands of Vermont, and DeBow threw it at the heads of his compatriots as a fact based on incontrovertible science. The editors' drumfire of argument and insult, their whiplash of scorn drove hundreds to the Virginia Springs who might have gone to alien pastures.

Larger events were casting shadows forward; the "inevitable conflict" was troubling the waters. Nor did it wait. Hostilities broke out on the spot with the Battle of the Belles. It was fought at White Sulphur in mid-July, 1856, precipitated by the unflagging efforts of a lady named Mary J. Windle.

Mary J. Windle came from Delaware. It was said her true name was McLane. She wasn't a professional *agent provocateur;* her regular job was to write a daily dispatch on Springs affairs for several of the larger Southern newspapers, and it was her distinction to be the first bona fide social reporter to invade the Virginia Springs, make copy of the private doings of Southerners, and live. She wasn't there to stir up fights, but the Battle of the Belles was her handiwork just as certainly as the brawls up North between Southerners and waiters were the handiwork of the abolitionists.

Miss Windle adored Southerners. She thought that Southern women, particularly if they came from South Carolina, were the most beautiful, the best dressed, the most charming, gracious and natural creatures in the world. Put her in a room with Southern girls and her vision swam with the heroines of Scott and Byron, with portraits by Reynolds, Titian, Raphael and Guido. Bring her face to face with a famous beauty like Sally Ward, the pride of Kentucky, and she made it clear that no one before her had ever done justice to that leading Southern product, the belle. Sally Ward's arrival at the White proved to be one of Miss Windle's golden opportunities.

"But the cynosure of all eyes, the nucleus round which all gathered, was the newly arrived bride from Louisville. We don't believe Tommy Moore found anything purer and fairer when he went angel hunting under the shade of the sumachs than the picture-like face of this child-like bride. She is evidently just from school, for the expression is bright with an early flush of youth, such as seldom survives the vigils and heart-burnings of a single season." (Sally was twenty-nine, had not been to school for at least eleven years, had been a bride for the second time five years before and was now well along in her second bellehood.)

"To our mind the chief charm of this young bride is the shy, sweet, tremulous tenderness, happy and bright, that seems to rest upon her face. Her diamonds and Point d'Alencon would have rejoiced the courtly pencil of Vandyke." That is the sort of effect Southern beauty had on Miss Windle.

Now it happened that the Northern ladies of fashion were coming to breakfast in silks and whalebone and loaded with trinkets, while their Southern sisters still clung to muslin and tarlatan, which they were wearing uncom-

monly long these days, just as their leghorn "flats" were uncommonly wide. Who could be blamed for finding them
irresistible? What with such a length of skirt to manage,
they were lifting it piquantly off the grass now, out of the
dew and the dust, so that more pretty ankles were seen
twinkling about the grounds than had ever rewarded the
gaze of man before.

One sharp-eyed old gentleman expatiated on this lifting
business and how it was becoming a habit. Every movement the dear things made they grabbed their skirts and
lifted them not only up but forward, he said, "giving full
expression to the entire rear outline." In the ballroom he
noticed they had taken up very low necks and "illusion,"
but never so much illusion that it was an impediment to
the eye. Another way of looking upon these things was La
Windle's way: the Southern girl, when she was so minded,
she said, could beat the Paris-gowned *élégantes* with their
own weapons.

Miss Windle was quite aware that the Northern beauties
were crowding on too much sail but she said nothing. In
fact she never by any chance in all her dispatches so much
as mentioned a lady from north of Baltimore, and that was
the trouble. The Northern ladies did their best to deserve
her attention. They kept putting Northern and Paris gowns
in her way to see what she would say of them, but she said
nothing and, considering what she thought of them, that
was a mercy. They charged her with prejudice; refusing to
take the hint she continued writing about Southern womanhood exclusively. Finally, in a fury, they challenged her to
write a sketch comparing the Northern and Southern girls,
and the fat was in the fire.

The scheme as proposed was that La Windle should write her essay under three headings, Beauty, Dress and Manners. It was to be submitted for analysis to a joint conclave of Northern and Southern belles, met together in a friendly way, and the authoress was to be called into the meeting after they had ironed out all their differences. Strange to say, this mad proposal was carried out to the letter.

The battle took place in one of the larger cottages and it was all fought and over with before the chief actress was called onto the field. When she got there, in response to the awaited summons, the Northern troops alone were holding the fort. The Southerners had grabbed up their long skirts and their leghorn hats and scooted to places of safety, leaving behind them the fumes of the smoke of battle: Windle sniffed the odor of smelling salts in the air.

The enemy general paced up and down. Behind her were her comrades drawn up in ranks and in her hand was the sketch. She pounded the table and berated the authoress. So! she said, they were the worst dressed ladies in America, were they, stiff mannered and never more than merely "pretty?" Never possessed of a high order of beauty, were they? Recommended to study the "exquisite demi-toilettes" of the Southern belles, were they, the simple muslins with flowing sleeves, and so on and so forth? Well, Miss Windle would see what they thought of her insults. Had she anything to say before they burnt the offensive thing, for let it be known that that was what they had unanimously determined to do.

La Windle could stand no more. The strain of the whole affair had been bad enough, but when she thought of her work destroyed, her subtle observations going up in flames, she was done in. She simply broke down and cried. That turned out to be the signal for a general emotional *crise;* the Northern general, taken unawares on the flank, whimpered and burst into tears and her forces behind her, their morale suddenly undermined, were overcome with the sniffles and drew their handkerchiefs. In a surge of womanly sympathy they returned the sketch on Beauty, Dress and Manners to its creator intact, and the Battle of the Belles was over.

But Mary J. Windle was not softened. She went right on in her chosen way, ignoring the gowns from above Baltimore and adoring the ones from below. She went farther, enlarging her field of operation. See, she said, what "pure taste" there is in the furnishings of the White Sulphur parlors, what a contrast to the gaudy styles up North; see the Southern planters in the stagecoach, so distingué in their loosely worn garments compared to the stiff Yankees. The black slaves at the Virginia watering places were far better treated than the white servants up yonder. Every sentence was a sledge-hammer blow to drive the wedge deeper. So far as Miss Windle was concerned the great separation had come, there was no turning back.

Hardly had the odor of smelling salts drifted from the battlefield before Edmund Ruffin came on the scene with that eagle's gleam in his deep-set eye. He had just dedicated what remained of his life to the proposition, generally speaking, that no Yankee was fit to lick the boots of a Southerner's body servant, and the sooner the South cut

The Lawn, White Sulphur

As it was in the mid-Thirties. Ballroom to the left, Paradise Row right, stables in the distance.

From a water color after the original by J. H. B. Latrobe

loose from such people the better. He was an avowed *agent provocateur,* he had no other job now, no other thought; he had given up farming, farm journalism, the preaching of fertilizer, those activities in which he had won fame and fortune he had put behind him now to throw his buzz-saw energy into tearing a body politic asunder.

Edmund Ruffin was sixty-two and looked an old man, what with his thin white hair falling down to his shoulders and his face aged with nervous collapse. From out two sunken caverns where his eyes were there flashed a fanatic fire, and the people he accosted found themselves fixed on two burning points. Few men except old actors ever acquired a mouth like his, made wide and thin and flexible with the continual passage of eloquence, set on a ruled line, tucked down at the corners. His chin was like a square headland and over his jaws there played the muscles of the avenger.

"In my visit to the Springs I used every suitable occasion to express my opinion . . . that the slave states should speedily separate as the only means of warding off the assaults of the northern people to destroy slavery and ruin the Southern states." Every suitable occasion indeed. And what occasion could not be suitable to this fearful enterprise? If Mr. Ruffin went with the crowds to the spring-house, it was not just to pass the time of day and add a straw to the light banter there but to buttonhole Governor Manning on the matter of reopening the forbidden slave trade with Africa. Did he go to the ballroom, it was not to watch the dancers but to talk earnestly with Judge Perkins of Tensas Parish (Louisiana) about disunion and the quickest way to have it over with. If he hustled over from the

Red Sweet to the Old Sweet, it was not the pleasant walk that drew him but the presence of more important men at the older resort for him to prod with the spearhead of action.

He was trying men out, he said, taking a poll of smouldering opinion. How many were there of his own mind who had not dared to speak? So he cornered James C. Johnston here and Jeremiah Morton there and Judge Hopkins at the Sweet and Judge Withers there too, and William B. Harrison and Isaac Hayne and Dr. Cocke and scores more into whose ears he poured his counsel of desperation summer after summer for four years. What a happy day that was when he and the rich young Judge Perkins formulated the idea of the Publication Society which, with several other conspirators, they founded to print and broadcast firebrand pamphlets. That meant concrete action and it brought joy to the old man's heart. He would write, write, write, night and day, an endless stream of passion's argument to keep the presses turning.

Ground was broken for the new White Sulphur hotel in the very month that a financial earthquake shook the North, bringing its bankers and merchants to their knees and their houses tumbling on top of them. A perverse fate had scheduled this catastrophe and the commencement of the long-awaited hotel for the same moment in history, but also something of the same perversity had made the South proof against this shock. They felt the tremors down there but hardly more. Total income instead of dropping went up. There had never been so many dollars' worth of cotton exported; the same was true of tobacco. The sugar plantations of Louisiana boiled twice as much cane as the year before and sold it at a good price. Figures could be marshalled to prove that, while the North was bogged, the South actually prospered.

The "outside" panic neither stopped nor slowed the building of the hotel and it was ready for guests the next summer, '58. Sprawling there in unprecedented length, financed by Southern money and completed by Southern energy at a time when building and enterprise in the North stood still, was it not further evidence that the South could get along very well by itself, that it had no need for the North at all?

The new building was all that the company had promised, dimensionally at least. It was indeed four hundred feet long and one hundred feet wide and it had the great parlor at one end and the ballroom at the other with the dining room between. The two floors above contained two hundred and twenty-eight chambers, and there was a basement floor with the bar, a "restaurant," the offices and a kitchen that was as dark as the Black Hole of Calcutta. No one, with the possible exception of the cooks, had been deceived by the glowing prospectus.

Not that it was very handsome or very Southern either. To look at it was not to know at once that one was in the South; it told no such story as the cottages did in the merest flash. And this was despite the arcaded basement which was Southern as a canebrake, an architectural fundamental dictated by mosquitoes and a damp and steamy earth. It was in truth a fine example of barracks design, and soon enough its deficiencies in the way of open verandahs became apparent and they began sticking them on, as they eventually stuck on a wing, too, of somewhat different architectural physiognomy. But the collective South regarded it with the eye of affection which makes all things lovely.

Perhaps the only person not supremely conscious and proud of this triumph was Edmund Ruffin. He was too busy even to mention it, writing seditious articles for Mr. Rhett's Charleston *Mercury,* correcting the proof of his forthcoming book, boring at the foundations of the Nation, capitalizing the little events of the Springs summer that had a curious way of playing into his hands as though he himself had just pulled them out of the hat.

There was at the White a bathkeeper named McIntosh, an intelligent darky and a freedman, not long returned from the emancipation colony in Liberia, where he had been a judge. Judge McIntosh made no secret of the fact that Liberia was a mess and a deathtrap, said he had been overjoyed to return to the land of slavery and that if there was a chance of his being banished from Virginia because he was a free Negro, he would ask Mr. Jeremiah Morton to make him a slave again. Fate threw Judge McIntosh into the arms of Mr. Ruffin, who made him a celebrity around the Springs and got publishers to broadcast his story. Hoch the blessings of slavery! shouted Mr. Ruffin. Down with the abolitionist meddlers and down with the sentimentally inept Colonization Society too.

A new Methodist Church had been built in the Springs grounds on a plot furnished by the owners, and the "Methodist Church North" had grabbed the deed through the Baltimore synod. Robbery! cried Mr. Ruffin. The money had come from the South and the deed belonged to the "Methodist Church South." (The church, setting an example to the Nation, had already split into two camps.)

Ably assisted by the fire-spitting Parson Brownlow, Mr. Ruffin kicked up a tremendous dust about it, persuaded men to withdraw their subscriptions and threatened to make things hot for the management by publicizing the "theft" throughout the Deep South. But his tongue was in his cheek. Whatever Brownlow wished to do with it was his own affair. As for himself, the matter was of no great moment, it merely served "to keep up this ferment."

The biggest prize that fell into Mr. Ruffin's hands was the new hotel, for now at the height of the season he had over sixteen hundred souls to work upon, where before his best audience had been four or five hundred less than that.

And the ambassador of destiny soon saw his handiwork taking on results: the clank of arms began to break through the laughter. The management at the White installed a pistol gallery where old and young were polishing up their marksmanship. Anyone could read in the Springs pamphlet that year the fire-tipped words that advertised the pleasures of shooting: "The keen report tells how promptly young America is preparing to avenge his insulted honor."

In miniature, too, the military note was struck. The little tots on the lawn were busy with their drilling and their battles, led on by Charley Bonaparte, great-grandnephew of Napoleon, putting his companions through their paces in front of Baltimore Row. Little Charles Joseph was an inveterate marcher, demonstrating a fine talent for strutting; he was a born commander, shouting at his troops in his shrill boy's voice. On his head was a little crimson undress cap, at his thigh a sabre. The Emperor would have been proud. Great-grandmamma, Betsy Patterson Bonaparte, drifted slowly by the martial scene on her walk to the spring, watching the workings of the Corsican strain. The Emperor's stamp in looks or action was on all of them: her son Jerome with his Napoleonic stance, her grandson, a soldier now in the service of Louis Napoleon, and now this latest Little Corporal.

Soon the sabre rattle and musket fire of grown men was heard on Copeland Hill, up back of Georgia Row where the cemetery was and where many a guest and the old man with the cue lay luckily asleep. Company F of the Richmond Volunteers was there in camp. It was the summer of '60 and Lincoln's star was rising, steadily, surely, above the horizon; "a house divided cannot stand" pounded fatefully in all their ears. Company F was drilling, eating the grub of war (it fancied), marching through the countryside, having the Richmond girls up to the officers' mess. Governor Letcher was up there with them, living the life of a soldier in a tent, not of a statesman down in the comfortable hotel. High and low, everyone must prepare.

Company F came down from Copeland Hill, bringing the electric current of militarism to the crowd. A ceremony had been announced; sixteen hundred people swarmed over the front steps, the galleries, the front lawn, face to face with the stiff ranks of the Volunteers. The occasion was the presentation of a handsome sword to Mr. Cary, the Company's captain. Mars was training at the waters, training and arming.

What was it Editor DeBow had written home from the White after drifting through the assembly taking samples of sentiment? "It is evident that the South is all right and moving together and will be ready to strike in the proper manner when the time comes, if come it does."

But it was not coming fast enough for Mr. Ruffin after all. He was discouraged, the temporizing of these people made him feel that all his preaching at the Springs had been wasted. These men of substance, these planters, bankers, merchants, judges and members of Congress were conservative, timid. It disheartened him to have Senator Chesnut condition his disunionist sentiments with an "if" here and an "if" there. It shocked him to find that Colonel Williams of South Carolina was an out-and-out unionist; he had thought the only unionist freak down there was James L. Petigru, the lawyer.

Mr. Ruffin was depressed. He was forced to admit, "I find myself alone as an avowed disunionist *per se*," feeling the pangs of a prophet without honor. Virginia was infested with unionists. He would give up his Virginia citizenship, he would go South where his blazing eyes could strike sparks in hotter heads.

But before he left the Springs a calm, sweet note sounded within the old man's jangled brain, a note of love. His son Edmund and the girl he had chosen for him had succumbed to the spell of the waters, which could practically be guaranteed. Jane had thrown aside her doubts and agreed to a marriage.

Ironically, that saved the old man from making a fool of himself. He had once imagined himself in love with her, and not as a father. Had he once followed his inclinations he might, he confessed, "be as great a fool as most other old men and seek to marry a blooming young girl." But to keep a fine woman in the family he had schemed for an alliance with Edmund, had brought them together here beside the romantic waters. It had worked. Now, relieved and happy, he could turn again to the prosecution of that other scheme.

That worked too. Eight months later, in the pale dawn at Charleston Harbor, who was it they gave the honor of firing the Palmetto Guard's first cannon shot at Fort Sumter? Who was that fiery old man with the mane of white hair pulling the fatal lanyard, looking eagerly after his shot as it struck the parapet of the fort? It was Edmund Ruffin, *agent provocateur*, blasting the last remaining tie between the South and the age of its glory.

Four years later, on the eighteenth of June, 1865, this same old man sat in the parlor of a farmhouse in Amelia County, Virginia. He surveyed his handiwork, the final outcome of his bitter Springs campaign, of the inflammatory pamphleteering. He who had had a tidy fortune was ruined. His sons were dead. The South was prostrate, bleeding, homeless, hungry, sunk in the ignominy of defeat. Turning to his diary he composed a long and final curse upon the conqueror, signed his name, wrote "The End," took up a pistol and blew out his brains.

XIII

Old Glory and New Fervor

LATE one day in July, 1867, those guests who happened to be on the turnpike side of the hotel saw two horsemen coming in from the East. One of them caught the eye at once. The whole effect of him was gray, gray clothes, gray horse, gray beard and gray wide-brimmed slouch hat; gray riding gauntlets too. He rode easily, as from immemorial custom, "arms swinging loosely by his side," but he was very erect just the same and his head was high.

"A stranger," said one of the onlookers, "would have taken him for a plain Virginia farmer," a farmer with his trousers tucked into his boot tops and still wearing, for economy's sake like many another Virginia farmer, an old officer's army coat.

As the bystanders watched him bring his horse smartly to a stop and dismount with military precision, a gasp of recognition passed among them. Many of them had not seen him since before the War Between the States, but he looked much the same as he had except for his hair and beard, gray and going on to white now, and the deep composed sadness of his face. It was Lee. He was "looking remarkably well," they said among themselves. He had ridden over from Lexington with Captain James J. White, once of the artillery but now a Professor of Greek in Washington College, of which Lee was the President.

The coach that came in after the two horsemen contained Mrs. Lee, incurably crippled with arthritis, her maid, her great handsome son, General Custis, her daughter Agnes and Miss Mary Pendleton. Somewhere, on the boot or on top, was Mrs. Lee's wheel chair. She had come to the White, the General said, "merely on the ground that she has never tried those waters, and, therefore, they might be of service to her." The Lee party was assigned the last cottage in Baltimore, which had once belonged to "Beau" John Barney and sheltered Captain Marryat.

A little later in the day, at suppertime, General Lee appeared with his charges (all except Mrs. Lee) in the door of the dining room. The hundreds already at table were seized with a fit of uncertainty. What should they do? Should there not be some recognition, some demonstration? None dared start it, well knowing how he shrank from demonstrations; for that very reason they had not sent out a reception committee to the foot of the Allegheny to bring him in. He might have bolted. Would he not prefer to go to his table quietly, to be treated as one of themselves, that most delicate of courtesies? But it was impossible. As he stepped into the room followed by his little band, a sudden spontaneous movement swept the whole company to its feet and all stood silently, with tears in their eyes, until he who bore defeat so nobly had taken his seat.

After tea he appeared in the parlor where, by the time he and Custis and Miss Agnes and Miss Mary got there, nearly the whole company was doing Treadmill. This was the postprandial exercise that had been inaugurated before the War in the great new parlor, an ideal show ring where they could troop round and round like so much cavalry, two and three abreast, sometimes four or five, winding in and out, breaking up, stopping, forming and starting again, trooping, trooping over the bare uncarpeted boards. All around the walls were chairs for the more sedate and those who could carry on a conversation without moving their feet. It was introduction time, when cousins from Virginia met cousins from everywhere else and it was the time before the ball when the beaux engaged their dancing partners.

At the edge of the whirligig the gray General appeared, very dignified and handsome and friendly. One of the young ladies said he "shone out as the handsomest man in the company," and his bearing was the most courteous she ever saw. At once the Treadmill stopped and there ensued a reception for the General, who bestowed kisses upon the cheeks of all the young ladies. But there was one who ducked, embarrassing for an awkward moment both the man of battle and herself. Miss Mary Jones, afterwards one of his favorites, was shy of the fatherly salute.

(With Colonel Thomas Carter, cousin to General Lee, it was the cousinly salute. He was observed one day when the coach came in from another Springs, to kiss each young lady as she stepped down, inquiring as he did so, "What might your name be, my dear? I think you are a kinswoman of mine.") *

* D. S. Freeman, "Lee and the Ladies."

He retired early to Baltimore Row but at midnight, after the ball was over, Professor Rosenberger and his band slipped across the lawn, formed up in the roadway under the General's high front porch and filled the night air with the soft melody of a serenade. That over, the band slipped back to the hotel again, permitting the travel-worn family to go to sleep.

❦

A fair company of General Lee's compatriots was already at the White when he arrived, like birds come back by sure instinct to an old shelter after the tempest. Here would be refuge, here would be kin and kind, here they might perhaps find some scraps of their former gaiety and forget for a while that they were Saturday's children, ruled over by white rascals and their former slaves in the name of "reconstruction," an ignominy devised by the victorious Republicans because it served their political designs. Slowly, having heard that the Springs were open again, they were coming in.

"This celebrated watering place is now fully open for the accommodation of ONE THOUSAND VISITORS. Rosenberger's celebrated Brass and String Band is engaged for the season. Charges for board: Per Day, $3.50; Per Month, $90. George L. Peyton & Co."

The advertisement had been appearing in the Southern papers for something over a month. The lessees, three Peyton brothers, had opened the doors about the first of June. The opening was on a subdued note. "We cannot expect to see there the society that once gave life and gayety and grace to that incomparably delightful summer resort," said the Richmond *Dispatch*. "The remembrance of the past days must sadden the feelings of many visitors the present year." They thought perhaps the natural beauties might cheer people up. Anyhow, the proprietors would do their best to accommodate the guests. "We anticipate a gay season." But it was an afterthought; they didn't believe it.

During the War the place had seen some rough service as barracks and as hospital. It had just escaped burning, the picturesque old Rows and the proud new hotel together. General Hunter of the Northern Army, in retreat, had given the order to put the whole village to the torch, and only the colossal nerve of Captain H. A. DuPont had saved it. Wouldn't such an act, he asked his superior, be a military mistake? In case they occupied the country again, might they not use all these buildings for winter quarters? Hunter looked at the Captain suspiciously for a moment, then countermanded the order. That was Captain DuPont's story.

After it was all over, rot and neglect and abuse had done their work: many of the steps to Paradise and Alabama and the other old Rows had crumbled, the lattice work under the porches was falling out, Hygeia atop the springhouse was missing altogether, riddled with bullets and carried away, roofs leaked, hangings were gone, furniture despoiled, paint was peeling. The once trig little village was out at elbow and down at heel but still sound. By the time the energetic Peyton brothers were ready to open up, two years after Appomattox, they had braced the steps and repaired the furniture and made the great rooms on the main floor festive with new draperies. The ballroom had been "tastefully decorated," said one; the ornaments therein "must be seen to be appreciated." Said another, it had been refurbished with large mirrors, floral wreaths and "glittering festoons." Very gay.

The crop of would-be belles was a new one entirely, new and fresh and starving for these pleasures. For four years their nourishment had been the terrors of war; they had grown from girlhood to young womanhood with cannon fire in their ears, trembling in attics, fleeing in the dreadful night, scraping lint, waiting helpless for the certain news of death. For two more years on top of that they had been salvaging what they could from the ruins.

During all this time the brightest stories they had heard were of the Springs, of the famous beauties and their beaux and their love affairs, of the waters that made young hearts beat faster. Would they ever be belles as their mothers were? Would the dreadful war be over and would people go to the Springs again before it was too late, before they were too old?

In a cottage close by General Lee's there was a little party of girls from Baltimore, typical of all the rest, bursting with excitement and expectancy. One of them was Christiana Bond, twenty-two and somewhat older than the others, a dark-haired and grave young lady, wistful and a little withdrawn, feeling that she was not cut out for belledom but nonetheless in quite as fine a fever as were her companions over the possibilities of this visit. They were all allured, she said, with the tales of the Springs; they were all breathless to meet the heroes of the War. They were starved for romance.

Soon the young ladies from Baltimore and from Virginia

and Louisiana and the whole South discovered that something was wrong. They went promenading in the sentimental labyrinth of Lovers' Walk all right, but they went with
each other. They climbed Kate's Mountain, too, but was
it with escorts or suitors or males of any description? All
too seldom. And the nightly balls were not what they had
been before the War. Instead of a close succession of polkas, waltzes, schottisches and lancers, there were frequent
pauses in the dancing while Professor Rosenberger played
selections from the *operas,* of all things. While it pleased the
old, it annoyed the young who knew that if there had been
enough dancing partners it never would have happened.

It was sad to have to face the truth: there were hardly
any beaux, lying as they were in shallow graves or slaving
on their farms to harvest a meager crop. Those that Mars
had spared poverty had taken over. Only a handful could
afford to go to the Springs at $3.50 a day, and most of that
handful were battle scarred and old before their time.

People were alarmed, old as well as young. The Richmond *Dispatch* complained that "the making of couples for
wedlock" had fallen off to pitifully small proportions and
that there had been "considerable inquiry." If the waters
had lost their potency it could not have been more calami-
tous. "The absence of the former abundance of eligible
beaux," reported a scout for the *Enquirer* was the subject
of universal sorrow. "All through the mountains a wail has
gone forth at the scarcity of young men." The cruelest blow
of war had struck home to the hungry hearts and it was
hard to bear.

But the little ladies of the lost generation soon found consolation. General Lee himself filled up the breach left by

the absent cavaliers; after his arrival their world began re-
volving around him for its center. They watched him as he
came and went, they coveted his conversation and the kisses
he bestowed upon their cheeks. After breakfast they way-
laid him in the parlor, but then it was all too brief; he was
soon mounted on Traveller and disappearing along one of
the trails into the mountains.

After dinner they gathered round to tell him their plans
for the afternoon; if there was an excursion afoot or a pic-
nic he could be depended upon to offer his services as escort. He was their host at a circus party the day Costello,
Barnum and Van Amburgh's Great Show came to Dry
Creek (though he himself did not go—too public) and he
had them in to a watermelon party afterwards. Someone
had sent him a sixty-pound watermelon from Mobile.

The best time was after tea, with everybody gathered for
the Treadmill. Then General Lee showed how willingly he
could submit to capture if only his captors were young and
lighthearted. The prettiest sight of the day was to see him
in the midst of the young ladies, and the finest lesson in
courtesy was the way he brought the shy ones into the
circle of his charm. Occasionally they bore him off to walk
in the Treadmill. The New York *Herald* reported him a
"great gallant."

Yet there was more than gallantry and more than diversion and more than his natural love for youth. For one
thing he found asylum among them, their cordon of loveliness shielded him from people full of weighty conversation.
For another and more important thing there was the task
of conciliator that he had set himself. After the old campaign there was this new one, to get his people to accept

the inevitable. Somehow this bitterness must be alchemized into something sweeter, if not love then at least courtesy. Behind the social charm the conscientious missioner was at work.

"Have any of you made the acquaintance of that group over there, have they been welcomed?" This he asked them during Treadmill one evening. The group "over there," sitting alone, was from the North, the party of Governor Curtin, War Governor of Pennsylvania. The manner of the Northerners, recently arrived, had not been inviting of courtesy, and on the Southern side, particularly among these young things, there had been animosity and suspicion.

Why should the Northerners come here? Was it to look upon their poverty, gloat over their defeat? Was it to smile at their make-shift dresses? No, they said, no one knew them. They knew it was Governor Curtin and his party and that no attempt had been made to welcome them. If the truth were known, they wished they would go away.

"Can no lady introduce me?" the General insisted. No lady could, indeed. It was their duty to be hospitable to strangers, he reminded them; this was their place, it belonged to the South, and they were its hostesses. There was no response. He told them: "I shall now introduce myself and I shall be glad to present any who will accompany me." No one volunteered, no one moved, until hesitatingly, dutifully, Christiana Bond said, "I will go, General Lee."

Halfway across the room Miss Christiana asked the question that was on all their lips. "But, General Lee, did you never feel resentment towards the North?" He had been preaching tolerance, telling them they must all go home and do the same; they must say General Lee wished it.

How, deep down, did he feel? They stopped under the radiance of one of the crystal chandeliers and the old gentleman told the young girl solemnly, "I believe I may say, speaking as in the presence of God, that I have never known one moment of bitterness or resentment."

And with that he proceeded to give a lesson in courtesy to the enemy.

❦

Miss Bond was a serious young lady, nourished on the poetic line and the code of chivalry, dreamy and artistic, prone to hide behind her poetry and her drawing. With the unerring instinct of so sensitized and shy a being she had found her knight, the one into whose keeping she would entrust her heart, found him and acknowledged it at once. Even before reaching the White, at a roadside tavern where they had stopped at midday, when he had stood above her on the stairs and spoken to her, she had known that this was her "realized King Arthur." Standing with him under the parlor chandelier, hearing the words of true nobility, she was doubly sure of it.

She made a drawing of his cottage in Baltimore Row, setting it down with delicately held pencil, thinking: I am not one of his favorites, I am too solemn for him, too grave. His pets are the gay ones, the light-hearted, irresponsible, carefree ones who make him forget the weight of memory that bears him down. But still, I love him best, I think. Have they, any of them, taken his image into their hearts as I have? How many of them say to themselves as I do, he is the pure in heart who shall see God?

Sketching, she thought of his other young friends, of the one who went into his cottage the other day and asked for some hairs of Traveller's tail. He had none of Traveller's hairs, he said, would she be satisfied with some of the hairs of his head? But she would not. "I don't want yours, I want Traveller's." And he had laughed.

She thought of her young Baltimore friend whose suitor was at the Springs, who was so busy getting herself engaged that she had no time to spend with a battle-weary old man. It seemed to be enough for her that he kissed her good-night.

Then there was another one, the flibbertigibbet who said, after listening to one of General Lee's little lectures on hospitality to the Northerners, "Well, General Lee, they say General Grant is coming here next week; what will you do then?" They could have slain her where she stood; they blushed for shame that there was a viper among them. General Lee replied gently that he would welcome General Grant as to his home and do everything he could to make his stay agreeable. But General Grant did not come. . . . No, she thought, these could not love him as she did. She adored and worshipped him, she knew he was the greatest man she had ever known or would ever know again.

The drawing came out a little crooked: the cottage leaned to the right and the trees leaned too. But it didn't matter. Those were the steps his feet had touched, that was the doorway he had passed through, that was the doorframe upon which his shadow had fallen. Always it would be the abode of her heart.

General Lee departed on August 15, when the crowd had reached its peak of seven hundred. The new managers, the

Peyton brothers, did not get the thousand they bid for, though forty of their most prominent guests signed a puff in praise of their fine management (even to the food), which was printed on the front pages of the newspapers. The food, they said, was equal to the best in what had receded far enough to be called "the palmy days of yore."

However, the same could not be said for the gayety, nor half the same. The *Dispatch* had been right. "We cannot expect to see the society . . . the gayety and grace. . . ." It was dull, but for most of them it was enough just to be back at the Springs once more, to go to the springhouse in the early morning, to sit in the circular colonnade and watch the belles come down.

"How daintily they trip down the hill," observed one of the gentlemen, "with skirts looped up to avoid the dew." Their cheeks were aglow in the misty morning air and their fleecy shawls were dazzling bright after the years of black alpaca and bombazine.

It was enough that one could while away the mornings on the benches under the great oaks and listen to the talk of the ex-Generals and the ex-Governors. It was enough that the ballroom was alight again, and what if Professor Rosenberger did splice the dance music with Verdi and Bellini, Mozart and Meyerbeer? Was not that the millennium after the roar of cannons and the shriek of dying men and horses?

❦

By the next season these muted pleasures were by no means enough. The younger generation that had shocked its elders during the War by giving ball after ball in Richmond while the carnage was going on would not be satisfied with such halting gaiety now that the carnage was over. Operatic selections indeed!

From the season's first gun the trains coming across Virginia were filled. The Virginia Central in a chivalrous gesture reserved special cars for the ladies, who promptly overflowed them. "The queens of society," said a traveller, had surrendered to an old vanity, carrying enough tackle for a regiment. "Their trunks are as large as ever, the bonnet boxes and other receptacles of apparel are as huge and countless as in the good old days before the deluge." Neither war nor poverty, he said, had changed them in the least. The debarkation at Millboro, the new railroad terminus not far from the Warm, was a scene of utter confusion, what with the avalanche of satchels, shawls, bundles and those terrors of a coachman's life, the Saratoga trunks.

By the first week in August there were a thousand people at the White Sulphur, twice as many as the year before. The Peytons said they were prepared to accommodate fifteen hundred. Come the middle of the month they gave a Grand Fancy Mask Ball which was so successful that they announced another Grand Fancy Mask Ball for the end of the month. The oldsters moaned and groaned and said it would be flying in the face of Providence; even in the days of the Flush Fifties such a thing had not been attempted. The belles of yesteryear shook their heads and could not imagine where a second set of costumes was to come from when it took such scratching and patching to get together enough made-overs for everyday.

The second Grand Fancy Mask Ball was every bit as successful as the first. That so many young ladies came in cos-

tume was widely laid to the presence of Generals Lee and
Beauregard; where in all the South was the young miss who
would not strive to look her prettiest for these two heroes?
Most of them came as European peasants, clad in bright
striped silks and so hung with jewelry (lately disinterred
from the gardens) that one gentleman thought their papas
must be "very well off in the world." Venerable Miss Clinch
of South Carolina, amazed at the outbreak of diamonds,
pearls, satin and velvet, exclaimed, "O that I had the jewels
and laces to sell for the poor of dear suffering Carolina!"

The Southerner's spirit leapt with new and sudden hope.
Was not this the old South resurgent, the old South of chivalry, social grace, sophistication, even wealth? Was this a
nation crushed in defeat? It was not only the two Balls in
such close succession; there had lately been other signs to
quicken the pulse of pride, a musical concert at which talents had come to light that would have done credit to pro-
fessionals (Mrs. Charles Huger, the beauty of the summer,
had sung a number of operatic selections), lectures by gentlemen who demonstrated the Southern genius for humor.
Dr. George Bagby convulsed everyone with his paper on
"Love." Colonel Farrar and Mr. Cowardin had them in
stitches with "Johnny Reb" and "The Humors of Reconstruction." Did a people shattered and without hope spring
so soon to life with singing and laughter?

❦

The affair that did most to revive their self-esteem was
the Peabody Ball. That came the next year, '69, and was
given to honor the king of philanthropists, Mr. George Pea-

body, the Yankee-born millionaire of London. Everything was ripe for the Peabody Ball, everybody was ready for just such a climax, the background was a perfect build-up; Mr. Peabody appeared at just the right time and lived just long enough. A few months later it would not have been possible, for Mr. Peabody would be dead.

The season of '69 had been a dance year as none other had ever been before. "One word," said Mr. Charles Pilsbury, "tells what people do here. Dance." They danced morning, noon and night, literally. Six nightly balls had proved insufficient to satisfy their hunger, so they had "morning germans." These matutinal hops began at eleven and lasted until it was time to dress for dinner.

Between dancing and treadmilling, which, after all, was the next thing to dancing, a belle had very little time for anything else. Of course she must make a sufficient number of trips to the photographer's gallery to be "taken" in her ball gowns; the new photography was the rage and infinitely superior to the pre-war daguerreotypes. Almost certainly she went to the new Japanese store to buy a fan which Generals Lee and Beauregard would autograph for her when she cornered them, and she might possibly have a try at the new game, croquet, particularly if she had come equipped with Godey's fashionable "croquet suit," of Swiss muslin with wide ruffles.

But these things were off her orbit; her day revolved around the orchestra for its center: she danced to it in the morning german (first costume), listened to it on the lawn between four and five (second costume) and came down to tea in full toilette (third costume) prepared to dance again after Treadmill.

Frivolity and vanity were fostered by the press; reporters were everywhere now taking down names and descriptions of gowns, listing a lady's jewels, even estimating costs. The old subterfuge of initials and dashes was abandoned for good and all, names in full emblazoned the paragraphs. When the old-school gentlemen cried out against these practices and called the reporters low fellows, the low fellows shifted the blame to the bare shoulders of the belles, whose modesty, they said, was a sham. They dressed for an audience as wide as the printed word would reach and they were in a panic if they thought they might be overlooked.

Talk of clothes filled the piazzas, of how so-and-so was wearing a dress she had last year, or the other wore her sister's hat, or a third had slept in her booties since they were so tight after the dance she couldn't remove them, or still another never appeared twice in the same gown, her husband being a whisky magnate with an income rumored at $6,000. "The overdressing is awful," cried the editor of the New Orleans *Times;* the ladies had lost all their becoming modesty, they were self-conscious and on parade.

The dress mania was whipped along by the battle of gowns between Kate Chase Sprague and Laura D. Fair. Kate Chase, as she continued to be known in spite of marriage, had come down from the North with her father and Simon Cameron, both rabid anti-Southerners and former members of Lincoln's cabinet, bringing trunks full of the most stunning Paris gowns, with which she proceeded to slay the simpler Southern belles. "She dressed exquisitely," said Miss Brockenborough, "and scorned the White Sulphur ladies."

Saratoga, Piazza of Congress Hall

Drawn by C. Burton

White G

Ground for the new h
artist, Ed. Beyer, projec
architect's drawing.

L

She was quite without competition until Laura D. Fair came along with equal trunkfuls of equally stunning Paris gowns. The White Sulphur ladies in their turn scorned Laura D. Fair with her California gold-mine millions (they said she had had seven husbands and that four of them were still alive), so the two gorgeously gowned creatures had the field all to themselves, appearing each day and evening in fresh creations of sartorial glory, fighting it out like foreign frigates, strangers to this shore, and finally sailing away when their ammunition was exhausted. What they left behind, according to the New Orleans editor, was a "very perceptible infusion of Northern styles and taste." It was distressing.

The hurly-burly was hard on the old men. Lee, who admitted to only "tolerable" health now, and Peabody, teetering on the edge of the grave, and their friend W. W. Corcoran of Washington, inheritor of Colonel Singleton's Colonnade, could retire to their cottages and talk of the future of Southern education in peace, but all were not so fortunate. There were quiet-loving old gentlemen in the hotel who thought the management might at least provide a reading room where they might escape the social maelstrom.

Nobody had time for the old men. Nobody had time for serious intent. General Magruder ("evergreen" Magruder) was itching to give his lecture on Emperor Maximilian and Carlotta, but it was postponed and postponed until he despaired of getting anyone to hear him, ever; Leo Wheat, the pianist, seemed daily to be getting farther away from his proposed concert. All they wanted him for here, he said, was as a partner in the german. So it went, most discouragingly for the would-be performers and the lovers of peace

[221]

but splendid as a background for a tremendous affair like the Peabody Ball.

It was scheduled for August 11 but long before the time people began coming in from other Springs and from the cities, Lynchburg, Petersburg, Norfolk, Richmond. What Southerner was not eager to honor the man who had given three and a half millions to the Fund for Southern Education, the greatest benefaction the South had ever known? What Southern woman was not ambitious to press a kiss onto the old man's sagging cheek in a fervor of gratitude? Who in all that broad land would not celebrate the name of Peabody at a ball, if only he had the time, the clothes, the legs and the railroad fare?

Everybody came by railroad now, all the way, the Virginia Central having extended its tracks to the very gate of the White Sulphur. The clerks in their office in the basement floor had to breast the mass attack of trainloads now in place of coachloads as of old. It was the difference between tens and hundreds. Anywhere between ten o'clock in the evening and four o'clock in the morning (for the train was always late) the weary clerks accommodated the clamoring mob as best they might, sending many of them to makeshift quarters hardly fit for common soldiers.

Each night a Negro with a lantern would lead a little company of men, women and children out of the office and across the lawn to the basement of the Methodist Church, which was divided off into apartments by sheets and furnished with cots. Every night the porters conducted little parties of five gentlemen each to the upper halls of the hotel where there were more of these "California apartments"; and there, behind their sheets and to the light of candles stuck in bottles, the gentlemen would disrobe. Cut-ups threw a comic pantomime on the sheets; modest girls rustling by on their way from the ball shrieked and ran for their rooms.

The ballroom was reckoned too small for the crowd; consequently the dining room was cleared of its tables and combined with the regular *salle de dance.* There, on the appointed night, from room to room, in and out among the double line of pillars that upheld the ceiling of the dining chamber, what remained of Southern society danced for the Northerner who had made a great fortune in London from dealer's discounts on American bond flotations.

The participants were estimated at anywhere between fifteen hundred and two thousand, "two thousand people," said the *Whig,* "the peers of the most gifted, distinguished and gentle-blooded to be found in either section of our vast country. Never has there been brought together a crowd of fair women and brave men which represented more largely the refined beauty, grace, worth and intellect of our country than that which did honor to Mr. Peabody." Sprinkled among the bright beauties from the South were a few from New York and Pennsylvania, more of them than usual, for the invasion that was to change the face of things here had begun.

Busily threading their way through the crowd were the reporters who had grown so bold, catching their glittering quarry on the fly: Miss Mary Thomas of Baltimore as "Daughter of the Regiment," the same Miss Mary who had appeared the year before as a German peasant, "decked with all the jewels she can consistently display without violating good taste"; Miss Skipwith Harrison of West Virginia as a "Persian Girl," in a dress of silver foil; "Rainbow," Miss Belle Campbell; "Moonshine," Miss Sallie Montague of Richmond; "Marquise," Mrs. Captain Connor of Louisiana in green satin over pink silk, à la Watteau, with a pearl necklace; "Shepherdess," Miss Thayer of New York; "Marie Antoinette," Miss Turner, also of New York.

A good half-hundred drew individual paragraphs: "Postilion," Mrs. Trigg of Memphis; "Mary Queen of Scots," Miss Keyser of Baltimore; "Light of the Harem," Miss Sutherlin of Danville in blue and crimson satin with diamonds and other jewelry; "Undine," Miss Lock of Georgia; Scott's "White Lady of Avenel," making a post-war appearance in the person of Miss Fox of Kentucky in white silk richly trimmed with lace, "one of the costliest dresses of the ball"; the handsome Miss Skiff of New Orleans as "Queen Elizabeth," in green velvet trimmed with ermine and elegant jewels to match.

Here was brilliance, proudly recorded for the world's eyes: costly lace, ermine, silk, satin, silver and jewels, jewels, jewels. Behold the South, they said, a phoenix risen from its ashes, renewed in loveliness, hung with precious stones and costly garments. Except Miss Agnes Lee, at the end, in "simple white tarletan."

At least twenty-five gentlemen rated individual praise, having paid Mr. Marshall, the costume man, anywhere from ten to twenty dollars for the hire of their resplendent court costumes: Charles II, Spanish Cavalier, Earl of Essex, Don Caesar, Pizarro and so on. And then there were the dowagers, listed under "Representative Ladies," and the imposing gallery of "Distinguished Gentlemen," including eleven Generals of the Confederate Army, whole troops of

Judges, Honorables, ex-Governors, Colonels, Majors and the bearded social lion of the season, Blacque Bey, Minister from Turkey.

Supper was served at eleven and nobody could praise it enough. Champagne flowed freely; so many empty bottles had not been seen since the Fifties, if then. At midnight the dancing was resumed and they kept it up until three in the morning. "The best order prevailed," said one of the reporters, though as a matter of fact a duel was narrowly averted between two correspondents because of some fancied slurs on the Baltimore girls.

At four o'clock the train started back to Richmond carrying some of the weary revellers and those ecstatic write-ups that were to fill columns of fine print in the newspapers of Richmond, Baltimore, Charleston, New Orleans and New York. The sad note of the evening was pretty well glossed over. The guest of honor, unable to cope with it, stayed in bed.

❦

The epidemic of dancing, the background of war, the sense of release, the universal gratitude for their new-found friend, everything had been right for the success of the Peabody Ball. Now that it was over, General Lee hoped for "more breathing space." Two weeks remained of his allotted time for drinking the water, and he wished to finish them out in peace.

The light-heartedness of two years before was all but gone now, what with illness and death in his family and the increasing pressure in his chest. Under his eyes the lines were heavy and in them was an intent look, baffled, far away. Regularly he made his three or four trips a day to the springhouse for the medicine that Providence gave out of the earth, the medicine in which doctors and men still put a desperate faith.

The crowd thinned out and General Lee got his breathing space, but the merry-go-round went whirling on. The war generation had struck its stride and there was no stopping the momentum. On the last day of August the dance fever culminated in a spasm called the Press Ball, a ball to honor the low fellows who bandied the names and apparel of ladies about in print. In spite of the predictions of the press itself that this would be "one of the great events of the times, and will doubtless draw such an assemblage of wit, beauty and gallantry as can only be seen once in a lifetime," the Press Ball was a fiasco. True, over seven hundred attended, but true also that the important people stayed away, including the Turkish Minister. When it came to honoring journalists in a world that still considered them a paltry lot, even an alien and a Turk could smell a rat. Things had gone too far, the daemon of worldly vanity had got out of hand.

The season of '69 was the climax, not alone of the postwar years but of all that had gone before, of the whole golden age of the Virginia Springs. It was a climax delayed, postponed by the years of strife and all the more frantic for the repression. The oldsters were there in force to give it their blessing, not to say *ton*. As John S. Wise said, some spontaneous impulse had swept a great galaxy of former stars together for this incomparable season; they were the symbols of the South's great day, revered and loved, and for a flash, under their guidance, that greatness seemed to be recaptured. It would never be like this again, the old stars would grow dim and fall away, new people would take their places, many of them from the prospering North, but for the moment they conjured up a bright mirage that excited and exalted them.

With this climax the Springs came into their own, all the Springs, as healing places for the Southern malady of defeat. No other watering places anywhere could have done as well; Professor Silliman had spoken better than he knew. Down at the Montgomery White Sulphur there was a splendid tournament, where some of Mosby's men rode at the ring and the old spirit of Southern chivalry reappeared in bright and shining garments, unsullied by the bucketing of a brutal war. Again it appeared at the Salt when they held a tournament there; knights were bold and ladies were fair as though the recent blood-letting had been only an interruption in Walter Scott's posthumous pageant, which was now resuming. It was the magic of the waters.

From the Sweet came the word that a "distinguished and aristocratic" company had rallied under their old banner and that they had given a Fancy Mask Ball such as only distinguished and aristocratic people could give. Simply to know these things was the finest kind of tonic. The guests at the Healing were preening themselves on their clever Tableaux Vivants; they were satisfied that their Springs, off the new railroad line where the mob could not penetrate, was "the gem of the mountains." How reviving that was to drooping spirits!

Everywhere they drank the tonic of self-esteem but nowhere more than at the White Sulphur. And why not?

These things were in the record: they had brought off successfully two Grand Fancy Mask Balls in the space of two weeks, they had raised at one of their musical concerts the sum of $805 for General Lee's church in Lexington, they had sent nearly $300 to the Reverend Mr. Broaddus for his Southern orphans fund, they had enjoyed for three seasons the incomparable presence of General Robert E. Lee, they had gazed upon the cameo beauty of Mary Triplett and they had staged the great Peabody Ball, such a send-off into eternity as few celebrities had ever enjoyed, in bed or out.

There in '68 the White Sulphur Manifesto had been signed. Engineered by General Rosecrans and written by A. H. H. Stuart, it was a summation of all that General Lee had been pleading with his countrymen to do, conciliate the vengeful elements in the North, accept defeat, appeal for justice, and he was the first of thirty-one Southern leaders to sign his name. Staggering importance was attached to this document at the time but it came to nothing.

There, the *Whig* said, was gathered a company that had "never been equalled in quality." There the ladies astonished everybody with such a wealth of costume and jewelry that a Southern matron was moved to cry out, "Oh, my dear Southern countrywomen, do not forfeit by frivolity and extravagance the world-wide reputation you so nobly earned during our struggle." All of it was mightily reassuring, particularly the frivolity and extravagance.

Once it had been the boast there that the atmosphere around the spring would tarnish a silver coin in the pocket, a silver buckle on the shoe. Now, by some other alchemy, it acted in reverse. Men and women came with the tarnish

Sweet Springs, 1868

The hotel with its three famous porticoes as Miss Christiana Bond drew it in her sketchbook.

Springhouse Levee

The world and his wife at the temple of Hygeia, White
Sulphur, 1870. At left, visiting Englishman and mountain-
eer. At right, gouty Cuban. Center, banker. Under the
dome, not-so-prosperous planters; also a little girl who has
just drunk the water.

Every Saturday, *October 29, 1870*

of defeat on their souls and went away all bright and shiny, hopeful of a new day as brilliant as the old.

There were no complaints. Everything was perfect: management, servants, food, music, beds, linen, dining room, everything. The Calwell System, that old dodge of charging for the water and throwing in the boot to eat, was buried so deep in the past that it was a matter for jest. The oldsters who had survived those times laughed and were proud, like veterans. Everybody was gay, everybody danced. After what they had known of hunger, humiliation, wounds, gangrene and death, this was the ultimate refuge, a grove in Elysium.

XIV

Young Man with Four-in-Hand

HAL DULANY drove his four-in-hand down to the Springs in the summer of 1877. It was a new four-in-hand because Mr. Dulany was a new millionaire and it was beautiful to behold. The leading pair were dark matched bays and the wheelers were the same but heavier. The vehicle was a "double drag" with a box for the driver and a rumble for the footman. In color it was jet black, striped and panelled in dark blue; harness gold mounted. Mr. Dulany, the New York *Herald* said, "leaves all in the shade."

Before he came down from Loudoun County some other turnouts had been cutting a dash around the White. The Peruvian Minister sported footmen and gold harness mountings too; Mr. W. W. Corcoran, venerable deity of the place, rode around in a most elegant phaeton; a gentleman by the name of Swepson had a drag which he kept filled with belles. And there was the wealthy young Mr. Schoolcraft with his Sterris side-bar, his "showy turnout." But none of them came up to Hal Dulany's four-in-hand and none other matched the "consummate skill" of his driving, which put a reckless faith in two wheels on all curves. Besides, he had recently inherited a great deal of money, he was a bachelor of twenty-three and he was a Virginia gentleman. Said the *Herald's* observer, "he was considered a great catch by the mamas."

At Saratoga there were many four-in-hands; praise of their splendor and of the wealthy sports who drove them rang through the land. August Belmont, William R. Travers, Leonard Jerome, all were in the daily parade there. Like mannekins to advertise the rich inventories of the North, they were the heroes of the gilded age. So the appearance of Hal Dulany at the Springs in the South was a bracer for everybody. They, too, needed a hero of the new era, a new-fashioned knight to play off against the Northern dashers. When he appeared they called him Hal, like a prince, and took him to their bosoms.

Colonel Richard Dulany of Welbourne had been left pretty well stripped by the War and the prospects for his son were anything but brilliant. When the windfall of about a million dollars came from England, the bequest of a Lady Hunter, the prospects changed. Hal became the catch of Virginia and his coach overflowed with young ladies who had inherited a stringent and necessitous post-war world.

The new hero was not handsome. His eyes were too prominent and their color was nearer lead-gray than blue; his blond hair was stiff and his features rather nondescript. But he was by nature a prince of good fellows and the money helped him give expression to his character.

While the golden boy was tooling his bays around the country, there was another young man of some prominence about the Springs. He might have been found at almost any hour in the ballroom, and his name was Jo Lane Stern. Jo Lane had been a telegraph boy in the last year of the War; now he was a lawyer, a notary public and a social engineer. He had two passions; one was the Virginia National Guard and the other was leading cotillions, and of all the young men who had landed on their feet in the post-war dance craze, he was the indefatigable one. "He would rather," someone said, "lead the german than the Old Guard at Waterloo," and by 1877 he had worked to the top of the heap. In that year he had opened the Lee Monument Ball at the White Sulphur (the second and largest of three) and he couldn't have done more to achieve fame if he had led a charge at Antietam.

In these two young men the old world of the Springs and the new met head-on. With a devotion only exceeded by his enthusiasm, Jo Lane Stern carried on the tradition of Colonel Pope in the ballroom while Hal Dulany and his cronies were whipping up a faster pace with their coaching parties, their horse races, their champagne suppers and their Clubs.

❦

A clamor arose for horse racing at the White Sulphur. Look at Saratoga, they said, how the lure of the track brought it prosperity. What is there to prevent the White Sulphur from being the "Saratoga of the South?" Some people even started calling it that. Down here, the argument ran, the breeding and racing of horses was in the blood, not just a diversion of the new rich. Moreover the White was central, midway between the Maryland-Virginia studs on the East and those of Kentucky on the West.

Now it happened that the very well-heeled William A. Stuart, of the cattle-grazing and salt-well Stuarts, had bought in the White Sulphur for his first lien of $300,000 at a court sale in 1879 and was now shovelling improvement money into the place like a ship's stoker. He formed a stock company and sold bonds. He became a princely purchaser of surrounding properties. He caught the enthusiasm for horse racing and put up $6,000 as a first payment on a near-by meadow that had been pronounced ideal for steeplechasing.

The horsey ones dreamed dreams and saw visions. "The best descendants of Lexington and the fastest steeds in the stables of Lorillard, Doswell and others will soon be racing before a brilliant crowd for glory and big purses." The next year (1881) they had their first meeting on the Jericho Steeplechase Course. The events were a half-mile hurdle race and a two-mile steeplechase. The purses were $260 and $380 respectively, about on a par with the smallest purses at Saratoga. Eight horses ran in the steeplechase and Colonel Dulany (Hal's father) won it with a horse named Fleet. It was not only the first meeting on the Jericho course, it was the last. The biggest purse went to the owner of the meadow, an Englishman, who got to keep the $6,000 and the property too.

That, however, did not kill horse racing. The very next year, beneath Lovers' Leap, they had a track for flat races, all under fence. The director of the initial meeting was Major Ferguson, Secretary of the Maryland Jockey Club, gesture toward the East. Gesture toward the West, they adopted the rules of the Louisville, Kentucky, Jockey Club. Everything was superior to the first attempt. Mr. Stuart *et al.* co-operated by contributing $4,000 to the purse; the railroad reduced rates to the White for the meeting, set for August 29 to September 7, with five days of racing all told.

People read in their papers that "The most noted stock of North, South and West is entered." The five days of racing went along as scheduled and the $4,000 purse money was distributed, plus the gate. There was nothing particularly notable in any of the races except the last, the Lovers' Leap Steeplechase, which was won by Hal Dulany's Colebrook with his cousin Rozier Dulany's Cyrus second. Purse, $200.

There were no more meetings on that course, either, unless we count a mule race of several years later, ten mules all programmed by the clever Miss Lena Jackson. "Bay Mule White Sulphur out of Funds by Tiger," was a sample. Still later, in 1886, some reckless amateurs were racing around the course and one of the equestriennes was thrown and badly hurt. That gave horse racing at White Sulphur its *coup de grâce*. It had been no good trying to make it the Saratoga of the South. The fast steeds in the stables of Lorillard, Doswell and others stayed away in carloads. There wasn't enough money and only the Southerners thought there was enough glory.

It was easier and cheaper and more up their street to dance, to give germans morning and evening, to have lawn parties and eat watermelon soaked in champagne, to pose after every party in large groups for the photographer, to ride around in the turnouts that came now for show only, in short to proceed with the giddy doings that had sent the blood to their heads after the War, giving them a pleasant fever that showed no signs of abating. Horse racing fitted neither the purse nor the mood. The Dulanys and their pals won the races and lost the round.

※

But the Clubs arrived. For any who felt the pangs of disappointment because the horses had departed, the Clubs were consolation, proof as they were that Saratoga had no monopoly on sports and dashers, and if the Southern gents of the Clubs did not, with one exception, have millions to throw about, they certainly went through some fine motions.

If we omit the Hey Rubes of Chicago (which we intend to do) there were four Clubs: the Irish, the Crowing Hen, the Nameless Five and the Presidents' Cottage Club. The Irish came together in 1885 like a lot of steel filings gathered to a magnet. There were seven filings, mostly from the Deep South, and the magnet was Miss Lena Jackson of New Orleans. It happened that summer that Miss Jackson was incapacitated for dancing by illness, an enormous handicap for the ordinary belle but something of an asset, as it turned out, for so lovely a creature as Miss Jackson. Hearing of her misfortune, seven gallant and quixotic gentlemen decided to make it up to the deprived lady. They would form a club, they said, and make her its Queen, such a Queen that she would be the envy of all the healthy belles who were dancing their legs off.

They called it the Irish Club because they could think of no other word so antipathetic to the word "german." Their meat was not to be this overdone vogue, but conversation, sociability; their specialties were déjeuners (new word), tea-time receptions with their Queen in fine red silk, champagne suppers. True, at their first lawn parties they did suffer "dancing on the lea" but it was mostly the *marche militaire* sort of thing. General Charles Anderson, a great beau, drilled the hundred happy guests up and down the lawn.

Most of the men around the New Orleans Queen were out of the Deep South. Judge Glenn and Willis Sparks were from Georgia, Will Curtis and Irwin Jamison from New Orleans and Charles Dudley came from Mississippi. The other two, H. G. Dennison and A. William Hamilton, were from Ohio and Kentucky respectively. Colonel Hamilton was President. There were no Virginians.

The Irish Club made the social pot boil. There was as much envy and excitement over one of its déjeuners as over a royal breakfast at a village inn. It really hit its stride the summer after the founding when it gave twice as many entertainments and stirred up twice as much *réclame* as the first year. "Cal" Nutt of Natchez, who lived by his wits and died by his pistol, seems to have been added to the group and it began to be whispered that the Irish Club was very "fast."

Soon the Springs heard of a rival club, a mysterious organization called the Nameless Five which burst into anonymity with the same line of goods as the Irish, stealing its thunder with déjeuners and champagne suppers. The dish of the Nameless Five, however, was spiced with an extra dash of hush-hush. The modus operandi was to give the guest list to the chaperones and let them do the inviting, so that the guests were kept in a froth guessing who their hosts were. The most knowing put a finger on the Springs' two

golden lads, Hal Dulany and Stilson Hutchins, Jr., son of
the owner of the Washington *Post,* and on Willie Eustis,
grandson of the rich Corcoran. One had only to figure who
might be footing the champagne bills and there was the
nucleus of the Nameless Five.

It all ended, the mystery and the thunder-stealing together, when the two Clubs merged and the Irish took in
the Nameless Five, the price of admission being an extremely swank dinner given by the upstarts to the en-
trenched Irish. They had the menus printed on "elegant"
white satin and they brought Small, the fashionable florist,
from Washington to do the decorating and make the ladies'
bouquets. Small made the bouquets smaller (the girls had
been toting great bucolic bunches of flowers) and the price
larger by something over $20 a head. From now on there
were five new and not so anonymous members in the Irish
Club, but still there was an air of mystery. Had the Irish
Club taken in the Nameless Five or had the Nameless Five
taken in the Irish?

❦

> Whistling girls and crowing hens
> Always come to some bad end.

The Crowing Hen was born out of an old couplet and
the combined inspiration of seventy-five gentlemen. These
gentlemen, including the members of the Irish Club and
the Nameless Five and others not so distinguished, invited
seventy-five ladies to a fête champêtre on the lawn. This,
too, was in reaction from too many polkas, schottisches and
waltzes, too many cotillion figures. Their first party was

featured by a doubles tennis match and a presentation of prizes, with speech, by an eminent Judge, which put it in direct line of descent from the tournaments. There was a Virginia reel as a concession to those who could not keep their feet still, and a collation of fruits, ices and the inevitable champagne.

The Irish Club and Crowing Hen may have started with the good intention of snubbing the ballroom, but it wasn't long before both of them were drawn into that vortex. Conversation wasn't enough, tennis wasn't enough, marching around the lawn behind the orchestra wasn't enough, the crowd was still happiest when whirling around a polished floor, so the clubs gave germans. When the Crowing Hen had its last blooming in 1892, brilliant and full of promise as the exuberance of a dying peach tree, they had a gymkhana in the afternoon with a quadrille on horseback (even the horses had to dance), but in the evening they gave a cotillion, showering prizes and favors on their guests as though this had always been their forte instead of gambolling on the lawn.

Nobody thought the Irish Club would fade from the scene as it did, it seemed so important, so permanent, engaging the large Calwell cottage for headquarters and fixing a fine of $150 for members who didn't show up by the first week in August. Its last important act was to clap this fine on Hal Dulany, who had taken to spending his time in Paris, and then, after its third summer in 1887, it was heard of no more. When the Presidents' Cottage Club was formed in 1890 there were only two survivors of the Irish Club on the roster.

There were new stars in the Springs firmament and a

new coach-and-four. On the box was Mr. Henry Fairfax and out in front were four of the finest hackneys in the country, of his own breeding, and up with him on the handsome "brake" was a new generation of belles.

This time, the Virginians were top dogs; Henry Fairfax and Henry Stuart were the ringleaders of the Presidents' Cottage Club. There were several new names from the Deep South, also, John Grant and Tom Paine. They installed themselves in the house that the sugar-rich Stephen Henderson had built and they had no traffic with outdoor entertainment at all. Their second and last summer was made memorable by a stag party that kept everybody in that section of the place awake until dawn. Next day it got round that the star of the evening had been the irrepressible Mr. Chiswell D. Langhorne who had them all in stitches with his plantation songs, his dancing and inspired high jinks, and except for a final cotillion that summer Mr. Langhorne's high jinks wound up the Presidents' Cottage Club.

The era of the Clubs, from 1885 to 1892, was proof, if such a thing were needed, that there was no longer any planter aristocracy. There were some surprisingly large blocks of Southern money but it was no longer planters' money. The men who now assumed the roles of Springs entertainers were lawyers like Judge Glenn and Charles Anderson, industrialists like John Grant (who had married railroad money), brokers like Tom Paine. Stilson Hutchins' money came from a newspaper, Hal Dulany's was manna from heaven. The wealth of the Stuarts was in stock raising and salt wells, railroad engineering had enriched Henry Fairfax and railroad supplies kept the heads of Chiswell Langhorne and his lovely daughters well above water.

Where were cotton and sugar and tobacco and rice now, where were the Hamptons and Singletons and Chesnuts and Mercers and Middletons and Hendersons? Emancipation and the torch had done for them. The sole survivor of this past magnificence, Wade Hampton III, still came to the waters but to an insignificant, inexpensive place called Dagger's Springs. He became so poor that friends had to band together to get him a house in Columbia. Occasionally he made a sortie from Dagger's to the White Sulphur, he and his flowing Dundreary beard, and his son and his brother with their Dundreary beards, too, and a great to-do was made over him as over the last of the panjandrums.

Their places had been taken by the lawyers, brokers, railway engineers and executives, tobacco factors, iron founders, those who had been adroit enough to turn their talents away from the soil. The middlemen ruled the roost now.

Add them all up, the swank of the four-in-hands, the horse racing fever, the imitative cry of "Saratoga of the South" and the swagger of the Clubs, put them all together and you get a Trend. It was toward a faster pace, toward unwonted display, toward razzle-dazzle. Something of what was going on up at the Northern resorts had seeped South.

In the way of the Trend were still some formidable obstacles: the dowagers rocking on the porches, ceaselessly vigilant; the deep and inviolable purity of the Southern girl, her rule against more than one glass of champagne per party; the law of the Springs that no girl might step off the piazzas after dark even with her own grandfather, the other rule that she had to scoot to bed after the ball, no loitering; the chaperonage system; the inborn gallantry of the Southern gentleman, who held that a whisky breath in the ballroom was a sacrilege on womanhood, even when it was his own. These add up to something, too.

Just the same, this splendid façade of traditional behavior sprung an ugly crack the night that George Morris drank champagne from Mrs. Padelford's slipper. Put it down to the Trend.

❧

The season of 1886, in its beginning, was hung with crape. People complained because the beaux stayed away; they complained equally of the beaux who came because they weren't up to snuff, not "White Sulphur's best." Beaux were so scarce in mid-July that children and older married people were desecrating the ballroom floor. Beaux-less girls sat around the piazzas toying with their sewing baskets.

They tried to whip up a Calico Ball, but only twenty couples danced the german and hardly anybody came in calico, a bad sign. The crowd began to feel better when Miss Susie Stuart gave her second huge eighty-couple german (she had given one the year before), but as her father owned the place the Stuart germans were, at least in part, managerial window dressing.

When things did hit a livelier pace after mid-August, the best parties were given by rich Northerners. The daughter of Shakespeare Caldwell, a New York millionaire, gave a large champagne supper. Another New York millionaire, George Kemp, distinguished himself with the season's most lavish ball-and-supper, importing New York florists and spending $1,500 on flowers alone. The Irish Club countered with two "brilliant" déjeuners.

People did not get excited now over Grand Fancy Mask Balls because there were none; they were old hat, in the discard. They did get excited over Mr. Kemp's stylish innovation of cutting out the usual cotillion altogether (they just danced) and his further innovation of serving supper from a long central table colorfully loaded with viands. Enthusiasms were *à la mode,* the new word for things was "swell." What background the season had was nouveau and stippled with gilt. Against this background the slipper episode was thrown like a spotlight.

Mrs. Bettina Ordway Padelford, the leading lady of the slipper act, arrived very opportunely. Virginia belledom, all summer, had been suffering a setback at the hands of a Northern beauty, Miss Nanine Cooper of Pittsburgh. The two foremost Virginia ladies were Miss Nannie Leary and Miss Page Aylett, both loaded with charm but under the handicap of having been belles rather a long time. In the '86 race it was said of them that they were "preserving the honor for Virginia." When Mrs. Padelford came and grouped herself with them, they were said to make a fine trio and it put more weight in Virginia's scales. The newcomer was eighteen, youngest of the trio, and aglow with that extra radiance of bridehood.

The former Bettina Ordway, daughter of the one-time Provost Marshall for the United States in Richmond, took naturally to dramatic entrances, to shining in public. She had a good voice and some theatrical talent and a flair for making the papers too. This had begun in her girlhood when, with an instinct for publicity beyond her years, she had bought the filmiest of Egyptian nightgowns at the Philadelphia Centennial and left it on display with her name on it. Inspired by this item, a newspaper editor warned her not to catch cold in this cobweb. Fame had begun.

Arriving at the White this summer, she was an instant success. At Miss Susie Stuart's german she was acknowledged by the Washington *Post's* observer to be "the most beautiful woman in the room." Her toilette was "an exquisite ivory tinted silk with rich embroidered panels," and she drew another notice from the press for dancing with the nonpareil, Hal Dulany.

Mr. George Morris, leading man of the episode, was an ornament of the Charlottesville bar. Twenty-eight now, he had graduated in law from the University at the tender age of twenty-one. His mother was the acknowledged queen of Charlottesville society and his step-father was Judge Robertson. Mr. Morris played around with the Irish Club at the height of its fame and, while he was not officially on the rolls, he more than made up for this by being a member of the Eli Banana, an outfit that was even more to the University of Virginia than the Irish Club was to the White Sulphur, as might be gathered from its marching song, which the membership shouted to the accompaniment of a large bass drum and a fife.

> Eli Banana, starry banner,
> We are drunk, boys, every one;
> 'Tis not the first time
> Nor yet the last time
> That together we've been on a hell of a bum,
> bum, bum.

In appearance, lawyer Morris suggested something of the corsair of romance; he was dark and his glance was piercing clear under heavy set eyebrows; his mustaches were fine and bristling, and he wore one of the new black derbies. His carriage was soldierly and he was an assiduous candidate for the hand of the beauty, Miss May Handy.

After the german one evening, the youthful bride and groom, Mr. and Mrs. Padelford, were on their way upstairs to bed when Hal Dulany rushed up and asked if they wouldn't chaperone a young lady who was to be his guest at supper and Mrs. Padelford said they would. In the course of the supper the talk turned to the custom of drinking wine out of slippers. The Poles did it at weddings, someone said; they drank wine from the bride's slipper. Hal Dulany avowed he wouldn't drink wine from any woman's slipper but George Morris said he wasn't so sure, it depended on the lady. According to some, he cast a tender glance toward Mrs. Padelford but as a matter of fact, a good Eli Banana wouldn't care what he drank out of.

"It struck me just then to do something shocking," said Bettina Padelford when she told the story. "I took my slipper off on the floor and said to Mr. Morris, 'There's your challenge.'"

Confronted with the actual slipper and a trifle of Mrs. Padelford's ankle the beau from Charlottesville took fright. His temptress said that he was obviously anxious to back out but that Hal Dulany and the others set upon him like a pack on a fox. They plagued and badgered him so that in desperation he caught the white satin slipper from the floor, poured champagne from his glass into the heel and tossed it off.

That was all there was to it, in Mrs. Padelford's own and most innocuous version (she had several). Other details were recalled by other witnesses. Major William Hale of

Hygeia is missing from the springhouse, casualty of the War.

Harper's New Monthly Magazine, August, 1878.

Paradise Row fell into disrepair in the "poor" Seventies but it was still Paradise to children, grownups and darkies.

Harper's New Monthly Magazine, August, 1878.

The White in Hal Dulany's Time

Spring=Going Types in the Seventies

From the New York Graphic, *August, 1877*

Natchez said that the lady in question did not just take her slipper off modestly, "on the floor," but held it up and ordered the waiter to fill it. The darky, sensing that nothing good was going to come of this, is said to have hesitated a long, long time. There was even a version in which Mrs. Padelford came dramatically to the door of the restaurant and held the wine-filled slipper up for the crowd outside to see. People confused it with musical comedy and even with the diplomatic set in Washington.

"Washington society," said one writer, "was deeply shocked when at a legation ball the young matron poured champagne into her white satin slipper and, holding it up, dared the young admirers about her to take a sip." The New York *Journal* even printed a large cartoon, years later, in which the lady herself was pictured as drinking from the fatal slipper.

The immediate repercussion at the Springs was terrific. "It almost demolished the moral and social structure of the famous resort," according to Major Hale. The next morning the indignation of the old guard rose in crescendo but the culprit had fled before the oncoming storm, in the early dawn. It was even said that he avoided for a time his haunts in Charlottesville, hoping it would blow over. It never did, becoming, instead, a national sensation. Why it did so, when any day in the week more valid scandals could have been picked up at Saratoga or the raffish Long Branch, is a mystery, but it was perhaps because it had happened at the White Sulphur, of all places, the old stronghold of pure womanhood and gallant manhood. A sprig of henbane had been discovered in a bed of tuberoses.

If it had been a shattering experience for Mr. Morris, it

was a godsend for Mrs. Padelford. Within a year she had walked out of the Hotel du Rhin in Paris with her five-weeks-old babe in her arms, leaving her wealthy husband forever. Returning to Washington and parents she finally decided to continue her dramatic career, but on the stage and for money, and she did it too. Her first part was in "The King's Fool," with Conreid's Opera Company and from that she went meteorically on to better roles and other managers.

The slipper episode was her press agent; for success in the theatre, she found, it was better to have had champagne drunk out of your slipper at White Sulphur than to have a good voice. As she toured in the Conreid and Duff companies from coast to coast, people were avid to see the champagne slipper diva and reporters besieged her for the story; sometimes she told it straight and sometimes she played it up for scandal, but she finally confessed to a writer for *The Critic* that "the novelty was wearing off and she must get something new."

There was very little she didn't get. She got six husbands after Padelford, most of them out of vaudeville. For nearly fifteen years she got the thrills and heartaches of the maddest, most wasteful, sensational, headstrong and tragic career on the American stage. None of her husbands was named Gerard, that was just the name she took. Her career swung in breathless arcs between stardom and the depths and back to stardom again, from jobs like the leading role in "In Old Kentucky" to the cheapest vaudeville. And then, the once vivacious bride who had tempted Mr. Morris died in 1905. The stuff in the slipper had been her undoing.

As for Mr. Morris, he became a most admirable Judge of

the Corporation Court in Charlottesville and a State Senator. He never married and he never liked the slipper business referred to. The social structure at the Springs was not put to such a strain again.

❦

None of the young ladies got Hal Dulany and his English fortune. After the score was in, his one great love was the matchless married belle, Mrs. Willie Allen. If this was the top romance of its day in Virginia (and it may have been) it could not be counted, being out of bounds. Mrs. Allen, despite her opportunities, remained Mrs. Allen and Hal Dulany went to live in Paris. At the Springs he was called a deserter and the Irish Club fined him, but he came back, more loyal to the waters than any of them. His loyalty will always rank beside that of Colonel Richard Singleton and William A. Stuart. It cost him a quarter of a million dollars.

In the late Eighties Hal Dulany propped Mr. Stuart's shaky fortunes with a loan of $200,000, then another of $50,000, for which his trustees took a first lien on the Springs. It was the largest and most expensive gesture of his openhanded career, and he was virtual owner of the property when he died in 1890. Many years later his heirs sold it to the railroad that passed by the gate for half the amount he had paid for it.

Hal Dulany died of tuberculosis. The Irish Club never met again and when the Presidents' Cottage Club took its place, social leadership had swung full circle, which is to say, it was right back in the ballroom and no foolishness about the superiority of conversation to dancing. The new club put its money on cotillions, better and fancier cotillions of which their new two-tone cotillion ribbons *with rosettes* were symbolic. Moreover, it was a member of the new club, Mr. Tom Paine of Atlanta, who began crowding the old hero of the ballroom for leadership, but the old hero was not to be crowded.

Hal Dulany was dead. Thirteen years before, he had first come down with his four-in-hand and thirteen years ago Jo Lane Stern was leading the opening figure in the second and most famous of the Lee Monument Balls. Now, in the same ballroom, the same gentleman was pursuing his joyful task, still carrying on the tradition of Colonel Pope. He was "General" Stern now, of the National Guard, and the mot that had passed round at the time of the Lee Ball was still good: He would rather lead the german than the Old Guard at Waterloo.

He was one with the time and he was at the apogee of his powers. Witness some of his masterworks: the National Figure, in which the ladies carried drums suspended from their shoulders and beat a tattoo while their partners waved flags; the Butterfly Figure, in which the ladies fluttered about waving their great wings of chiffon and the gentlemen pursued them with nets; the Slipper Figure in which the favors were tiny silver slippers filled with candy and *not* with champagne; the Coach-and-Four Figure, with the gentlemen driving the ladies, harnessed four abreast and covered with jingle bells, around the ballroom.

The price of General Stern's success had been patience, ingenuity and an almost incredible devotion to the art. By the exercise of these qualities a cotillion leader rose and stayed up. When other men of flashier habits and fatter pocketbooks had passed from the scene he might easily be left the keystone of the social structure. It might be said of him, as the ladies said of General Stern now, in the early Nineties, that only when *he* appeared the first of August could the season be said to have begun.

But the decade of the Eighties had gone to the young man with the four-in-hand.

XV

Belledom: the Golden Age

NOW was the very heyday of belledom. All that had gone before had been in preparation for this, including the War, and all that came after was imitation, disillusion and decline. Roughly, the period of belledom's high crest lay between the end of the War and the end of the Century. For more exact limits take for a beginning the entry of Mary Triplett at the Grand Fancy Mask Balls of '68 and, for an end, Irene Langhorne's engagement in '95, the event that removed the last of the great belles from circulation.

During this stretch of nearly three decades belledom was the beau ideal of life, and every Southern girl stretched every means to get herself to the Springs where she proceeded to throw herself into the race with a zeal and abandon later to be associated with having a career. If straightened circumstances kept their parents at home, young ladies grouped themselves under a chaperone, three to half a dozen at a time. Many of them became newspaper correspondents and wrote ecstatic reams in exchange for board and lodging. Or they might be subsidized like the girl who wrote to Mr. Corcoran, the banker. "Please, Mr. Corcoran, send me $100 so that I can go to the Springs and be a belle as my mother was." He sent her the $100.

In Miss Snead's opinion, these girls were simply fabulous. Their equals were certainly not to be found at Saratoga, for Miss Snead, crack society correspondent for the New York *Daily Graphic,* had just come down from Saratoga. "They are such girls as you read about in novels," she said; they were "born in idleness" and the one compulsion of their lives was to have "a real good time." It was a half truth only. There was another compulsion in their lives and that was to get a real good husband in a post-war world of stringencies and stratagems. There was more to this belledom, Miss Snead, than summer madness.

What amazed the correspondent of the *Daily Graphic* was the stamina of the Southern belle. Evidently, she was made of some "non-wearying stuff." She could dance until three o'clock in the morning and be up for a seven o'clock horseback ride with one of her beaux. After breakfast she kept hourly (sometimes half-hourly) engagements to walk about the lawn or through Courtship Maze; in the parlor she paraded with her admirers both before and after meals and she still had the legs to carry her through a morning german that lasted from eleven to one and an evening german that lasted into the morning again. "This is literally true," said Miss Snead, expecting nobody to believe it.

In the parlor these ladies of iron constitution passed in review before the old guard, without whose approval their energies were wasted: lovable Mrs. Thomas Carter, the queen-pin, who had mothered so many of the beaux at

Pampatike, her husband's school; Mrs. Roger Pryor, handsome, entertaining, literary, down from New York where her husband had a judgeship; Mrs. Wilkins Bruce, perennial fixture in the same chair by the door, heavily enameled to the eyes; Mesdames Branch and Anderson of Richmond and dozens more. And of course there was the Grand Old Man, Mr. Corcoran, passing no judgments but content to come summer after summer and sit at his accustomed table in the corner, playing whist as the parade flowed by over the new red carpet and under the new crystal chandelier, liberal gifts of the latest proprietor, Mr. Stuart.

Miss Snead's head swam. "The procession moves round and round until it makes one fairly dizzy," she said. "The effect produced by so many colors in perpetual motion beneath a strong light is very bewildering. There is light in the girls' faces and eyes; they seem elated with enjoyment." Carrying the huge bouquets that their beaux gave them, they were often oversupplied, and when they had more than two of these floral trophies, they parked the extras with their chaperones, picking them up seriatim as they came around again. Some had as many as six.

❦

The golden age of belledom divided itself into three nearly equal decades, each with its undisputed queen or queens. The first span, from 1868 to 1876, was dominanted by Mary Triplett and Mattie Ould. The South, in its contemplation and adoration of these two ladies, got as much satisfaction as the North got from counting the cost of Cornelius Vanderbilt's horses or Jay Gould's yacht.

From the time that Mary Triplett, with her chiselled, rose-tinted beauty, stepped into the ballroom at the first Mask Ball of 1868 as a Marquise and at the second Mask Ball as Undine, her white gossamer dress appliquéd with ferns and her blonde hair sparkling with diamond dust, she was "the fairest of the fair," and no arguments. The North was advised, by the *World,* that in face and figure Miss Triplett was the South's "unrivalled beauty." Through that summer and the summers following until her marriage in '74, all eyes were trained on her blonde perfection as she sailed through parlor and ballroom or down the wide steps to the lawn.

The hearts beating fast for her beauty beat faster still because she was a creature of high romance. A duel had been fought for Mary Triplett, and a man had died, one Mordecai, mortally wounded on the field of honor by her defender, Page McCarthy. Journalists both, they wasted their talents (Mordecai had "insulted" her in a poem) and their powder. Belles of such a stature weren't marrying poor journalists and sure enough, Miss Mary soon betrothed herself to one of those rare Southerners of substance, Mr. Philip Haxall, a gentleman with mills.

During the whole of the 1880's Mrs. Haxall was back at the Springs, either at the Rockbridge Alum or the White Sulphur, stirring nostalgic memories. At first the role she played was not that of the married belle but of the handsome matron with new belles under her wing. For these debutantes she gave great dances and lawn parties, with champagne flowing and an orchestra playing operatic selections, though the Haxall mills had burned and the Haxall fortunes were not what they had been. Foolishly extravagant in her advancing years, some people said. In the summer before she died, 1890, she went out in a blaze of glory, as she had come in, leading the grand march at a spanking big german with Colonel Castleman of Kentucky and recapturing the thrills of her youth.

"Grace, wit and beauty, these make a Triplett." So had Mattie Ould once toasted her brilliant rival (and the toast held over for an epitaph when the time came), though when Mattie Ould called anyone else witty it was like the first clown in the circus referring to the camel driver as an extremely funny fellow. *Noblesse oblige.* Mattie Ould herself was the wit of wits and knew it. There was a difference between them in beauty, too, for hers was not carved at all but moulded, and the stuff was warm and soft. Her nose was delicately retroussé, her lips ripe and full, and her eyes extraordinarily wide and appealing. To this considerable equipment she added a mind of quicksilver, a flashing wit that she kept constantly in play.

The audiences that hung onto the Grecian beauty of Mary Triplett hung with equal fascination onto every word that came from Mattie Ould's pomegranate lips. Her sallies became household words, the joke currency of the day, infinitely re-told. Everybody had heard of the time she laid her head on the shoulders of a Mr. Young, saying it was a case of "Ould head on Young shoulders." Everybody got his fun out of the skirmish of the rhymed couplets. It seems that she had dropped her glove and an elderly and unwelcome admirer had recovered it. Handing it to her, he said,

> If from your glove you take the letter "g,"
> Your glove is love and that I bear for thee,

and she shot back

If from your name you take the letter "P,"
Your Page is age; that will not do for me.

She could use her wit as a Turk used a scimitar and she
cut down another nuisance with the remark that "ill weeds
grow apace"; the gentleman's name was Pace. Asked by a
young girl whether she would marry a Mr. Wise or a Mr.
Morrison, she said, "Oh, hasten, sinner, to be wise, stay not
for tomorrow's sun." Like an actress at a luncheon she felt
she owed them a continuous performance.

In the parlor she turned on another of her talents, a small,
tear-laden voice. Every afternoon a crowd gathered around
her at the piano and there wasn't a dry eye in the house as
she sang through the four verses of "Under the Daisies,"
her favorite. Her forte was expressiveness. What her voice
lacked in polish it more than made up with "feel"; it spoke
straight to the tear ducts.

Bemoaning her departure for another Springs, the *Enquirer* said, "Her absence will be felt, especially in the spacious drawing room, where she reigned unrivalled as the
queen of belles and beauties." "Throngs of admirers," they
said, had been drawn by her "personal charms, rare intel-
ligence and sparkling wit." She had everything, she was the
answer to the Southerner's dream of a complete belle.

All around her the girls were taking older husbands from
among the older beaux, that being the order of the post-
war day. But Mattie Ould rebelled, it was not to be the
order for her. Was she not different, a genius, a law unto
herself, or what did all the applause and adulation mean?
In the summer of '76 she was to have been found down at
the Montgomery White Sulphur, belle of belles as usual. In
mid-August there she scandalized society by eloping to

nearby Salem with Mr. Oliver J. Schoolcraft, a Northern-born "editor" in very good standing at the bank, a Richmond resident and not old at all. He was twenty-four; she claimed twenty-three.

At nine o'clock in the evening, in the Salem home of Captain John McCaull, the belle and the "editor" were married. Hardly any detail of this proceeding was as it should have been, and Judge Ould never forgave his daughter, would not go to her on her deathbed. He had selected for her another husband altogether, an older man.

Retribution for this rash rebellion caught up with her too soon; she died in childbirth. Instead of hymns at her funeral they sang the four verses of "Under the Daisies," and they planted daisies on her grave. The following August her widower was back at the Springs, driving about the White Sulphur in his Sterris side-bar, behind a "neat little team."

That summer it didn't seem to matter that Nellie Hazeltine, the St. Louis beauty, was there, nationally famous and trailing the glory of a Saratoga success, making a great splash, blowing the whistle at the Ladies' German and calling the figures; it didn't matter that Lilly Norton, the Kentucky wonder, and a whole regiment of Kentucky satellites were there, too, showing off their superior horsewomanship and their superior wardrobes. ("Virginia girls have such bad style," they said.) The Kentucky-St. Louis invasion did not impress the referees of belledom as it should have. With Mattie Ould's place empty they were in no mood to award the crown of "first belle" until the memories of "Under the Daisies" became a little less poignant. "No reigning belles," was the word that went out.

This belledom was like a never-ending horse race; a large gallery was always crowding the rails and cheering its favorites. Now one entry pulled ahead, now another; new ones ran in from the sidelines and old ones dropped out. No sooner was Nannie Leary, a blonde of fine proportion, thought to be in the lead than Page Aylett was declared "the belle," or the title was conferred on Lena Jackson or on one of the Petersburg beauties. There were always Petersburg beauties, they raised them down there as other places raised cabbages.

Years of painful indecision followed the Triplett-Ould regime, years when the course was as crowded as usual but no one got the palm, as the saying was. It was a belles' world, belles were what the gallery came to see, belledom was what the newspaper reporters came to judge and when no one of the contestants stood more than a curl's width above the others and that never for long, the referees suffered from frustration. "There is no reigning beauty," one would say, or another, more hopefully, "The belle of the season is yet to come." "Sallie Ould is a belle after two seasons," sounded hopeful, too, but the great Mattie's sister was a trifle disappointing: she preferred the parlor's whist tables to the ballroom.

In periods of dilemma, the reporters would poll the gentlemen, hoping for a popular decision, and one beau would say Miss Nannie Leary, another Miss Page Aylett; later on they would vote for Miss Virgie Brock or Miss Gertrude Rives or Miss Anne Carter or Miss May Handy, depending on where they had placed their hearts, like bets. That got a referee nowhere.

When, inevitably, two undisputed queens did emerge in

the mid-Eighties, it was the same as it had been before; they were remarkable for the disparity between them. One was an orthodox beauty toeing the line, the other was a rebel beauty blithely stepping over it; one was a virgin belle, the other had a husband; one was gracious to the members of her sex, the other didn't care a straw for them and showed it. These two were May Handy and Mrs. Willie Allen.

May Handy was the prime product of her age. As a girl she had absorbed belledom from her step-sisters in the same house, Mattie and Sallie Ould, and what she did not get from them she got from her mother, who schooled her for a belle's career as a thoroughbred is schooled for the track. She had a schedule which specified a morning constitutional and an afternoon nap. She had a dietary regimen and, except on the nights of balls, she was allowed no late hours. Nobody ever saw her looking fatigued or a hair of her head out of place.

At the Springs she was first noticed as "one of the prettiest misses," in 1880, a "miss" being a sub-deb. Even after she was out she came along slowly and some laid it to mistaken notions of what constituted becoming dress and coiffure. In Baltimore, one of her swains (Robert Chamberlaine) dropped hints and strove to simplify her style, which did indeed become strikingly simple, if that could be any consolation to a rejected suitor.

But soon the little girls of Richmond were running out to see her as she walked down Franklin Street, scooting around the block to meet her again and drink in her beauty.

"She smelled delicious," one of the little girls remembered. "She always wore a large bunch of 'May Handy' violets. A florist had named them for her." The little girls drew in her fragrance and swooned a little.

They had run around the block for Mary Triplett too. In Richmond, that was the final test of a great belle. Nationally, there was another test: Had she starred at the Eastern resorts, at Bar Harbor, Newport, Lenox or Saratoga? Had she made a North-and-South tour as Nellie Hazeltine had done or Madame LeVert long ago? That gave a belle the final cachet and, in due course, both May Handy and Mrs. Allen passed that test. In fact, before they appeared for the White Sulphur season in 1886, both had been laying them in rows at Bar Harbor, "dividing the honors between them," it was said.

Six years after she was listed as a "pretty miss" May Handy had distanced all her rivals. She was described at a White Sulphur german in simple muslin, her hair brushed back and coiled far up on her head. "Her face is rich in coloring and clear-cut like a cameo," said the *Dispatch*. "The fashion of her form is most divinely moulded and her carriage graceful. She reigns as undisputed queen of love and beauty."

This beauty of hers was electric. When she entered the parlor and glided across its new red carpet people forgot what they were saying and stared. At Mrs. McKim's Beauty Luncheon in Baltimore ("Beauty Luncheon" fairly describes the age), she was the only guest whose appearance quite stopped the chattering. They were all suddenly aware that *en*trance and en*trance* were the same word.

A path was being worn to the North by the feet of the premier belles, bound for the better marriages of bonanza land, and May Handy followed it, but her marriage to the divorced Mr. Potter rather shocked the young ladies back in Virginia. To them, there was still something unholy about divorce.

As for Mrs. Allen, the beautiful Savannah-born Minnie Anderson, the other belles knew with what light disdain she regarded them, but they had to admit her to the front rank of belledom because, for one thing, she had all the beaux. For other things, in no particular order, (1) she had taken the "catch of Virginia," Hal Dulany, away from all rivals; (2) she was a *femme fatale* under a coating of soft Southern graces; (3) she scandalized and delighted everybody by keeping a court of rich admirers about her; (4) she never divorced Willie Allen, a true Virginia gentleman whom everybody liked. Of all errors, that would have been unforgivable, locking the gates of this Eden behind her before she knew she was out of it. She remained Mrs. Allen to his end, though not much beyond. Acknowledged the first married belle of her time, the reporters always bracketed her with the virgin belles just as though she were one of them.

At the White Sulphur encomiums flew about her head: "one of the loveliest ladies at the Springs," "the beauty of the White Sulphur," and the barrage of praise kept up until she took her charms and her husband northward to larger arenas. After the end of the Eighties she did not return to the Springs, but the echoes of her daring did.

She dared, out of spite, to publish *The Love Letters of A Liar*, the outpourings of a Virginia lawyer-poet and as torrid a collection of amorous epistles as ever found their way into print. (He later published a poem whose last line ran, "Thank God that I lost you, Bonny Lorraine.") She dared

At the Zenith of Belledom

MISS MATTIE OULD   MRS. WILLIE ALLEN (Minnie Anderson)
(Mrs. Oliver Schoolcraft)   *Matchless married belle*
Witty Rebel   *Photograph by H. P. Cook*

MISS MARY TRIPLETT
(Mrs. Philip Haxall)
"Grace, wit and beauty"

MISS MAY HANDY   MISS LENA JACKSON
(Mrs. James Brown Potter)   (Mrs. William Warren)
Belledom's finest handiwork   *Queen of the Irish Club*

They Called the Hotel "Grand Central"

The Old White at the height of its development, in the
1880's. The extreme right wing is imaginary.

From J. G. Pangborn, The Picturesque B. and O.

to dedicate this crimson booklet to "the men who wouldn't, couldn't and didn't write these letters." She dared, when Mr. Allen died, to spend the gravestone money, so the story ran, for a jewel that hung about her neck. "This," she would explain, "is Willie's memorial stone." She dared to bring her next husband, a musician, to play sad airs over Willie's grave. On her rare visits to Richmond the little girls stole from their homes to peek at her through the windows of the boardinghouse where she stayed. She had been a great belle.

❦

Other Springs, other races. The White Sulphur was not by any means the only course. The Rockbridge Alum and Jordan Alum, the Alleghany, the Montgomery White Sulphur, the Blue Ridge Springs, the Yellow Sulphur, Capon, Amelia, Huguenot and a dozen more, to say nothing of the old stand-bys like the Warm and the Sweet, were all assiduously setting belle traps. Like prideful provincial capitals they boasted that they were more accessible, more select, more comfortable, more friendly, cheaper and socially more brilliant than the cosmopolitan White Sulphur. The newspaper editors allowed their columns to be filled with inflated puffs from all of them. The Rockbridge Alum in second place and the Alleghany in third (its rise had been phenomenal) got nearly as much newspaper space as the White itself.

Spring-going since the War had not decreased, it had increased. The railroads, penetrating everywhere, facilitated marvelously the transfer of whole families to the mountain resorts for their holidays. Everywhere the owners of these

Springs were throwing up new cottages, new dining rooms, new ballrooms and hotels (the Jordan Alum had a new hotel with bells and hot and cold water in every room), just as though the words "In Chancery" written several times over the portals of the leading Springs were not a warning.

There was no use pretending that as arenas for belledom they were equal to the White Sulphur, and yet stars of the first magnitude were on every provincial stage: Lizzy Cabell (whom many people ranked with Triplett and Ould) at the Alleghany, Lena Jackson there, too, Mattie Ould at the Montgomery White, Mary Triplett Haxall at the Rockbridge Alum and always a bevy of Richmond's best at the elegant Capon. Alleghany got such a reputation for harboring pretty girls, particularly from the Deep South, that at one time there were nine Generals of the Confederate Army there to see what they could see.

If you wanted to view the Memphis belles, blessed with what Dr. George Bagby described as "fuller and more perfect lines of form" than the Virginia girls, you went to the Blue Ridge Springs; or if you were after New Orleans beauty you would most likely find it at the Montgomery White, where Jeff Davis went and important meetings were held and the Southern Historical Society was founded, all before a tremendous cloudburst roared down the narrow valley and washed out five hundred guests overnight. After that the Montgomery was never the same.

The Rockbridge Alum held onto that second place, in point of size and popularity, which it had gained before the War. It was particularly favored by the professional classes, the doctors and judges and professors, and socially it was always on its toes. No sooner did the White Sulphur have

Pink Teas and Pink Dinners and Pink Germans than the Rockbridge had them, too, everything pink, dresses, window drapes, bandstand, candles, badges, pink icing on the cakes, pink ribbons on the boxes of Huyler's candy. Did the White Sulphur have military encampments to furnish beaux for the girls? The Alum had them, too, even more of them. Was the White the only place a belle might make a good match? Not at all, cried the Alum, loudly and clearly. "The place offers as good an opening as can be found anywhere in the mountains of Virginia for such of our young ladies as desire clever husbands."

The Alum acquired something of a left-handed fame toward the end of the century, to the effect that all that went on there was not in belledom's purest code. On the surface, said James Branch Cabell, a beau of the day, all was according to Thomas Nelson Page but underneath there was comedy by Casanova. Fondly and nostalgically, Mr. Cabell afterward remembered slippered feet treading cautiously through the long dim hallways, appointed doors ajar, kerosene lamps left burning at their dimmest on the yellow and black striped maplewood dressers. Outside, his youth lay buried under every bush.

But it is the report of a fictioneer making notes on the cuff. Even then he wandered in the never-never land of Poictesme (every cliff and tarn and blue hill of which was purloined from the Rockbridge Alum); even then he was conjuring up the amours of his hero, Jurgen, and those frail demoiselles who, saying "No" meant "Yes." Let not the belles of the Rockbridge turn uneasily in their graves or in their sleep. Their historic purity is unassailable. The adventures of "Jurgen," as all the world knows, are out of a wanton imagination, the frail demoiselles of the low-burning kerosene lamps shameless inventions.

❦

So Minnie Allen did not return to the Virginia Springs. Instead she became a society correspondent and went to Narragansett and boasted of the money she was making with her pen and with *The Love Letters of a Liar*. At the White a new star arose. She was launched into belledom from a window sill.

It was the custom for the sub-debs to sit in the deep window embrasures of the ballroom during the first half-hour of the ball, to gape at the fashionable kaleidoscope, to chatter, to envy the arrived belles, to sigh with impatience before their parents sent them to bed. One evening in July, 1889, the "starry-eyed" Irene Langhorne was sitting in one of the window embrasures with several of her fellows, legs dangling under her modest long muslin dress, when Billy Wright of Philadelphia, one of the married beaux, sailed up before her.

"How old are you, Irene?" he asked.

"Sixteen," she said.

"Then it's time you were out," and he pulled her from her perch and whirled her into the dance. The last of the great belles had made her debut.

As a girl of fifteen, Miss Langhorne had been noticed around the place, now at a bowling party, now at a candy "stew." She was a vivid girl and it was plain she was to be a beauty. As a belle, she was a "natural," not the product of ambitious grooming. That strenuous, populous, highly individual household of the Langhornes, father and mother, Irene and Phyllis and Nannie and young Buck and several darky nursemaids, all crowded into a small cottage in Virginia Row, was not the milieu for grooming a belle. That team of goats and the goat cart that their diverting father managed to transport to the Springs for the children was not an adjunct of belledom, either. Out of such a stirring and crowded nest a belle would have to "take to it," as a scarcely feathered bird takes to the air.

Miss Irene took to it with spontaneous flight from the window sill, though she seems not to have been totally unprepared for this coming out. On the 9th of August that year she was noted at a "full dress" german in a crimson satin ball gown. At sixteen. She was "the bewitching Miss Langhorne" and "her eyes glowed with liquid fire." From then on the regal Miss Handy had a new rival with whom she had to divide the honors.

Mr. Dam, sent down by the *Times* of New York to write about these fabulous creatures, drew what he considered to be a composite. Whether Mr. Dam knew it or not, his composite contained a great deal of Miss Langhorne.

"She is slender and strong and well modelled," he said. "Her nervous personality is of value in making her eyes bright and her perceptions quick. As a rule she is high spirited and self willed and when she makes up her mind to get married she usually carries out the program if it takes a saddle horse and a train. She talks in a high-keyed voice, rapidly, speaks of her escort as her 'man' [Mr. Dam didn't get *that* from Miss Langhorne] and is never visible in public without one." Dancing, he added, is her specialty and she does it superbly.

Where was the languorous Southern belle of popular conception, the slow-drawling lady, limp as a conjuror's rabbit, reclining on sofas and being eternally fanned? No, the South was not cutting its belles to pattern, though the pattern could be found if a man were to hunt around in the wake of these strenuous Kentucky and Virginia girls.

Before the crest of belledom began to break, an exceptionally handsome lot was riding it: Irene Langhorne, the ineffably lovely Ellie Bosher, Anne Carter, Anne and Eugenia Tennant of Petersburg, Martha Bagby, Judith Carrington. Every one of them made a brilliant match. Four of the seven followed a path to the North; two of the four married millionaires.

Upon the announcement of Miss Langhorne's engagement in '95, the Richmond *Times* gave her the proper send-off: "Miss Langhorne is one of the greatest beauties in the South and, excepting Miss May Handy, it may be said that she stands unequalled and unrivalled in her regal beauty." She married the most accomplished and popular young artist of his day, Charles Dana Gibson, and went on to greater fame and into every household as his model of the Gibson Girl, the symbol of an era.

※

Something happened to belledom the afternoon that Miss Gertrude Rives jumped her horse over every tennis net on the lawn, to win a bet. Something happened when Miss Hamilton of Kentucky was observed driving her span of thoroughbreds as skillfully as any man. Something happened when the lovely creatures came out of those muslin and tarlatan party dresses in which they had futilely tried to play tennis in the early Eighties and got into more serviceable cottons.

Something happened to belledom when the shocked piazza brigade heard a young lady exclaim, "Oh, that's rot!" Something happened when the belles were pushed into the minor roles of scorekeepers at the matrons' euchre parties. Something quite definite happened when the married ladies gave themselves *bals poudres* and the belles sat on the sidelines "playing chaperone" in sober black and with spectacles on their noses, tricked into thinking that this significant charade was just a bit of fun.

Something happened to the whole romantic tradition when apparently bibulous young men made a mockery of serenading and caterwauled around the grounds until four-thirty in the morning. Something happened when the serenadees abandoned their old modest ways and tossed out hasty notes of acknowledgment.

At the time it didn't look as though anything was happening; it merely looked as though the belles were adding to their repertoire. Besides just strolling through Courtship Maze and dancing germans and talking the "language of the thimble" with their beaux over sewing baskets, they wielded tennis rackets, they did quadrilles on horseback, they drove smart tandems. Were they not more bewitching than ever in their new outfits, their pink and white striped cotton skirts, cut bell-shaped, their blue and white striped silk shirtwaists, their white silk ties? And so sensible. Around their waists were the inevitable blue silk belts with gold or silver buckles, and on their backs were white flannel blazers with blue pin stripes. Their beaux were all in these new blazers, too, with even broader stripes, and the lawn was dazzling, full of animated peppermint sticks.

Such was the renown of Virginia Springs belledom that rich Northerners were bringing their daughters down to make Southern belles of them, the Reinharts of Plainfield, the Hillhouses, Onderdonks, Shakespeare Caldwells and George Kemps of New York, the Carlisles of Washington, the Ingalls of Boston and Cincinnati. To provide ever fresh starring vehicles, the cotillion leaders busily turned out a stream of new german figures: the Cornstalk Figure, the Chinese Lantern Figure, the Post Office Figure, the Champagne Cocktail Figure.

A reporter wrote, "All wholly surrender themselves, soul, body and business to unconfined jollity and joy." What with one thing and another, it looked as though belledom might go on forever.

Gamblers in the Daylight

Occasionally a Tiger operated on this hill at the White
but the real Tiger was on the other side of the springhouse.

From a water color after the original by J. H. B. Latrobe

XVI

Who Killed Cock Robin?

JUST prior to mid-August, 1892, Mr. Henry Walters' private Pullman car came down on the New York train. In it Mr. Walters was bringing the favors for Mrs. Pembroke Jones' german, on the sixteenth. Never had there been such favors, either in number or value: jewellers' boxes with gold and silver trinkets, cuff buttons, bangles, silver and gold mounted hair combs, gold match boxes, silver card cases and belt buckles. All previous germans paled beside this one: variegated ropes of fringed tissue paper radiated from the central chandelier to the walls on all sides, massed with foliage. The tall mirrors were crowned with floral garlands and gay lanterns, the band was hidden behind greenery. All, all had been made possible by railroad money. In Mr. Walters' waistcoat pocket was fifty-one per cent of the Atlantic Coast Line, and Mr. Pembroke Jones was his protégé.

Prize euchres were the rage and of all the prize tables that year none surpassed Mrs. Reinhart's. She had ordered

Tiffany's to send down a box from which she might make her selections. They were: (1) a silver repoussé hand mirror, $30, (2) a silver repoussé bonbon dish, (3) a silver and gold punch ladle, as well as numerous silver souvenirs for the young ladies who kept score. Railroad money made that possible too; Mr. Reinhart was President of the Atchison, Topeka and Santa Fe. Railroad money brought down from Plainfield, where the Reinharts lived, extra furnishings to brighten up their Tansas Row cottage: bamboo tables and chairs, grass portieres, bamboo awnings, a piano. Their horses were numerous, their turnouts stylish, the Reinhart girls had a T-cart. Railroad money.

Mr. George Warren Elliott was a song bird. Stout, jolly, a non-dancer but filled with music, Mr. Elliott was ringleader of the gang that stomped around porches and lawn single file, hands on shoulders in front, singing "Who Killed Cock Robin?" Day and night they wanted to know who killed Cock Robin. Mr. Elliott brought his family in *his* private car. He was President of the Wilmington and Weldon Railroad.

The place became a mecca for railroad mandarins, President Scott of the Pennsylvania, President Stevens of the Ohio and Mississippi, President King of the Erie, all sporting private cars. President Ingalls of the Chesapeake and Ohio (also President of the Big Four) brought his numerous family from Cincinnati and they at once bounced into social leadership from a springboard of railroad money, bouncing from there into springs ownership. The Springs was the Hot.

Mr. Ingalls had become enamored of making the Hot into the Aix-les-Bains of America and he dangled the rather decrepit old place before the eyes of the syndicate (of which he himself was one) that had bought the Chesapeake and Ohio from Collis P. Huntington. The others were J. P. Morgan, George Bliss, the Brown Brothers and W. P. Anderson of Cincinnati. The syndicate swept into its collective pocket not only the Hot but the Warm and the Healing as well. Mr. Morgan's proportion was forty per cent. As a syndicate owning a spa they floated, in 1891, a bond issue of a million dollars; then as a syndicate owning a railroad they took $385,000 of their own paper.

Which is to say, railroad money and dizzy business had moved in on the Springs, titans of the industrial age were reaching down from the North. These were the bold and shrewd men who had enriched themselves by turning the railroad wrecks of the Seventies and Eighties into gold mines by a financial legerdemain known as "reorganization." And it happened that they and their families fancied buying in on Southern charm, a little battered and shaken, to reorganize that too.

※

As a lottery fever sweeps over a nation, prize euchres swept over the Springs, large and small. The smaller the Springs the less expensive the prizes. A hostess could give hand-painted glove boxes and the like at the Alleghany or the Sweet but at the White Sulphur and the Rockbridge Alum she dared not have a "stop" party or a Newmarket party or a progressive euchre without an array of sterling.

No longer ago than the mid-Eighties this prize business had started modestly enough, with pistache green silk sashes, trinkets from the Japanese store, occasionally an ostrich feather fan, but now all was silver and gold. Nor was it just a strange infection to which only Northerners were susceptible. The euchres of Mesdames Rutherfoord and Starke (Richmond) and Bate (Louisville) glittered with precious metal as well as those of a Reinhart (New Jersey), and Mrs. Pembroke Jones, an extravagant dispenser of costly bibelots, was none other than Sadie Greene of Wilmington. Her friend Mr. Walters, who brought that haul of german favors in his car, was a son of Baltimore.

A gentleman at the Rockbridge Alum lifted his voice in protest. Why could no simple game of cards, he wanted to know, be played without a costly lot of prizes for the winners and one even for the booby? Was it lust for gain that had seized upon all these good people? Mrs. T. E. Ford of Kentucky staged a one-woman rebellion. Having herself won Mrs. Reinhart's thirty-dollar silver repoussé hand mirror, she was aghast. She would play no more cards at the White Sulphur, she said, she would no longer make one at the money changers' booths that had moved into the old temple of Hygeia.

Cards and gold were buying out belledom. Inveigled into playing mere bell-boy roles at the matrons' circuses, the belles distributed tallies, kept score and had their palms crossed with minor silver: silver hat pins, glove buttoners, scissors and pens and such trifles to indemnify them for this betrayal. Drawn out of the limelight, they made way for the "stags," as matrons without men came to be called, who battled for Tiffany's latest repoussé.

The season of 1892 had the look of one of those revels before the crash. Far away, the Homestead strike blazed up, ugly and ominous; shots were fired and men lay dying but the cloud of industrial strife cast no shadow in this vale of happiness. The fun went on. To the Jones-Walters silver-plated german there were added that "last-burst" party of the Crowing Hen, subscription germans that were oversubscribed, a Columbian Bal Poudre to ballyhoo the coming Chicago Exposition and a yellow fever scare in the lowlands that kept the frolic in the mountains going well into September.

Things were cutting loose from their old moorings. Someone gave a mixed pool party, to the horror of the old guard. Stories went round of mint juleps floating on boards during the ladies' hour at the pool. Women had started going to Mr. Hill's gambling house, something unheard of even at Canfield's Saratoga Club House, but at Mr. Hill's they were always in parties and they went more for the pheasant and turkey poult dinners than for the roulette and baccarat tables. Mr. Hill looked anything but a gambler. He was a quiet, soberly dressed, almost ministerial personage and no gentleman would have thought of eating his food before sacrificing at least ten dollars to the spinning ball.

The next year a national panic broke in all its fury. Entertainment at the Springs went dry like a desert water course and the following summer, 1894, the White Sulphur did not open its doors.

❖

Another Springs was all ready to leap into the breach. Since floating that million-dollar bond issue in 1891, the Morgan syndicate under Mr. Ingalls' direction had been

busy at the old Hot. They had built a new and excruciat-
ingly fancy hotel at the railroad terminus in the manner of
the European spas and a new $100,000 bathhouse. They
had spruced up the old hotel, enlarged it and re-christened
it The Homestead. None of the Virginia Springs had ever
been improved to the tune of a million dollars before. The
Hot was ready to capitalize on anyone else's calamity, and
capitalize it did.

When the news spread that the old habitués of the White
Sulphur were flocking to the Hot, the headline that ap-
peared in the papers was, "It's An Ill Wind That Blows
Nobody Good." New Yorkers could read in the *Mail and
Express* that "Hot Springs, so long a favorite resort for
Southern people is now largely patronized by Northerners."
Largely but not altogether. Mr. Tom Paine, the demon co-
tillion leader from Atlanta, and Mr. Edward Hanewinkle,
a rising star from Richmond, were on hand to show them
how it should be done.

Fortune smiled. Seven private cars of seven railroad mag-
nates were on the siding at one time. Six Harvard men, also
all at once, took everybody's breath away. Miss Irene Langhorne stayed overnight on a riding trip, giving it her blessing. Said the Richmond *Dispatch,* "It bids fair to be a dan-
gerous rival to the White Sulphur when the famous hostelry
shall again open its doors." Railroad money had passed a
miracle. The ancient Hot, so long shunned by the pleasure
bent, had been transformed into a stylish spa. The words
"water" and "cure" had been restored to the Springs vo-
cabulary. During the dancing decades they had been well-
nigh forgotten.

The panic and the strikes and the angry threats of the poor put only a temporary check to Springs gaiety. The White Sulphur re-opened in '95 and by the time Teddy Roosevelt marched on Cuba everything was booming again, in the country and at the Springs. There were more silver match boxes, more silver picture frames and bonbon dishes and cut glass toilette bottles than ever before. Pink parties took up where they had left off, everything pink from window hangings to cake icing. There were more champagne suppers and more prize euchres to fill more columns of fine print in the Sunday papers of Virginia and papers of the East and North as well. The editorial eye still saw these social minutiae through the romantic tradition of the Springs as through a great magnifying glass, and the endless dull detail still had the look of splendor and importance.

Golf came in like a new madness. (As early as 1884 some Englishmen and Scotchmen had introduced golf to America on America's first golf course not four miles away, and then the White Sulphur-ites had gone out to watch and jeer.) Hard, white, gutta-percha balls whizzed by the ears of old-fashioned card players under the trees as the new era stabbed at the old. Girls in red jackets swung golf clubs as well as tennis rackets. It was reported from the Rockbridge Alum that they were at it as early as seven o'clock in the morning. Would-be belles played baseball. At the White Sulphur in '97 a nine of fair maidens defeated a nine of gentlemen over fifty. Belledom reeled under the blow. In 1900 Mrs. Sorlls, a former Virginia girl, appeared as the Women's Golf Champion of New Orleans. Belledom was dead. It was the end of something, too, when *Town Topics* turned one of its serpents loose in this once sacred grove.

Though he was run to earth and thrown out by some Richmond cavaliers, his contaminating work had been done.

The final year of the century brought a spate of four-in-hands; the roads teemed with them, à la Saratoga: Mr. George Ingalls at the Hot, Messrs. Fairfax and Clendennin at the White, Mr. Sprague of New Orleans at the Warm. Another four-in-hand dasher of the time was Mr. Alfred D. Cushing, a new playboy from Washington, but in 1900 it appeared that Mr. Cushing came without his hackneys. The reason why got round soon enough and it was with extreme impatience that he and the entire Springs with him awaited the arrival by freight car of his automobile.

Idyll on a Cottage Verandah

These two are married, of course, else no such abandon.
A drawing by the popular artist, C. S. Reinhart.

Harper's Weekly, *August 4, 1888*

The Old White Hotel

At the end of the century.

From the painting by Carolyn van Bean

Afterword

OF ALL those happy rendezvous, only two survive as going concerns, the White Sulphur and the Hot, wholly modern spas equipped to cope with modern demands. Nowadays they are known as much by the names of their splendid hotels, The Greenbrier and The Homestead, as they are by their old Springs names. The Healing, an adjunct of the Hot, opens its ancient doors each summer for the nostalgic souls who like to regard the face of things as they were, if they can do it under a good mazda lamp. And to that list, come to think of it, must be added a small resort known as the Craig Healing, not far away.

So all has not vanished utterly. True, the once brave Montgomery White Sulphur has been swept off the earth to the last brickbat and many another with it, but a sentimental journey would reveal a surprising lot of old Springs buildings still standing, in a manner of speaking. Berkeley has been returned by the State of West Virginia to its original uses as a bathing spring for invalids. Recent architectural rehabilitation has spruced up the Old Sweet. The much beloved "Old White" hotel is gone but most of the cottage rows still stand there. The waters taste about the same.

Chevron
January, 1941

Appendix

THE medicinal effects for which the Springs were noted were best summed up by Joseph Martin in his *New and Comprehensive Gazetteer of Virginia,* published in 1835.

"The White Sulphur acts, when taken in doses of two or three glasses at a time, as an alterative, exercising on the system much of the salutary influence, without the evil effects of mercury,—used in larger quantities is becomes actively diaretic [*sic*] and purgative. The Salt Sulphur is more remarkable than the White, for the latter property; but not equal to it in the former. The Red Sulphur, in addition to the qualities which it has in common with the last mentioned springs, is remarkable for its action on the pulse, which it reduces considerably in a short time. The Sweet springs . . . are of the class of waters called acidulous, and are valuable as a tonic in cases of debility, and in all varieties of dyspepsia which are unaccompanied by inflammation. The Hot springs are celebrated for their efficacy in cutaneous, rhumatic [*sic*] dyspeptic and liver complaints. Dr. Bell . . . observes,—all that has been performed by the Bristol, Buxton and Bath waters in England may be safely claimed . . . by the Virginia springs just enumerated. If to the Hot, Warm and Sweet Springs,—we add the White, Salt, Red and Blue Sulphur, we may safely challenge any district of country of the same extent in the world to produce the same number and variety of valuable waters.

In an age when poetry sprouted indigenously from every other citizen, it was inevitable that much verse should have been written at, or about, the Springs. Besides some pedestrian stuff on the life at the White Sulphur, Francis Scott Key wrote a poem about the death of a pet bear at Red Sulphur, which was recited to music by Benjamin Judah, with great effect. It is long and tedious. There were poems to lady loves, to the fountains of health (that of Lord Morpeth has been mentioned in the text) and about the legend of the waters, one of them involving a drowned wolf. Because they capture the dual atmosphere of gaiety and physical wretchedness that hung over these resorts, particularly in the early years, the following verses are printed here. They first appeared in the *Southern Literary Messenger* for October, 1834, anonymously.

Stanzas

Written at the White Sulphur Springs of Virginia

With spirits like the slacken'd strings
Of some neglected instrument
Or rather like the wearied wings
Of a lone bird by travel spent,
Ah! how should I expect to find
Midst scenes of constant revelry,
A solace for a troubled mind,
A cure for my despondency?

There was a time when mirth's glad tone
And pleasure's smile had charms for me—
But disappointment had not strown
My pathway then with misery;
Health then was mine—and friends sincere—
Requited love—and prospects bright—
Nor dreamt I that a day so clear
Could ever set in such a night!

This is Mrs. Cabell's poem to Colonel Pope * in its entirety:

To William Pope, Esq.

Oh the White Sulphur Spring! the White Sulphur Spring!
How pure, how limpid, how cool are its waters!
Every year, thither borne upon hope's buoyant wing,
Hie the brave and the fair and the rich from all quarters.

Some go to seek pleasure and some to woo health,
And others like "Cœlebs in search of a wife,"
Whose virtues and charms, though unaided by wealth,
Shall solace their cares and enrapture their life.

But others there are, the base sordid elves!
Who sigh not for these—their object is *money!*
Ye favored of fortune, take care of yourselves!
Ah! list not their love-tales, though melting as honey.

Oh the White Sulphur Spring! the White Sulphur Spring
Can cure every evil that ever was known—
Gout, fever, dyspepsia, and each horrid thing
That e'er worried the flesh or tormented the bone.

How verdant its lawns in the depths of the mountains;—
How snug are its cabins, all ranged in a row—
What spruce beaux and belles daily quaff at its fountains,
So gay and so stylish, they make quite a show.

When the bell sounds to dinner, what throngs sally forth,
Of bachelors, maidens, of husbands and wives!
There tories and whigs, from the South and the North,
Talking and walking as if for their lives.

At table what scrambling, and bustle and clamor!
Here gentlemen calling, and there servants running!

* See Chap. VI, p. 82.

Vulcan's stout myrmidons, wielding the hammer,
  Could not have occasioned a clatter more stunning.

But enough of *terrestrials;* now haste we to *Paradise,*
  Where dwell the bright houris, whose soft silken chains
Have entwined many hearts, and led them to sacrifice
  Friendship's sage feelings to love's silly pains.

There you'll find sweet Miss C. and Miss B. and Miss W.,
  And some other belles who in R——d reside;—
But beware of their charms, they have power to trouble you,
  And cause what is much like *an ache in the side!*

From Baltimore, Boston, Philadelphia, New York,
  From Louisville, Lynchburg, and Edenton City,
There are fair ones and rare ones—just look in that walk!
  'Tis filled with the graceful, the beauteous, the witty!

There are songstresses also among the blithe train,
  Whose soft notes enchant as they fall on the ear—
And Havana can boast of a nymph whose sweet strain
  It delights every lover of music to hear.

At night you must wend to Terpsichore hall;
  You'll see there assembled a brilliant collection,
Who form every evening a sociable ball,
  Where cotillons and waltzes are danced to perfection.

There are judges and gen'rals, whose names I could mention,
  And lawyers and doctors all worthy of fame;
But to lengthen this ballad is not my intention,
  Such time would it take every one to proclaim.

Yet ere I conclude, lo! a paradox hear!
  Though protestants all, yet obey we a POPE,
Whose mandates give pleasure, whene'er they appear—
  That long he may reign most devoutly we hope!

Acknowledgments

IT GIVES me great pleasure to acknowledge the generous contributions of many people and institutions in the matter of research. The following list is in no particular order nor does it pretend to be complete, for I have received assistance from so many more kind people than I can name in a limited space. My gratitude extends to all of them.

At the University of North Carolina, Dr. J. G. de Roulhac Hamilton and Librarian Robert B. Downs gave me the run of their rich manuscript collection, and Mrs. Lyman A. Cotten made my work as easy as possible. Dr. J. P. Breedlove, Librarian at Duke University, and Professor J. H. Easterby, of the College of the City of Charleston, were equally generous with their collections at those institutions.* The South Carolina Historical Society, at Charleston, turned over their Singleton and Chesnut papers.

My grateful acknowledgments are extended also to Miss Clelia Porcher Missroon, of Charleston, for permission to use material from the unpublished memoirs of her great-uncle, Professor Frederick A. Porcher; to Mrs. W. L. Jett of Memphis for much valuable Chesnut material; to Mrs. M. L. Parler of Wedgefield, South Carolina, for information which she had collected on the Singleton family and for ex-

* The following items have been quoted by express permission of Duke University: Letter of Richard I. Manning (Chap. IV, p. 54); letter of Andrew Stevenson (Chap. IV, p. 65); and letter of James Chesnut (Chap. VIII, p. 116).

[283]

cerpts from the DeVeaux diary; to Mrs. LeRoy Halsey for her store of letters and articles on the Singletons; to Mr. Robert Lancaster, Jr., President of the Virginia Historical Society, for permission to use the Clay letters; to Mr. Thomas P. Martin of the Library of Congress, Division of Manuscripts, for his sympathetic assistance in the matters of letters and diaries. The diary of Ann Price has been used by the kind consent of Miss Mary Overton Haw. Permission to reprint Chapter I and various additional paragraphs has been granted by *Town and Country,* which first published them.

I wish to thank the following people for their generous co-operation in various ways: Lucile Kellar of the McCormick Historical Association, Mrs. E. D. Friedricks of the New Orleans Archives Library, Mrs. William D. Duke, Mr. Loren R. Johnston, Mrs. Frank D. Williams, Mrs. Victor Barringer, the late Mr. Harry Frazier, Mrs. George Gordon Battle, Mrs. Bradley S. Johnson for her rich reminiscences, and most especially Miss Christiana Bond, author of *Memories of General Robert E. Lee,* who so unstintingly supplemented that charming book with many letters and reflections on the post-war years.

The Messrs. John and Raphael Semmes of Baltimore have kindly given permission to use unpublished Kennedy and Latrobe material and to reproduce the Latrobe water colors owned by the Semmes estate; and Miss Florence Kennedy has made available material of the Maryland Historical Society.

For her skill and patience in making copies of five of the Latrobe water colors (the originals of which were unavailable for reproduction by the ordinary methods) my heartfelt thanks are due my wife, Ashton W. Reniers, whose assistance in the preparation of this book has been invaluable.

BIBLIOGRAPHY

INDEX

Bibliography

I

Books and Pamphlets on the Springs

A Trip to the Virginia Springs, or Belles and Beaux of 1835, by A Lady. Lexington (Va.), 1843.

Bell, John, m.d. *Mineral and Thermal Springs of the United States and Canada*. Philadelphia, 1855.

Burke, William, m.d. *The Mineral Springs of Western Virginia*. New York, 1842. Also, *Red Sulphur Springs* (pamphlet). 1860.

Cowan, Robert. *Guide to the Virginia Springs*. Philadelphia, 1851.

Horner, William E., m.d. *Observations on the Mineral Waters of the Southwestern Part of Virginia* (pamphlet). 1834. First published serially in the *National Gazette*, 1833.

Huntt, Henry, m.d. *A Visit to the Red Sulphur Springs of Virginia* (pamphlet). Washington, 1838.

Moorman, J. J., m.d. *A Directory for the Use of the White Sulphur Waters* (pamphlet). Philadelphia, 1839. This pamphlet was later enlarged into a book, *The Virginia Springs*, 1846, and this book went through many editions, each one larger and more comprehensive than the one before it, between 1846 and 1873. The 1873 edition was called *Mineral Springs of North America*.

Mütter, Thomas D., m.d. *The Salt Sulphur Springs of Monroe County*. 1840.

Pencil, Mark (Mary M. Hagner). *The White Sulphur Papers, or Life at the Springs of Western Virginia*. New York, 1839.

Perkins, Col. T. H. Introduction to reprint of Dr. Huntt's pamphlet on the *Red Sulphur Springs*. Boston, 1839.

Prolix, Peregrine (Philip Houlbrooke Nicklin). *Letters Descriptive of the Virginia Springs, the Roads Leading Thereto and the Doings Thereat*. New York, 1835. Second (enlarged) edition, 1837; third edition, 1844.

Rouelle, John, m.d. *A Complete Treatise on the Mineral Waters of Virginia, Etc*. Philadelphia, 1792.

Selden, John. *White Sulphur Springs*, a play.

Six Weeks in Fauquier Etc., anon. (pamphlet). New York, 1838.

TINDALL, P. B., M.D. *Observations on the Mineral Waters of Western Virginia.* 1858.

WINDLE, MARY J. (MARY J. McLANE?) *Life at the White Sulphur Springs, or Pictures of a Pleasant Summer.* Philadelphia, 1857.

There are many other books and pamphlets on Springs and Mineral Waters of the United States and Canada. For the most part they are medical treatises and they are not listed here because they have not been used in this book.

II

MAGAZINE ARTICLES ON THE SPRINGS

American Magazine of Useful and Entertaining Knowledge, "The Mineral Springs of Virginia." June, 1835.

American Turf Register, "Phenomena," article on the Singleton house and stud. Vol. XI, Charleston, 1840.

Annals of Medical History, "John Jennings Moorman, A Biographical Note," by Guy Hinsdale, M.D. Vol. VI, No. 4, 1934.

DeBow's Review. September, 1859.

Harper's Magazine, "The White Sulphur Springs," by John Esten Cooke. August, 1878.

Harper's Weekly, "Virginia Summer Resorts." October, 1885.

Knickerbocker Magazine, "A Trip to the Virginia Springs," by Viator (David Hoffman). 1852–53.

Lippincott's Magazine, "Virginia in Water Colors," by Mary B. Dodge. July, 1872.

The Nation, Letter on the Virginia Springs, unsigned. September, 1877.

New England Magazine, "The White Sulphur Springs," by Viator; sub-title, "An Excursion from Cincinnati, Ohio, to the White Sulphur Springs in Virginia." September, 1832.

New York Times Magazine, April 12, 1936, an article by R. L. Duffus. The author is indebted to this article for information on Edmund Ruffin.

Potter's American Monthly, "A Southern Watering Place," by C. A. Pilsbury. October, 1880.

Southern Literary Messenger:
  "Another Visit to the Virginia Springs or the Adventures of Harry Humbug, Esq." 1835.
  "Journal of a Trip to the Mountains, Caves and Springs of Virginia," by a New Englander. 1838.

BIBLIOGRAPHY

"The Sweet Springs of Virginia and the Valley Which Contains Them," by Byrd Powell, M.D. 1835.

"Visit to the Virginia Springs," anon. 1835.

West Virginia Review, article on Berkeley Springs, by Roy Bird Cook. February, 1935.

III

GENERAL BIBLIOGRAPHY

ALLSTON, JOSEPH BLYTH. "Life and Times of James L. Petigru," *Sunday News*, Charleston, S. C. January-June, 1900.

Appleton's Handbook of American Travel, Southern Tour. 1873.

ARESE, COUNT FRANCESCO. *A Trip to the Prairies and in the Interior of North America, 1837–38*, translated by Andrew Evans. New York, 1934.

BAILEY, ROBERT. *Life and Adventures of Robert Bailey* (autobiography). Richmond, 1822.

BAYARD, FERDINAND M. *Voyage dans l'interieur des Etats-Unis*. Paris, 1797.

BEYER, EDWARD. *Edward Beyer's Cyclorama*. Dresden, no date.

BLANTON, WYNDHAM B., M.D. *Medicine in Virginia in the Nineteenth Century*. Richmond, 1933.

BOGART, ERNEST LUDLOW. *Economic History of the United States*. New York, 1922.

BOND, CHRISTIANA. *Memories of General Robert E. Lee*. Baltimore, 1926.

BRADLEY, HUGH. *Such Was Saratoga*. New York, 1940.

BUCKINGHAM, JAMES SILK. *The Slave States of America*. London, 1842.

CABELL, BRANCH. *These Restless Heads*. New York, 1932.

CARSON, JAMES PETIGRU. *Life, Letters and Speeches of James Louis Petigru*. Washington, copyright, 1920.

Confederate Veteran, Vol. XXI, No. 2 (February, 1913), p. 53.

CRAVEN, AVERY. *Edmund Ruffin, Southerner*. New York, 1932.

DREWRY, WILLIAM SIDNEY. *The Southampton Insurrection*. Washington, 1900.

DUPONT, H. A. *The Campaign of 1864 in the Valley of Virginia*. New York, 1925.

FEATHERSTONHAUGH, GEORGE W. *Excursion through the Slave States*. 2 vols. London, 1844.

FREEMAN, DOUGLAS. *R. E. Lee*. 4 vols. New York, 1936.

———. "Lee and the Ladies," *Scribner's Magazine*, October-November, 1925.

GILMAN, CAROLINE. *The Poetry of Travelling in the United States.* New York, 1838.

HOWE, HENRY. *Historical Collections of Virginia.* Charleston, 1845.

KENNEDY, JOHN P. *Swallow Barn; or a Sojourn in the Old Dominion.* 2 vols. Philadelphia, 1832. Also editions of 1895 and 1929.

LEE, CAPTAIN R. E. *Recollections and Letters of General Lee.* New York, 1924.

LeGrand, Julia, Diary of. Edited by Kate Mason Rowland and Mrs. Morris L. Croxall. Richmond, 1911.

LUDY, ROBERT. *Historic Hotels of the World.* Philadelphia, 1927.

MACKAY, ALEXANDER. *The Western World.* Philadelphia, 1849.

MACKIE, J. MILTON. *Cape Cod to Dixie and the Tropics.* New York, 1864.

MARRYAT, CAPTAIN. *A Diary in America.* Philadelphia, 1839.

MARTIN, JOSEPH. *New and Comprehensive Gazeteer of Virginia.* Charlottesville, 1835.

MARTINEAU, HARRIET. *Society in America.* London, 1837.

MAURY, GENERAL DABNEY H. *Recollections of a Virginian.* New York, 1894.

MORRISON, A. J., ed. *Travels in Virginia in Revolutionary Times.* Lynchburg (Va.), 1922.

MORTON, OREN F. *Annals of Bath County, Virginia.* Staunton (Va.), 1917.

NEVINS, ALLEN. *American Social History as Recorded by British Travellers.* New York, 1923.

PACKARD, JOSEPH, D.D. *Recollections of a Long Life.* Edited by Thomas J. Packard. Washington, 1902.

PAULDING, JAMES K. *Letters from the South.* New York, 1817.

PHILLIPS, ULRICH B. *Life and Labor in the Old South.* Boston, 1929.

———. "The Literary Movement for Secession," *Studies in Southern History and Politics,* Inscribed to William Archibald Dunning. By his former pupils, the authors. New York, 1914.

POLLARD, EDWARD. *The Virginia Tourist.* Philadelphia, 1870.

RAVENEL, MRS. ST. JULIEN. *Charleston, the Place and the People.* New York, 1912.

REED and MATHESON. *A Narrative of the Visit to the American Churches,* by Andrew Reed, D.D., and James Matheson, D.D. New York, 1835.

ROBERTSON, ALEXANDER F. *A. H. H. Stuart, a Biography.* Richmond, 1925.

ROYALL, ANN. *Southern Tour or Second Series of the Black Book.* Washington, 1830.

SAXON, LYLE. *Old Louisiana*. New York, 1929.

SEMMES, JOHN E. *John H. B. Latrobe and His Times*. Baltimore, 1917.

SIMPSON, W. D. "Col. Richard Singleton of Home Place," *The State*, Columbia (S. C.), April 26, 1931.

SINGLETON, MRS. ELIZA GREEN. *The Singletons of South Carolina*. Columbia (S. C.), 1914.

SMEDES, SUSAN DABNEY. *A Southern Planter*. New York, 1890.

SMITH, SUSIE M. H. *The Love That Never Failed*, a biography of Mary Kelly Watson. Charlottesville, 1928.

WATKINS, JAMES L. *Production and Price of Cotton for One Hundred Years* (pamphlet). U. S. Dept. of Agriculture, 1895.

WEYBRIGHT, VICTOR. *Spangled Banner: The Story of Francis Scott Key*. New York, 1935.

WISE, JOHN S. *The Lion's Skin*. New York, 1905.

In the last years of the century, the newspapers superseded all other sources in value. The best dispatches have been found in the Richmond *Enquirer*, the Richmond *Whig*, the Richmond *Dispatch*, the *State* (Richmond), the Charleston *Mercury*, the Charleston *Courier*, the Baltimore *Sun* and the New Orleans *Times*.

Index